Women in Africa and the African Diaspora

Edited by

Rosalyn Terborg-Penn
Sharon Harley
Andrea Benton Rushing

Howard University Press
Washington, D.C.   1989

First paperback edition 1989.

Printed in the United States of America

Library of Congress Cataloging-in-Publication Data

Women in Africa and the African diaspora

   Includes papers presented at the meeting, Women in the
African Diaspora: an Interdisciplinary Perspective, sponsored
by the Association of Black Women Historians, and held June
12–14, 1983 at Howard University.
   1. Women—Africa—Social conditions—Congresses.
2. Feminism—Africa—Congresses. 3. Afro-American
women—Social conditions—Congresses. 4. Women,
Black—Social conditions—Congresses. I. Terborg-Penn,
Rosalyn. II. Harley, Sharon. III. Rushing, Andrea Benton.
IV. Association of Black Women Historians (U.S.)
HQ1787.W65 1987   305.4'2'096   87-22784
ISBN 0-88258-177-5

We dedicate this anthology to women of African descent throughout the world—past and present.

Contents

Foreword

In recent years the conceptualization of the historical and contemporary relationship between Africans residing on the continent and African descendants living throughout the world has occupied the attention of a growing number of scholars, writers, and others, especially in the United States and in Africa. Persons of African descent living outside of Africa have felt the need to establish ties with Africa both physically and spiritually as a way to affirm their identity. One therefore is not surprised that Africans in the Americas, since their arrival and their subsequent transformation into Afro-Americans, have sought to comprehend more clearly the nature of their African roots, the extent of their African continuities, the influence of their adopted societies, and the meaning of that bicultural experience.

Although the African presence abroad resulted from both voluntary and involuntary migrations, the slave trade and slavery most accounted for the African diaspora. That dispersion of Africans overseas should be conceptualized as part of the African heritage. Whether Africans were slaves or free persons in Asia, Europe, or the Americas, they confronted pervasive and consistent efforts, direct and indirect, to bleach their Africaness; but not only did the Africans survive physically and culturally, they adapted to their host settings and developed societies, and, over the centuries, they have made significant contributions to their adopted countries, Africa, and indeed the world.

How this occurred and with what consequences are major research agenda for a small but significant group of Africanists and Americanists, whose emergence was demonstrated at the First and Second African Diaspora Studies Institute, which met at Howard University in 1979 and at the University of Nairobi, Kenya in 1981. Those two meetings of scholars and writers from Africa, Europe, and the Americas not only assessed the current status of teaching and research in the field; they also clarified the concept and methodology and projected guidelines for future activities.[1]

A major caveat in the field is the place and role of women of the African diaspora. Thus, the Association of Black Women Historians organized the conference, "Women in the African Diaspora: An Interdisciplinary Perspective," which convened at Howard University, June 12–14, 1983. We are fortunate that many of the papers presented at that conference are included in this volume.

These papers are not simply attempts to fill in the gaps; they boldly address the issue of feminism in history and its relevance for the reconstruction not only of the history of African and Afro-American women, but of the African diaspora generally.

The task of reconstructing the history of women in Africa and the African diaspora is enormous, and the systematic investigation of such a neglected area of study undoubtedly will raise as many questions as it answers; such is the role of any pioneer study. Thus, this volume makes a significant contribution to the field. An array of established and younger scholars, by their seminal papers in this volume, have set upon a course which will unearth and present the facts of the past and shape the future perspectives of research on and by women in Africa and the African diaspora.

Joseph E. Harris
Professor of History
Howard University

NOTE

1. Several of the papers presented at the First African Diaspora Studies Institute appear in *Global Dimensions of the African Diaspora,* ed. Joseph E. Harris (Washington, D.C.: Howard University Press, 1982).

Acknowledgments

This anthology is the result of the efforts of various people, especially those members of the Association of Black Women Historians who remained committed to the research conference that produced the papers in this volume. In addition, this collection was made possible through the assistance of a research grant from the National Endowment for the Humanities.

Special thanks go to Shirley A. Patterson Morrell, Administrative Assistant for the project, who continuously volunteered time to see that the manuscript would be completed. Furthermore, we extend our appreciation to the conference participants—those who presented stimulating papers, those who responded with enlightened questions and comments, and those who chaired the sessions or recorded data. We also thank Theodore Cassell and Michael Terry for assisting in the circulation of the manuscript among the editors. In addition, we thank the Rhode Island Black Heritage Society for permission to publish data found in the Bertha Higgins Papers. Finally, we appreciate the librarians and archivists who assisted us in collecting our data.

Overview—
Women in the African Diaspora: An Overview of an Interdisciplinary Research Conference

Rosalyn Terborg-Penn

Since the early 1970s, African diaspora studies has become a research frontier among scholars in history and other disciplines. Considerable interest has been generated among academics, as indicated by the two successfully convened African diaspora studies conferences organized by historian Joseph E. Harris in 1979 and 1981. In addition to scholarly meetings, there have been several cultural gatherings aimed to involve people of African descent cross-culturally. The four Carifesta festivals are good examples. Held in Guyana, Jamaica, Cuba, and Barbados, these cultural gatherings included popular and scholarly activities. The Smithsonian Institution African Diaspora Program, coordinated by historian-performer Bernice Johnson Reagon, from 1972 to 1976, highlighted the performing arts, the cultural artifacts, and the rituals of people of African descent found throughout New World societies. Visual artist Marta Morena Vega focused upon the religious connections in the diaspora when she organized the world conferences on Orisha at Ife, Nigeria, in 1981, and in Rio De Janiero, Brazil, in 1983.

Until recently, there has been little effort to organize African diaspora scholarship and cultural activity which focuses primarily upon the experiences of women. Just as black women's studies has grown out of the experiences of black studies and women's studies programs, women as a focus in the diaspora is emerging as a distinct area of inquiry as well. The publication, in 1981, of Filomina Chioma Steady's anthology *The Black Woman Cross-Culturally* indicated growing interest for this perspective among scholars.

Similar concern has developed among lay groups as well. The Missionary Department of the Bethel AME Church in Baltimore, under the leadership of Cecilia Williams Bryant, the minister to women, organized two conferences on black women and religion—one in 1978 and one in 1980. Each conference stressed the experiences of women in Africa and in the African diaspora.

For several reasons it is important for scholars—those who research black women's lives and those who research people of the African diaspora—to be pioneers in the scientific study of women in Africa and in the African diaspora. Because the scholarly evolution of African diaspora studies about women is in its infancy, a forum to present, discuss, and examine the scholarship is crucial to future conceptual and methodological issues. Because the scholarship that is evolving crosses disciplines and cultures, there is a need to provide guidelines for exchanging theories and sources for investigation. An important reason for the study of women of African descent throughout the world is the common nature of their struggles and the similar ways used by black women to deal with the problems and the joys in their lives. Finally, analyzing how women of African descent view themselves and provide their own cultural parameters is crucial to future research in the social sciences and the humanities.

With these objectives in mind, the Association of Black Women Historians (ABWH) initiated a research conference, "Women in the African Diaspora: An Interdisciplinary Perspective," held for three days in June 1983 at Howard University. Nell Irvin Painter, professor of history at the University of North Carolina and then national director of the ABWH, opened the conference. Scholars and interested participants discussed what scholarship is being produced and what research needs to be developed in the future to broaden the female perspective in African diaspora studies and to encourage cross-cultural studies of black women's lives. Three themes were originated to illuminate some of the many experiences and common concerns among women in the African diaspora, whose world view is rooted in traditional African cosmology.

The first theme, "Developing a Theoretical Framework for the Study of Women in the African Diaspora," was designed to probe how scholars can develop research theories and techniques that provide not only interdisciplinary perspectives, but a cross-cultural framework. Historian Mary F. Berry, formerly a member of the United States Civil Rights Commission and now a professor at the University of Pennsylvania, opened the first plenary session by discussing the diversity of problems minority women encounter dealing with economic and political barriers placed in their paths. Specifically making reference to her experience as a member of the Civil Rights Commission, Berry was encouraged by the audience to continue her fight against gender and race prejudices. She then introduced Filomina Chioma Steady, who presented a keynote address that centered upon African feminism as a worldwide perspective. A Sierra Leonian anthropologist, Steady describes herself as a product of the African diaspora, because her ancestors had been African slaves transported to the New World, then repatriated by the British and returned to the African continent, where they were resettled in Sierra Leone. For Steady, African feminism may be the key to liberating humanity from various forms of oppression. As a pioneer in the emerging field of African diaspora women's studies, she provided for the conference participants a theoretical foundation, from a black woman's perspective, as well as from an anthropologist's point of view.

The first of two sessions organized around the first theme provided a theoretical framework for African diaspora women's studies—"Conceptual Frameworks for the Study of Women in the African Diaspora." The session was chaired by folklorist Mildred Hill-Lubin, professor of literature, University of Florida. My paper, "African Feminism: A Theoretical Approach to the History of Women in the African Diaspora," was designed to apply the Steady concept to the historical discipline and to review the theoretical approaches historians have used to assess black women's history in the United States. Using my past research and experience teaching African-American women's history as an associate professor of history at Morgan State University, I argued in favor of the African feminist model. I attempted to demonstrate why Steady's theory was best suited for cross-cultural black women's historiography. Daphne Duval Harrison, who heads the African–Afro-American Studies Program at the University of Maryland–Baltimore County, gave the second theoretical paper. A specialist in the music and the experiences of black women blues singers in the United States, Harrison, whose paper was entitled, "Theoretical Approaches to the Study of Culture and Women in the African Diaspora," called for theories that focus on the way black women define their experiences through various genres. William Alexander, assistant professor of history at Hampton University, was the recorder for this session.

The second session, "Research Techniques for the Study of Women in the African Diaspora," was chaired by John Henrik Clarke, emeritus professor of history at Hunter College. The session included three scholars who have worked inside and outside of academic institutions. Beverly Lindsay, policy analyst, National Institute of Education and Policy, has written extensively about women and education in Africa and in the United States. Her paper, "Comparative Educational Research Methods and Literatures: Perspectives on African and African-American Women," included a critique of the way in which recent women's studies of black women suggest ameliorating conditions that prevent social and economic independence. Saundra Rice Murray directs the Office of Field Services Operations for the United Planning Organization in Washington, D.C. A psychologist, Murray is among the few in her field to promote the study of black women. In her paper, "Psychological Research Methods: Women in the African Diaspora," Murray assessed the current research and literature on black women in her discipline and called for new research techniques that consider the "social context" of the women to be studied, rather than the standard psychological instruments that are often biased against them. Similarly, A. Lynn Bolles, the director of the Afro-American Studies Program at Bowdoin College, called for the application of John Gwaltney's term, *native anthropology*, when researchers attempt to collect data about black women in the Caribbean. An anthropologist who has researched black women in Jamaica, Bolles presented "Anthropological Research Methods for the Study of Black Women in the Caribbean," which reflected her call for responsible research that takes into account the cultural milieu of the women under study. Cynthia Neverdon-Morton, professor of history, Coppin State College, served as the session's recorder.

The general consensus among the scholars who addressed the conference was that theories and research methods should be developed for studying women in the African diaspora. Applicable techniques require understanding the cultural context and acknowledging black women's definitions of themselves, as well as their means of expression. In essence, the pursuit of this method will facilitate comparative, cross-cultural studies—the ultimate goal.

The second theme of the conference was "Cosmology or World View: Women in the African Diaspora." The two sessions that examined this theme sought to explore women's roles in traditional milieus, like religion and the family, in order to investigate the relationship between African and African diaspora cosmologies. Historian Bettye Collier-Thomas, director of the Bethune Museum-Archives, opened the second day and introduced the keynote speaker, Cecilia Williams Bryant. The Reverend Bryant addressed the plenary session with a traditional, New World, African-American sermon, which demonstrated the spiritual and instructive functions of sermons in black culture. Her topic, "Woman: Apocalyptic Hope of the Diaspora," exemplified the diversified character of black Christian sermonic form in its poetry, call and response, and spontaneity, as Bryant and members of the audience became overcome with the Spirit. A major theme in her presentation was the "chosen" women, who are called to lead their communities despite their will. Women as independent leaders of secular and spiritual movements are common in the history of Africa and the African diaspora.

The first session organized around the second theme was "Religious Experiences of Women in the African Diaspora," chaired by Franklin W. Knight, professor of history, the Johns Hopkins University. Bennetta Jules-Rosette, professor of sociology at the University of California–San Diego, gave the initial paper, "Privilege Without Power: Women in African Cults and Churches." A specialist on African religions, she began with a discussion of visionary African women in sixteenth-century Central Africa. Jules-Rosette provided an analysis of the large roles women have played and continue to play as members of African cults and churches. She found that African women have limited power and access to top positions in church hierarchies, as do black women in the United States. Black women missionaries were highly visible in Africa during the Christian missionary movement of the nineteenth and early twentieth centuries. Sylvia M. Jacobs, professor of history at North Carolina Central University, has published extensively on the African-American missionary presence in Africa. In her paper, "Afro-American Women Missionaries Confront the African Way of Life," she concluded that black American women went to Africa as second-class missionaries but with prejudices similar to those held by white American missionaries. However, she found that their concern for African women, their often second-class status as missionaries, and their experiences on the continent helped to amend their preconceived Western notions about the "dark continent." As a result, they often formed networks to assist African women and their children. Two recorders served for this session, Maricela Medina Cruz, assistant professor of history, Howard University, and Janette Hoston Harris, associate professor of history, the University of the District of Columbia.

The second session, "Family Structure and Women's Roles: Perspectives from Within the African Diaspora," focused upon how African family structures are related to family life in the African diaspora. A. Lynn Bolles chaired this session. Niara Sudarkasa, president of Lincoln University in Pennsylvania, delivered the first paper. An anthropologist with extensive experience researching West African women and their family roles, she has been a pioneer in the study of Yoruba women. Sudarkasa contributed a theoretical base, which can be used for looking at contemporary African-American families as well as West African Families. In her paper, "The Changing Roles of Women in West African Families," she concluded that extended family structures, so common in traditional West African societies, continue to provide the networks needed for women and family in rapidly changing Africa. Similarly, in the United States, extended family systems provide kin-help networks essential to survival in the modern world.

Extended family networks was a major focus in Harriette Pipes McAdoo's study, "Extended Family Involvement and Roles of Urban Kenyan Women." A professor of social work at Howard University, specializing in the black family, McAdoo found similarities in the range of responsibilities professional Kenyan and African-American women held as mothers. Despite the kinship networks among Kenyan women, which relieve much of the time spent on chores and child care, professional Kenyan women experience high degrees of stress as they coordinate large households of kin and meet their financial needs. Robert Hall, assistant professor of history and Afro-American studies, University of Maryland–Baltimore County, has researched black families in the South. He raised questions about how best to analyze women's roles in traditional black southern families of the past and compare them with the women in black families returning to the South from northern urban communities. In his paper, "Extended Family Networks Among Black Southern Women in the United States," Hall asked whether these families are in search of the traditional extended family networks that emerged among black families during and immediately after slavery. Noralee Frankel, special assistant for women and minorities, the American Historical Association, served as the recorder for this session.

Notwithstanding the diversity of topics related to the second theme, most of the papers explored the ways in which black women organize networks of family, friends, or associates to provide support for daily survival. Support networks were evident among African as well as New World communities, where black women held prominent roles in religious and familial institutions. In addition, the findings of most speakers revealed the low status of black women cross-culturally and through time, as well as their burden of inordinately difficult and numerous responsibilities. Further cross-cultural studies, especially of various New World societies, were among the priorities identified for future research.

The purpose of the third theme, "African Women in the

Culture of New World Societies: Past and Present," was to focus upon slavery, as a theme of the past and of literature and, therefore, as a vehicle for assessing the present. Johnnella E. Butler, director of the Department of Afro-American Studies at the University of Washington, chaired the plenary session. Bernice Johnson Reagon, director of the Program in Black American Culture, Smithsonian Institution, and the founder of the vocal group "Sweet Honey in the Rock," gave the keynote address. Her paper, "Women and the Culture of New World Societies," complemented Bryant's sermon in that Reagon spoke of "chosen" women also. In her discussion of the various women leaders who attended the first African diaspora program held during the Smithsonian Institution Folk Festival in 1972, Reagon noted the importance of their ritual roles, as well as their leadership in the cultural process being shared. These characteristics could be observed among these diverse bearers of culture from Brazil to Jamaica to the United States.

The first of the two sessions organized around this theme was "Women in Slavery," moderated by Monica Schuler, professor of history, Wayne State University. The three scholars who presented papers in this session were all historians. Tiffany R. Patterson, research fellow, Frederick Douglass Institute, University of Rochester, began with her paper, "Slavery and Women in New World Societies." She felt that before New World slavery and its impact upon women could be fully analyzed, an examination of women enslaved in Africa at the time of the New World slave trade was needed. The role of Christian and Muslim slave traders as well as the status of women in African societies, both free and enslaved, must be considered along with the diversity of attitudes toward slaves and their descendants found in the various New World cultures. Patricia Ann Mulvey, associate professor of history, Bluefield State College, presented a paper entitled "Black Sisters in Slavery in Brazil." She raised several questions about the various subordinate positions of women, free or enslaved, in colonial Brazilian society. Focusing mainly upon Brazilian cities, Mulvey noted that no complete picture of slave life for women in Brazil can be gathered from colonial records and only recently have other sources, such as the records of black burial societies, been used to clarify the sketchy picture that currently emerges. Thavolia Glymph, formerly assistant professor of history, University of Texas–Arlington, presented the final paper in this session, "Slavery and Afro-American Women." She raised significant questions about the way enslaved black women's lives have been and need to be assessed. Glymph concluded that the relationship of slave women to the economies of New World societies awaits analysis, as does the relationship between enslaved men and women and the impact of variables such as the type of work, the size of the slave community, and the organization of plantations or other work sites. Sharon Harley, assistant professor of history, Afro-American Studies Program, University of Maryland–College Park, served as recorder for this session.

The second session in this series was entitled "Images of Black Women in New World Literature," moderated by Karen Smyley Wallace, an associate dean of Liberal Arts at Howard University. The three panelists who presented papers are all literary critics. Andrea Benton Rushing, professor of English and black studies at Amherst College, gave a paper entitled "Images of Black Women in Afro-American Literature." Rushing, whose research and publications reflect a diaspora perspective, chose to explore how black poets have honored their women singers—from the late nineteenth-century poetry of Paul Laurence Dunbar to the more contemporary work of poets in the black arts movement of the 1960s. She argues that both the honorific titles given to the singers and the powers ascribed to them echo West African attitudes toward female deities. "Images of Black Women in the Literature of Spanish Speaking New World Societies" was the title of Annette Ivory Dunzo's paper. An associate professor of Spanish in the Department of Romance Languages at Howard University, she looked at the development of female images in Spanish-speaking Caribbean literature, where until recently, women of color have been described passionately and exotically through the filter of European culture. Nonetheless, she explains that African traditions and sounds can be found in Afro-Hispanic poetry. Martha K. Cobb, emeritus professor, Department of Romance Languages at Howard University, presented a comparative study that reflects her expertise in Spanish, French, and English literature. "Images of Black Women in New World Literature: A Comparative Approach," treated the work of an American novelist, a Haitian novelist, and a Uruguayan poet, all of whom explore their identity as black women. Cobb found that female consciousness among black women writers developed earlier in the United States than it did in the Caribbean and in South America. Nevertheless, she finds new themes in the literature of women—women's identity quest, feminine self-perception, and black self-awareness—which were missing when black women's images were created by male writers of the past. Deborah McDowell, University of Virginia, served as the recorder for the session.

The scholars who participated in the two aforementioned sessions raised many questions that have not been answered because the cross-cultural study of black women in the New World is still in its infancy. All called for more cross-cultural studies that deal with a variety of factors often difficult to compare across New World societies. For example, languages and skin color perceptions vary throughout the New World. Although Africa as the common source of early experiences can be analyzed, the impact of various European cultural exchanges presents diversity that complicates cross-cultural studies.

The final plenary session, "Research Priorities for the Study of Women in the African Diaspora," was opened by Arnold Taylor, professor of history in the Department of History at Howard University. Sharon Harley moderated this session, wherein the six recorders from the previous sessions gave highlights and detailed the questions and priorities raised by the audience participants. Following the panelists' presentations, the audience was asked to share, in addition to their general comments, their reasons for attending the conference and their priorities for the future study of women in the African diaspora. Over all, conferees called for more networking, especially through professional and scholarly conferences, and the consensus was that more cross-cultural, comparative studies are the priority.

Two documents were promised as a result of the conference—a diaspora women's networking directory and the publication of papers delivered during the conference. The directory was the result of a questionnaire completed by more than fifty conference participants, outlining their research and professional interests to be shared with others. I compiled this directory, which was printed and distributed to listees. This anthology is the second document promised. It contains ten of the original essays presented during the conference, two essays by presenters on topics not presented at the conference, and a concluding essay that examines the state of the field and suggests where we should go from here.

The anthology focuses upon three themes—theoretical approaches and research methods, women and new roles in African societies, and black women in folk culture and literature. Our hope is that this collection will stimulate additional research in various disciplines, especially using comparative methodology. The essays in this collection are pioneer efforts. They are not designed to be definitive works but to serve as formative studies on the cutting edge of the emerging field of African diaspora women's studies.

Part I

Theoretical Approaches and Research Methods

African Feminism: A Worldwide Perspective

Filomina Chioma Steady

THE NEED FOR A THEORY
OF AFRICAN FEMINISM

Various schools of thought, perspectives, and ideological proclivities have influenced the study of feminism. Few studies have dealt with the issue of racism, since the dominant voice of the feminist movement has been that of the white female. The issue of racism can become threatening, for it identifies white feminists as possible participants in the oppression of blacks. In the main, the accusation of universal male oppression through the system of patriarchy has been politically advantageous to white women.

From the perspective of some black women, evidence of racism during the precarious period of affirmative action policy can cause a certain uneasiness. Upwardly mobile black women and those who have been co-opted to serve the interests of the white power structure may find the issue of racism provocative and threatening to their professional survival as individual "tokens." They may also be under various pressures to demonstrate allegiance to feminist, rather than racial, causes.

Significantly, the issue of racism combined with sexism is explosive and potentially revolutionary. It threatens to destroy the existing power base of the world economy, which is dominated by whites. Maintaining an inequitable and unjust world economic order is most profitable to the strongest, richest, and most powerful men and women in the world. The subordination of the majority of black men and women has been vital to this world order, for the productive and reproductive labor of black women

3

have served and continue to serve as necessary prerequisites for capital accumulation on a world scale. By being at the bottom of this structure, poor black women, not the mythical Atlas, hold up our unequal and unjust planet. For this reason, primarily, an African feminism that encompasses freedom from the complex configurations created by multiple oppression is necessary and urgent.

In Africa, as well as in the diaspora, the black women engaged in research on the black woman are involved in a process of liberation, as well as in a scholarly endeavor, since research, being essentially a product of the power structure, has sometimes been used as a tool of domination.[1] The increasing involvement of African women in research can lead to redefinitions and critical examinations of concepts, perspectives, and methodologies used in research and inspire a vital change that will render research activity as a basic human right and a process of liberation for oppressed groups.[2]

African feminism combines racial, sexual, class, and cultural dimensions of oppression to produce a more inclusive brand of feminism through which women are viewed first and foremost as *human,* rather than sexual, beings.[3] It can be defined as that ideology which encompasses freedom from oppression based on the political, economic, social, and cultural manifestations of racial, cultural, sexual, and class biases. It is more inclusive than other forms of feminist ideologies and is largely a product of polarizations and conflicts that represent some of the worst and chronic forms of human suffering.

An inclusive feminism can signal the end of all vestiges of oppression, including those glossed over by revolutions based primarily on class conflicts. It can be argued that this type of feminism has the potential of emphasizing the totality of human experience, portraying the strength and resilience of the human spirit and resounding with optimism for the total liberation of humanity. African feminism is, in short, humanistic feminism.

The world we inherited generates polarizations at an alarming rate and now faces the possibility of total annihilation through nuclear war. African feminism does not need the threat of nuclear war to initiate a struggle for the preservation of life, for survival has always been a central issue for the African woman. In seeking total liberation, African feminism is intrinsically a moral and political statement for human survival and well-being.

By using historical and global perspectives, this paper illustrates the way in which various economic, social, cultural, and political elements have interacted to produce a special brand of African feminism, despite differences in nationality and class among African women on the continent and in the diaspora.

THE ROOTS OF AFRICAN FEMINISM

Tensions and conflicts exist among all social groups, and African societies are no exception. The intention here is not to romanticize the African past but to draw on those features in traditional tribal societies that promoted complementary values—the essential framework for African feminism.

Precolonial African societies, in general, developed self-reliant social systems, as well as favorable and ecologically safe environments. These ensured the physical, emotional, and spiritual well-being of the population, despite droughts, floods, diseases, and wars. Postharvest preservation techniques, as well as intercommunity exchanges, provided some insulation against seasonal variations and natural calamities. Societies endeavored to achieve balance with the physical and metaphysical world by being in tune with, rather than in opposition to, nature.[4]

Men, women, and children were cooperatively involved in production in a social, rather than individual, context. Economic activities such as farming, fishing, hunting, and gathering were geared toward subsistence so that access to land, the vital resource, was determined, primarily, by rules of common property usufruct, rather than by private ownership. Communal values stressed cooperation and distribution, rather than individualism and accumulation.

The household was an economic unit generating use values through production and reproduction. For the most part, communal ownership facilitated women's access to land and ensured a certain degree of control over their labor, as well as some decision making about their labor input. The sexual division of labor was essentially along parallel, rather than hierarchical, lines, thereby giving, in general terms, equal value to male and female labor.[5]

Social organization was based on the principle of patrilineal or matrilineal descent or a combination of both.[6] Socialization of children took place in a group, rather than within the context of a nuclear family, with men being actively involved in the socialization of boys. Polygamy, as an economic system, promoted communal and cooperative values and ensured the economic security of the members of the household. It also facilitated the shared mothering of children and guaranteed women some autonomy, personal freedom, and greater mobility than would be possible in a monogamous, nuclear family. Women had more time to themselves, developed strong bonds with other women, and experienced a more limited, rather than absolute, form of patriarchy. The emphasis on communal living, cooperation, and peaceful coexistence with cowives necessitated the development of good interpersonal skills, diplomacy, and responsibility for men and women. It can be argued that despite the implication and manifestation of female subordination, polygamy provided several safeguards against male domination and female destitution. This may partly explain why it is still practiced today, even though its economic usefulness in production is increasingly becoming obsolete.

Adolescents played an important role in the socialization of younger children. In some societies, particularly in East Africa, peer group socialization was institutionalized through units composed of "age" mates. In the West African nations Sierra Leone and Liberia, secret societies like the Poro (male) and Bondo (female) were mainly responsible for the collective socialization of adolescents into adulthood. They also provided institutionalized means of mutually sanctioning the behavior of members of the opposite sex.

A woman's status changed throughout the life cycle, rising significantly during her reproductive years and reaching its zenith during old age, when she became an elder eligible for certain political positions. It also signaled her approaching entry into the world of the ancestors; old age and ancestors were always revered and respected.[7]

Regardless of the forms of social organization, the dominant ideology was group preservation and well-being ensured by institutionalized checks and controls to reduce tension, especially between the sexes. In patrilineal societies, all men and all women worked to preserve the patrilineage. In matrilineal societies, the preservation of the matrilineage by all men and all women was a supreme value. Sanctions were imposed through ritual expression, ridicule, supernatural interventions, and male and female pressure groups.[8]

African women had definite social, political, and economic roles that induced them to achieve a measure of independence and autonomy and to develop their self-reliant capabilities through participation in production and reproduction.[9] In a number of societies women held executive positions as chiefs, paramount chiefs, and monarchs.[10]

Since production was primarily for use, it can be argued that the question of differential valuation between production and reproduction was not an issue. The basis for valuation of reproduction was more metaphysical and symbolic than purely materialistic. As a result, a woman's role in reproduction often received supreme symbolic value, since it strengthened the human group, ensured continuity of life, and became equated with the life force itself. The bond between the mother and child surpassed all other human bonds and transcended patrilineal rules of descent. In patrilineal societies, the structural position of women as those who perpetuate the patrilineage served to modify the undue male control made possible by the strong corporateness of localized patrilineage groups. Among the Swazi and the Ashanti, representing a patrilineal and a matrilineal society respectively, this principle received supreme political value through the institution of the dual monarchy in which a king ruled jointly with his mother—often referred to as the Queen mother.[11] The role of women as mothers operated at the symbolic level, where the very essence of female biology could be used to sanction the behavior of men. Some male secret societies, such as the Gelede among the Yoruba of Nigeria, capitalize on the reproductive power of women to the extent of effecting cures for some illnesses among men. Women's power to give birth and their role as healers make them awesome figures in a sex-oriented culture.

Parallel autonomy, communalism, and cooperation for the preservation of life are more useful concepts in developing an appropriate framework for examining African feminism than the frameworks of dichotomy, individualism, competition, and opposition, which Western feminism fosters. Men and women in traditional African societies had spheres of autonomy—in economic, social, ritual, and political terms—ensured by various mechanisms of checks and balances. Women's ability to utilize these mechanisms was an important aspect of their feminism. They had the added advantage of being intrinsically central to the preservation and continuation of life through their reproductive role.

African patterns of feminism can be seen as having developed within a context that views human life from a total, rather than a dichotomous and exclusive, perspective. For women, the male is not "the other" but part of the human same. Each gender constitutes the critical half that makes the human whole. Neither sex is totally complete in itself to constitute a unit by itself. Each has and needs a complement, despite the possession of unique features of its own.

Sexual differences and similarities, as well as sex roles, enhance sexual autonomy and cooperation between women and men, rather than promote polarization and fragmentation. Within the metaphysical realm, both male and female principles encompass life and operate jointly to maintain cosmological balance.

AFRICAN FEMINISM WITHIN
A WORLD ECONOMIC SYSTEM

The exploitation of Africa's resources, as well as the productive and reproductive labor of African men and women, and the subsequent appropriation by the West of the enormous wealth this generated, contributed greatly to the rapid development of Western countries and families.[12]

These modes of exploitation took the form of oppression of whole groups of people and gave rise to the ideology of racism to justify oppression on the grounds of fabricated notions of racial inferiority. The role of the black woman in ensuring the survival and well-being of her people was significant and added other dimensions to her feminism—namely, liberation from white oppression and destruction of the ideology of racism.

The incorporation of Africa into the world economic system has made the continent a battlefield in an on-going struggle among world powers for economic, cultural, and ideological domination. This struggle has produced some of the most devastating effects on the African family. The processes of slavery, colonialism, imperialism, neocolonialism, and apartheid have resulted in chronic underdevelopment.

Slavery

The slave trade constitutes part of the beginning of a complex system through which the continent of Africa has been dominated for centuries. The single most important historical event responsible for the massive dispersal of Africans was the transatlantic slave trade. Some fifteen to twenty million Africans were shipped regularly across the Atlantic over a period of about four hundred years, from the seventeenth to twentieth centuries, to work as slaves in the Americas, the Antilles, and, to a lesser extent, in Europe.[13] The majority of black women in the African diaspora are descended from African women brought to the New World as slaves. Black women from Africa became a key factor in the production of capital because of their capacity to reproduce slave labor.[14]

Some of the ideas of African feminism developed on the continent no doubt had relevance in the New World. Though parallel autonomy (or any autonomy for that matter) was impossible to achieve under slavery, self-reliance was a closely related concept and became a necessary ideology. African ideas stressing male-female cooperation, as well as belief in the totality of male and female beings, no doubt became enhanced under conditions of slavery, which threatened survival and fragmented social life.

African feminism in the New World, as in Africa, also took on activist dimensions, involving protests against the system of slavery, which exploited female slave labor in production and reproduction and abused female sexuality and biology. African women were involved in several acts of resistance to slavery and in revolts, both in the Caribbean and in the United States.[15]

Female personalities like Harriet Tubman and Sojourner Truth became legends because of their role in the struggle against slavery in the United States. In the Caribbean, among the Maroons of Jamaica, for example, the myth of Nanny as an invincible warrior fighting against slavery became an ideal and inspiration and a cornerstone of Maroon feminism.[16] Other forms of resistance involving subtle and subversive acts of rebellion like sexual abstinence, abortion, and infanticide, were not uncommon in the United States.[17] These acts of protest, resistance, and rebellion were to continue through the Civil War and into the modern civil rights movements, in which black women played an important part in the struggle against racism.[18]

Colonialism

Colonial penetration in Africa in the nineteenth and twentieth centuries produced the most profound changes in the lives of the African woman on the continent and disrupted the traditional system of production. It also reinforced existing systems of social inequality and introduced oppressive forms of social stratification, including racial segregation, through the machinery of the state. Other devastating effects of colonial penetration included the disintegration of self-provisioning agricultural systems, through the introduction of commercial agriculture and exploitative wage employment.

Long before European colonial penetration, Sub-Saharan Africa came under the influence of patriarchal Islam, but its societies never became as intensely orthodox as those in North Africa. Except among groups like the Hausa of Nigeria and the Swahili-speaking Muslims of Kenya, Islam never became entrenched as a way of life. In fact, the effects of colonial administration have been of greater significance on African societies. The impact of Islam on the majority of African women in the diaspora has been minimal.

Through colonization by European powers such as Britain, France, Italy, Germany, Belgium, and Portugal, Africa was brought into the world economic system as a major target for exploitation. Surplus was drawn from its great reservoir of natural resources in the form of raw materials, food crops, mineral resources, and cheap labor. The colonial machinery ensured a conducive political climate for the exploitation of the continent through a system of taxation, coercion, and military administration.[19]

The process of incorporation involved releasing male labor from agricultural and other subsistence activities, often by direct coercion in the form of forced labor. This produced a supply of cheap male labor which was often migratory and seasonal. The household continued to support the wage-earning male through unpaid family labor, creating a differential process of incorporation for women. Women served primarily as a labor reserve and as a mainstay for the subsistence and reproductive sectors.[20] If and when necessary, they became marginally proletarianized as cheap sources of labor.[21]

Colonialism was also established in the Caribbean with exploitative and oppressive consequences. In post–Civil War United States, many of the features of institutional racism have been viewed as forms of "internal colonialism." In all of these processes the productive and reproductive labor of women of African descent served to bolster capital accumulation by economically dominant white men and women.

Independence and Neocolonialism

In Africa, independence did not bring about significant changes in the social, sexual, and racial inequalities perpetuated by colonialism mainly because many of the economic structures of colonialism remained intact and, in some cases, became even more exploitative. Contemporary Africa is marred by its dependency on the West and its adoption of exploitative models of development. Tensions are apparent not only in political ideology but also in the conflict between traditional African views of women's roles and European sexism. The minimal participation of African women in contemporary political institutions, as opposed to their complementary participation in traditional political institutions, is only one of the numerous examples of the continuing cultural domination of the West.[22]

Postindependence processes have thrown into sharp focus the unity of the world economic system, characterized by the development of some countries and some groups at the expense of others. It also reveals the tenacity of imperialism, through which a subjugated people remain in an economically subjugated position, perennially linked to their former, alien rulers.[23]

The present inequalities in the global division of labor which continue to favor countries less dependent on primary products as their major resource are aspects of imperialism. The African economy has functioned, essentially, to develop countries outside of Africa and to make profits, primarily, for people with white skins; racism remains an important aspect of this subjugation. Bernard Magubane writes, "the ideology of racism . . . became a permanent stimulus for the ordering of unequal and exploitative relations of production along 'racial lines' and further demanded justification of these relations."[24]

There are several examples of African women's resistance to the colonial system which, like slavery, exploited both their productive and reproductive labor. The Women's War of 1929 in Nigeria is probably the best known. This was a direct form of resistance against the colonial system of taxation and an indirect protest against the differential integration of women into the world economic system. The British plan to tax women as well as men provoked Ibo women to attack a British colonial station.[25]

Apartheid

African women have also been very active in the struggle against the racial ideology, policy, and practice of apartheid in South Africa. Apartheid poignantly illustrates the most extreme form of monopolistic accumulation of wealth by whites at the expense of blacks, with the black woman as the worst victim. The subjugation of the black woman, who is considered a minor by law in South Africa, is the foundation of the apartheid system. Forced to live in reserves, or "homelands," the black woman reproduces the cheap black labor force. She also cares for the old and sick, as well as the economic rejects who are discarded into the homelands when they cease to be productive.

The majority of African women who work for wages do so as agricultural laborers, domestic servants, and menial industrial workers, in a desperate attempt to save their families from starvation. African families are systematically separated, harassed, and forcibly moved into designated settlements. The destruction of the African family is only one aspect of the systematic attempt to eliminate the black race in South Africa. Other activities in this regard include forced settlement in non-arable homelands, man-made malnutrition, aggressive family-planning policies for blacks, and outright murders.

Under the system of apartheid, African men, women, and children in South Africa and Namibia are constantly subjected to oppression, imprisonment, tortures, and killings if they oppose apartheid, the most diabolical political system ever fashioned by the human mind.[26]

Liberation from colonialism and racism has been an equally important dimension of African feminism on the continent, as well as in the diaspora. For example, the liberation battles of Mozambique, Angola, Guinea-Bissau, and Zimbabwe, as well as the civil rights battles in the United States and the Caribbean, were fought by both men and women.

Chronic Underdevelopment

One of the consequences of the disintegration of the self-provisioning agricultural system in Africa has been rapid urbanization. The urbanization process in Africa contains all the features of asymmetrical development characteristic of Third World countries with a colonial history.[27] Inequalities based on race, class, and sex are most marked in urban areas.

High rates of rural and urban migration, chronic unemployment, and the proliferation of shanty towns and extreme poverty characterize large sections of cities in the developing world and in Third World sections of the United States. A large number of the urban poor, particularly migrants and women, eke out a living in the informal labor market as service workers, laborers, artisans, prostitutes, petty traders, and unskilled factory workers. By all indications, the condition of the urban poor in many Third World countries is worsening, and women, particularly black women, are among the most vulnerable victims of poverty, a persistent feature of chronic underdevelopment.

In Africa, urbanization far exceeds the rate of industrialization, which is often capital-intensive, foreign-owned, and oriented toward production for an external market, rather than an internal one. Because industrialization was inspired, primarily, by colonization, the dominant pattern has been the establishment of mines, plantations, and export-oriented industries. Male labor was made cheap and plentiful, but female proletarianization has become effective in a number of situations, such as in the case of male absenteeism as a result of male migration. In Swaziland, for example, where men migrate to South Africa to work in the mines, women constitute 60 percent of the labor force in the sugar plantations and 95 percent in the citrus industries.[28]

The precarious, casual, and seasonal nature of industrial employment applies to both men and women in Africa, as do the low wages paid. However, some agro-industries with monopolies have been known to exploit women further by hiring them at lower wages than men. In the Ivory Coast, for example, women in the sugar industry are paid wages that are 40 percent lower than men's wages.[29]

Significant, and even more ominous, is the tendency of agro-industries to take over the best land for cultivation of cash crops. Intensification of cash-crop production can seriously threaten the ecological health of the society by undermining the quality of the soil. Livestock industries can produce similar effects when their objective is the intensification of production for export. In Botswana, for example, heavy grazing and pressure on the land for the export-oriented livestock industry has undermined the production of the staple crop, sorghum.

Similar, negative trends of urbanization and industrialization are apparent in the African diaspora. In the Caribbean, the use of black women in conversion and export-oriented industries as cheap sources of labor is now becoming a tradition. The same is true of the majority of black women workers in Europe, particularly in England and France. In the United

States, urbanization and industrialization have also had several deleterious effects on the black woman.

In an illustrative study of the United States by Rogers-Rose, migration to the urban areas continues to keep the majority of black women in poverty without the benefit of access to rural land. Furthermore, the urban environment imposes a structure that tends to separate wives from their husbands. The poorer the family, the more likely it is to be headed by a woman, and the number of children living with both parents has been drastically declining since 1940. The welfare system fosters this by supporting dependent children, rather than struggling families.[30] What we learn from this is that the urbanization process in the United States is reproducing cheap black labor at the lowest possible cost.

RESISTANCE AND THE CREATION OF SURVIVAL IMPERATIVES

As a reaction to conditions and processes of economic marginalization and racial oppression, African women developed various means of resistance and survival, despite the fact that these processes sometimes created conditions that were unconducive to traditional family life. Men were often rendered peripheral to the family and household unit through male migration, unemployment, imprisonment, and wars. In developing coping mechanisms for these disruptive conditions, African women added other dimensions to their feminism. Female-headed households developed as a survival mechanism among black women not only in Africa but also in the diaspora, as this form of social organization was adaptive to precarious and subsistent economic and military situations.[31] In some instances also, notably in the English-speaking Caribbean, the female-headed household became an important aspect of resistance to processes that threatened the survival of the black race, and it provided a base for the development of female independence and autonomy.

South Africa, through its policy of apartheid, provides the most extreme example of making adult males peripheral to black family life. Through a pass system, migration to urban areas is strictly controlled. Men who migrate to work in the mines and in other industrial complexes often are not permitted to bring their families with them. Women, children, and the old are left behind in the homelands. Consequently, long periods of separation of family members inevitably leads to the breakdown of the family. The imposition of the Bantustans can be seen as reinforcing this destructive pattern. One study by Sibisi that has dealt specifically with the effect of male migration on black women in South Africa poignantly illustrates the difficult adjustment of black women to male absenteeism.[32]

Male peripherality in the Caribbean and the United States, as in African societies undergoing industrialization, is also the result of economic marginalization and imposed poverty. The controversial theory of the black matriarchy in the United States is increasingly being viewed as a form of imposed male peripherality. Because of the high rates of unemployment among black males in the United States, black women, the majority of whom are poor, often lack the economic support which society deems to be the responsibility of males.

Black women in the New World have used the strong bonds among female kin,[33] in addition to an ideology of self-reliance, to reinforce their survival strategies. In Africa, as well as in the diaspora, black women have consistently had to ensure not only their economic, political, and social survival but their physical survival as well. Because of poverty, racial and sexual discrimination, and a generally low status in society, most black women are constantly exposed to health hazards. As a result, black women generally have a lower life expectancy than white women. Black women also suffer child loss more frequently than do white women. In Africa, the mean infant mortality rate is 147 per thousand live births. In the United States and the Caribbean, there is a higher mortality rate for black infants than for white infants. Nevertheless, black women have been the targets of aggressive population control activities worldwide. Black women are also among Third World women used in experiments with new contraceptives and dangerous drugs, and they lose more children through marasmus, an often fatal disease related to infant formula feeding.[34]

The work patterns of the majority of black women usually

involve long hours of strenuous physical labor; often, they work without receiving adequate nutrition, particularly in the rural areas. The majority of black working women in the United States perform heavy physical tasks in the lower ranks of industry and as domestics.[35] The remunerative and nonremunerative aspect of women's work has been a dominant paradigm in feminist analyses. For the black woman, the framework of analysis also should seek to demonstrate the link between women's work and their health, nutrition, and well-being.

In order to ensure their physical survival, black women have had to develop survival imperatives, one of which is the provision of health care. During slavery black women performed healing roles, including midwifery. This is also true in Africa, the Caribbean, and South America, where women traditionally provide primary health-care services and deliver babies. Also during slavery, infectious diseases and gynecological problems due to biological and sexual abuse were prevalent, and black women had to rely on a number of home remedies for survival. Some of this knowledge, particularly of the value of medicinal herbs, was derived from Africa.[36]

The struggle against modern forms of oppression, economic hardship, illness, and unethical marketing practices adds new dimensions to the configuration of African feminism, which is resulting in increasing political awareness, grass-roots organizing, and political action at the national and international levels. One important aspect of African feminism, which is both an aspect of the coping with inimical historical processes, as well as a feature of African societies, is the overlap, rather than the dichotomy, between the public and private spheres. Sudarkasa has argued that in precapitalist societies in West Africa this dichotomy was not marked nor did it correspond to masculine and feminine domains,[37] as most Western feminist theories have suggested.[38]

It can be argued also that in societies where survival is critical, as in many black societies, the exigencies of survival would militate against dichotomies between the private and public spheres. In the United States, for instance, men were depicted in slave narratives as performing roles of cooking, serving, and child rearing. As Perkins points out, the disenfranchisement and oppression of all blacks during slavery left little room for male chauvinism.[39] For the Caribbean, a study by Mathurin has observed that during slavery, men and women were equal both in production outside the household context and also "under the whip."[40]

In recent times, some neo-Marxist interpretations of female subordination have shown the dichotomy between the private and public domains to be only a superficial one in capitalist societies when, in fact, the public sphere maintains powerful organic links with the private sphere as an important feature of the exploitative relations of production.[41]

For the black woman, the global processes of capital accumulation ensure that she is unpaid for her labor in the reproductive, private domain and is paid very cheaply in the productive, public domain. To survive and to ensure the survival of her family, she *must* operate in both domains. Racism ensures that she *does* operate in both domains under the most exploitative and oppressive conditions. For the black woman, then, these powerful, organic links become even more exploitative.

CONCLUSION:
TOWARD HUMANISTIC FEMINISM

For the majority of black women poverty is a way of life. For the majority of black women also racism has been the most important obstacle in the acquisition of the basic needs for survival. Through the manipulation of racism the world economic institutions have produced a situation which negatively affects black people, particularly black women. Various forms of domination have resulted in a situation in which black women reproduce and maintain a steady supply of cheap labor and become available as cheap sources of labor themselves. Poor black women in Africa and from Africa not only reproduce the labor force for free but reproduce a labor force that is significantly and qualitatively different from the mainstream labor force in economic and political terms.

In structural terms black women and black men under conditions of domination, economic exploitation, and racial oppression share a similar position of subordination in relation to the dominant group. What we have, then, is not a simple issue of sex or class differences but a situation which, because of the racial factor, is castelike in character on both a national and global scale.

Within the present unequal socioeconomic structure between and within nations, a campaign for sexual equality without class equality would benefit women in more privileged classes. This is particularly true of white women of these classes in Western societies, who already raise, nurture, and comfort the white male oppressor and share with him a bond of privilege.

The struggle for class equality is impossible without racial equality, since the ideology of racism, though often ignored in class analyses, has been a very potent and expedient method for maintaining class inequality. Even when changes seem apparent and inevitable, the ideology of racism can rebound with tenacity to maintain the unequal character and global imbalance in the world economic system.

Many questions remain unanswered in current theoretical approaches in feminist studies when the racial factor is included. For instance, much has been written about the reproductive role of women as a common denominator of their oppression, but not enough analysis has been made of the vastly different contexts of reproduction for different groups of women. Among important research questions to be asked are the following:

1. What are the structural relationships of social and racial groups to the reproduction of the labor force? How do these produce and reinforce social inequality, discrimination, exploitation, and the oppression of one group by another?
2. How is the reproduction of the labor force qualitatively different in different social contexts? Is the reproduction of Prince William by Princess Di in a posh medical suite, for example, the same as the reproduction of Mary by Jane in the black ghetto? Or of Fatu by Geneba in a Freetown slum or of Buntu by Martha in Soweto? How are these linked?
3. What roles have women in structurally subordinate racial groups played, and what roles do they continue to play in the

reproduction of structurally dominant racial groups when they serve as childminders, wet-nurses, domestics, and emotional shock absorbers and tension relievers?

4. How are the profits generated from male labor expropriated in various racial and social groups, and what role do economically dominant women play in its expropriation?

5. If and when women from racially dominant groups become politically powerful, will the exercise of their power be qualitatively different from that wielded by racially dominant men? What form will the new, reinforced partnership between economically dominant white men and women take?

6. Using the family as the unit of analysis, might not the additional material gains of some white women, in terms of total family income, create even greater marginalization of black families within the current racial and unequal distribution in the world economic system?

To summarize, one can say that because of the need for male-female complementarity in ensuring the totality of human existence within a balanced ecosystem, and because of the negative and destructive effects of historical processes and racism on Africa and its people, values stressing human totality, parallel autonomy, cooperation, self-reliance, adaptation, survival, and liberation have developed as important aspects of African feminism. These are important concepts in developing a framework for the study of women in Africa and in the diaspora.

To some extent, elements of African feminism have a reality sui generis in the diaspora. Nevertheless, the cultural roots of African feminism have survived and become important in the ensuing development of the global division of labor and its concomitant unequal class, racial, and sexual manifestations. From a worldwide perspective, the oppression of the black woman is complex, structural, and sexual. For the majority of black women, liberation from sexual oppression has always been fused with liberation from other forms of oppression, such as racial and class oppression, as well as liberation from slavery, colonialism, neocolonialism, and imperialism. African feminism, therefore, has a practical aspect linked to social action and change.

In my introduction to *The Black Woman Cross-Culturally,* I

concluded that the African woman was the original feminist. I also indicated that the continent of Africa as the birthplace of human life must also be the birthplace of human struggles. One can optimistically conclude, then, having examined the evolution and constitution of African feminism within a world perspective, that by virtue of its inclusive and humanistic character, the emergence of African feminism no doubt signals a major step in the intellectual and pragmatic struggle for societies devoid of class, caste, racial, and gender biases.

NOTES

This paper continues the discussions initiated in my introduction and overview to the pioneering anthology on the black woman in Africa, the United States, the Caribbean, and South America. Some of the ideas presented there have been repeated for emphasis. See Filomina Chioma Steady, ed., *The Black Woman Cross-Culturally* (Cambridge: Schenkman Publishing Company, 1981).

1. Numerous studies have demonstrated this. A critique of the promotion of racism and sexism through research is Inez Reid, "Science, Politics and Race," *Signs* 2 (Winter 1975): 397–422.

2. Some of these ideas and principles have been adopted by the Association of African Women for Research and Development (AAWORD), of which I am a founding member. See "The Experience of the Association of African Women for Research and Development," *Development Dialogue*, 1982: 1–2, 101–13.

3. Steady, "The Black Woman Cross-Culturally: An Overview," in Steady, *The Black Woman Cross-Culturally.*

4. References from oral and written histories, ethnographies, biographies, and African literature are too numerous to mention. For an understanding of the general philosophical tenets of African societies, see John S. Mbiti, *African Religions and Philosophy* (New York: Anchor Books, 1970.)

5. See *Women in Food Production, Food Handling and Nutrition: With Special Emphasis on Africa* (New York: United Nations, Protein Advisory Group, 1977).

6. A. R. Radcliffe-Brown and D. Forde, eds., *African Systems of Kinship and Marriage* (London: Oxford University Press, 1950).

7. See, for example, Harriet Sibisi, "The positions of a Zulu married woman in relation to her ancestors and to her natal family" (Mimeographed paper, 1975).

8. See, for example, Jean Borgatti, "Songs of Ritual License from Midwestern Nigeria," *Alcheringa,* n.s. 2 (1976): 66–71.

9. Filomina C. Steady, "The Social Position of Women: Selected West

African Societies" (Unpublished B. Litt. thesis, Oxford University, 1968).

10. Carol P. Hoffer, "Mende and Sherbro Women in High Office," *Canadian Journal of African Studies* 6, no. 2 (1972): 151–64.

11. Harriet Ngubane, *Body and Mind in Zulu Medicine* (London: Academic Press, 1977).

12. This is now a firmly established, central, and pertinent explanation and demonstration of global imbalance and inequality. The theoretical leadership for this position has been provided mainly by Third World scholars such as Walter Rodney, Samir Amin, among others for Africa, and Andre Gunder Frank for Latin America.

13. For a general history of the slave trade, see Philip Curtin, *The Transatlantic Slave Trade* (Madison: Wisconsin University Press, 1969).

14. For a comprehensive study linking slavery with capitalism see Eric Williams, *Capitalism and Slavery* (New York: Capricorn Books, 1944; reprint, Chapel Hill: University of North Carolina Press, reprinted 1966).

15. See, for example, Lucille Mathurin, *The Rebel Woman in the West Indies During Slavery* (Kingston, Jamaica: African Caribbean Publications, 1975).

16. A. Tuelon, "Nanny-Maroon Chieftainers," *Caribbean Quarterly* 19 (1973): 20–27; E. K. Braithwaite, *Wars of Respect: Nanny and Sam Sharp* (Kingston, Jamaica: Agency for Public Information, 1977); and Kenneth Bilby and Filomina Chioma Steady, "Black Women and Survival: A Maroon Case," in Steady, *The Black Woman Cross-Culturally.*

17. Darlene C. Hine and Kate Wittenstein, "Female Slave Resistance: The Economics of Sex," in Steady, *The Black Woman Cross-Culturally.*

18. Michelle Wallace, *Black Macho and the Myth of the Superwoman* (New York: Dial Press, 1979).

19. Walter Rodney, *How Europe Underdeveloped Africa* (Washington, D.C.: Howard University Press, 1974).

20. Marie-Angelique Savanne, "L'Emploi des femmes dans une perspective de changements sociaux et de liberation des femmes: Le cas de L'Afrique," *IFDA Dossier* 25 (September/October, 1981).

21. Filomina Chioma Steady, "African Women, Industrialization, and Another Development: A Global Perspective," *Development Dialogue: A Journal of International Development,* 1982, 1–2.

22. See, for example, Kamene Okonjo, "Women's Political Participation in Nigeria," in Steady, *The Black Woman Cross-Culturally.*

23. See, for example, Samir Amin, *Neocolonialism in West Africa* (New York: Pathfinder Press, 1976).

24. Bernard Magubane, *The Political Economy of Race and Class in South Africa* (New York: Monthly Review Press, 1979).

25. See Caroline Ifeka-Moller, "Female Militancy and the Colonial Revolt: The Women's War of 1929, Eastern Nigeria," in *Perceiving Women,* ed. Shirley Ardener (London: Malaby Press, 1975).

26. Studies and reports documenting the effects of apartheid on African women and the struggle of African women against apartheid are quite numerous, and only a few examples are offered here: Elizabeth Thaele Rivkin, "The Black Woman in South Africa," in Steady, *The Black Woman Cross-Culturally;* Hilda Bernstein, *For Their Triumphs and for Their Tears* (London: International Defense and Aid Fund, 1975); United Nations, *The Effects of Apartheid on the Status of Women in Southern Africa* (World Conference on the United Nations Decade for Women, 1980); and United Nations, *The Struggle of African Women Against Apartheid* (World Conference on the United Nations Decade for Women, 1980).

27. See Filomina Chioma Steady, "Urban Malnutrition in West Africa: A Consequence of Abnormal Urbanization and Underdevelopment," in *Towards a Political Economy of Urbanization in Developing Countries,* ed. Helen Safa (New Delhi: Oxford University Press, 1982).

28. Patricia McFadden, "Female Employment in Agro Industries in Swaziland" (Paper presented at the Dag Hammarskjöld Foundation [AAWORD] Seminar, *Another Development with Women,* Dakar, June 1982).

29. Aminata Traore, "Agro-business and Female Employment in the Ivory Coast (Paper presented at the AAWORD conference on *Women and Rural Development,* Algiers, September 1982).

30. La Frances Rodgers-Rose, "Some Demographic Characteristics of the Black Woman," in La Frances Rodgers-Rose, ed., *The Black Woman* (Beverly Hills, Calif.: Sage Publications, 1980), 40.

31. See, for example, Edith Clark, *My Mother Who Fathered Me* (London: George Allen and Unwin, 1957); Fred Strodbeck, "The Poverty-Dependency Syndrome of the ADC Female-Based Negro Family," *American Journal of Orthopsychiatry* 34 (March 1964): 216–17; and Bilby and Steady, "Black Women and Survival," in Steady, *The Black Woman Cross-Culturally.*

32. Harriet Sibisi, "How African Women Cope with Migrant Labor in South Africa," *Signs,* vol. 3, no. 1 (1977).

33. Carol Stack, *All Our Kin* (New York: Harper and Row, 1974).

34. Filomina Chioma Steady, "Infant Feeding in Developing Countries," *Journal of Tropical Pediatrics,* vol. 27, no. 4 (August 1981).

35. See Jean Noble, Chapter 4 in *Beautiful Also, Are the Souls of My Black Sisters* (Englewood Cliffs, N.J.: Prentice-Hall, 1978); and La Frances Rodgers-Rose, *The Black Woman.*

36. Todd Savitt, *Medicine and Slavery: The Diseases and Health Care of Blacks in Ante-Bellum Virginia* (Urbana: University of Illinois Press, 1978).

37. Niara Sudarkasa, "Female Employment and Family Organization in West Africa," in Steady, *The Black Woman Cross-Culturally.*

38. This is a position that received one of the earliest theoretical formulations, in *Woman, Culture and Society,* ed. Michelle Rosaldo and Louis Lamphere (Stanford: Stanford University Press, 1974).

39. Linda Perkins, "Black Women and Racial 'Uplift' Prior to Emancipation," in Steady, *The Black Woman Cross-Culturally.*
40. Mathurin, *The Rebel Woman.*
41. See Claude Meillassoux, "From Production to Reproduction: A Marxist Approach to Economic Anthropology," *Economy and Society* (1975); Zillah Eisenstein, ed., *Capitalist Patriarchy and the Case for Socialist Feminism* (New York: Monthly Review Press, 1979); Special Issue: "Development and the Sexual Division of Labor," *Signs,* vol. 7, no. 2 (1981).

The "Status of Women" in Indigenous African Societies

Niara Sudarkasa

INTRODUCTION

Long before the women's movement ushered in an era of renewed concern with the "status of women" in various societies and cultures, a number of writers had addressed the question of the "status of women" in various African societies.[1] Some writers characterized women in African societies as "jural minors" for most of their lives, falling under the guardianship first of their fathers and then their husbands. Other writers stressed the independence of African women, noting their control over their own lives and resources.

From my own readings on Africa and my research among the Yoruba in Nigeria and other parts of West Africa, it appears that except for the highly Islamized societies in Sub-Saharan Africa, in this part of the world more than any other, in precolonial times women were conspicuous in high places. They were queen-mothers; queen-sisters; princesses; chiefs; and holders of other offices in towns and villages; occasional warriors; and, in one well known case, that of the Lovedu, the supreme monarch. Furthermore, it was almost invariably the case that African women were conspicuous in the economic life of their societies, being involved in farming, trade, or craft production.

The purviews of female and male in African societies were often described as separate and complementary.[2] Yet, whenever most writers compared the lot of women and men in Africa, they ascribed to men a better situation, a higher status. Women were depicted as saddled with home and domesticity; men were

25

portrayed as enjoying the exhilaration of life in the outside world. For me, the pieces of the portrait did not ring true. Not only was there an obvious distortion of the ethnographic reality—women were outside the home as well as in it—but there was also something inappropriate about the notion that women and men were everywhere related to each other in a hierarchical fashion, as was implied in the most common usage of the concept of status of women.

The *status* of women is often used simultaneously in the two conceptual meanings that it has in social science. On the one hand, the term is used in Ralph Linton's sense to mean the collection of rights and duties that attach to particular positions. According to this usage, *status,* which refers to a particular position itself, contrasts with *role,* which refers to the behavior appropriate to a given status.[3] On the other hand, the concept of the status of women is also used to refer to the placement of females relative to males in a dual-level hierarchy. In this sense, the term *status* connotes stratification and invites comparison with other systems of stratification. It was this notion of sexual stratification that seemed inappropriate for describing the relationships between females and males in most of the African societies I had studied.

Martin K. Whyte concludes his cross-cultural survey, *The Status of Women in Preindustrial Societies,* with a similar observation. After discussing the status of women in the hierarchical sense used above, Whyte's first major finding is that there is a general absence of covariation among the different indicators of status in this hierarchical usage. He notes that one cannot assume "that a favorable position for women in any particular area of social life will be related to favorable positions in other areas." Similarly, there is no best indicator or key variable that will yield an overall assessment of the status of women relative to men.[4]

More to the point of the present argument is Whyte's observation that this lack of covariation in the indicators of the status of women signals a difference between this area and other areas where stratification is a known feature of the social structure. "This lack of association between different measures of the role and status of women relative to men still constitutes something of a puzzle. . . . In the study of stratification we ordinarily expect indicators of status at the individual level to be positively, although not perfectly, associated with one another." Drawing on Simone de Beauvoir's distinction between the position of women and that of oppressed national or racial groups, Whyte concludes that "powerful factors" in all preindustrial societies lead to the perception by females and males that women's statuses differ from those of men but in a manner that does not imply the hierarchical relationship characteristic of those linking occupational and ethnic groups. Going further, Whyte states that "the lack of association between different aspects of the role and status of women relative to men is due largely to the fact that women as a group [in preindustrial societies] are fundamentally different from status groups and classes."[5]

This observation by Whyte seems to make sense of the data from most African societies. Although his cross-cultural study dispels a number of treasured notions about "*the* status of women," it points to a critical research problem that should be pursued, namely, the problem of determining the conditions under which women's relationship to men *does* take on the characteristics of a hierarchical relationship. I should hasten to point out that conceptually, this is a *different* problem from that which seeks to ascertain when an egalitarian relationship between the sexes gives way to a subordinate-superordinate relationship. The very concept of an egalitarian relationship between women and men implies that the female and male are unitary categories that are measured, or "sized-up," one against the other in the societies described. Here, I will attempt to show that there are societies for which such a conceptualization does not accurately reflect the social and ideological reality of the peoples concerned. The data gathered from some African societies suggest a reason for this. As I will attempt to demonstrate, female and male are not so much statuses, in Linton's sense, as they are clusters of statuses for which gender is only one of the defining characteristics. Women and men might be hierarchically related to each other in one or more of their reciprocal statuses, but not in others. Because contradiction, as much as congruence, characterized the status-clusters termed female and male, many African societies did not or could not consistently stratify the categories one against the other, but, rather, codified the ambiguities.

The argument put forth in this article suggests that Engels and a number of his adherents may have missed the mark in arguing that private property and production for exchange served to lower the status of women. It also suggests that Karen Sacks's reformulation of Engels, which, in any case, rests on a controversial interpretation of the African data, also misses the mark by arguing that the critical, or key, variable in the subordination of women in class societies was their confinement to production within the domestic sphere and their exclusion from "social production for exchange."[6] I am suggesting here that various conditions, including most probably the development of private property and the market or exchange economy, *created conditions where female and male became increasingly defined as unitary statuses that were hierarchically related to one another.* Such conditions appear to have been absent in various precolonial African societies and possibly in other parts of the world as well.[7]

In recent years, the postulation of separate, nonhierarchically related—and, therefore, complementary—domains for women and men has been disputed by anthropologists who argued that women occupied the "domestic domain" and men the "public domain" and that, because power and authority were vested in the public domain, women had *de facto* lower status than men.[8] It has always seemed to me that in many African societies a more appropriate conception (and by that I mean one that makes sense of more of the realities of those societies) was to recognize two domains, one occupied by men and another by women—both of which were internally ordered in a hierarchical fashion and both of which provided personnel for domestic and extradomestic (or public) activities. I have already argued in another article that there was considerable overlap between the public and domestic domains in preindustrial African societies.[9]

In the remainder of this paper, I will examine the roles of women in families and descent groups, in the economy, and in the political process in West Africa. Potentially nonhierarchical models of relationships between females and males are indicated and contrasted with ones that are hierarchical. The data are used from stateless societies, such as the Ibo and Tallensi, and from preindustrial state societies, such as the Asante (Ashanti), Nupe, and Yoruba.

Before turning to the data, note that there is no question that status, in the hierarchical sense, attaches to sex (or gender) in contemporary Africa. Ester Boserup is the best known exponent of the view that the forces of modernization and development have denied African women equal access to formal education and have undermined their contribution to the political and economic arenas of their countries.[10] Annie M.D. Lebeuf was one of the first writers to make this point and was the one who demonstrated it most conclusively for the political sphere.[11] Other scholars have taken up and elaborated the same theme. The fact of the present-day linkage between gender and stratification in West Africa and elsewhere on the continent and the realization that most of the studies from which we have to take our data were carried out *after* the onset of the colonial period, should be borne in mind as the following discussion unfolds.[12]

WOMEN IN AFRICAN KIN GROUPS

In West Africa, as in most parts of the continent, the three basic kin groups to which females and males belong are (1) corporate unilineal descent groups, which we term lineages; (2) domiciled extended families made up of certain lineage members and their spouses and dependent children; and (3) conjugally based family units that are subdivisions of the extended family and within which procreation and primary responsibilities for socialization rest.[13] Within their lineages, African women have rights and responsibilities toward their kinsmen and kinswomen that are independent of males. As far as their responsibilities are concerned, female members of the lineage are expected to meet certain obligations in the same way that males are. For example, women offer material assistance to their sisters and brothers; they also do their part (that is, they make the appropriate financial or material outlay) at the time of important rites of passage such as naming ceremonies, marriages, and funerals. Within patrilineages, women, as father's sisters, sisters, and daughters, generally do not hold formal leadership positions—although they do take part in most discussions of lineage affairs—and the more advanced in age they are, the more influence they wield. As mothers, sisters, and daughters within the matrilineages, some women hold leadership positions and exercise authority equivalent to that of men.[14]

In both patrilineages and matrilineages, interpersonal relations on a daily basis tend to be regulated by seniority as determined by order of birth rather than by gender. Hence, senior sisters outrank junior brothers. Where males prostrate before their elders, they do so for females, as well as males.

In the extended family, women occupy roles defined by consanguinity, as well as conjugality. They are mothers and daughters, as well as wives and cowives. The position of "wife" refers not only to the conjugal relationship to a husband, but also to the affinal (or in-law) relationship to all members—female as well as male—in the husband's compound and lineage. (Among the Yoruba, for example, female members of a lineage refer to their brother's wives as their own "wives," a formulation which signals that certain reciprocal responsibilities and behavior are entailed in the relationship of the women to each other.)

If there is one thing that is conspicuous in discussions of "the status of women" in Africa (and elsewhere in the world), it is the tendency to assess that status only in relation to the conjugal roles of wife or cowife. Interestingly, in Whyte's cross-cultural study of the status of women in ninety-three societies, of the twenty-seven indicators of status as related to gender and the family, twenty (74 percent) of the variables had to do specifically with behavior or rights within or related to the conjugal (marital) relationship. The focus on the conjugal roles of women to the near exclusion of analyses of their functioning in consanguineal roles derives, as I have tried to show elsewhere, from the obsession of Western scholars with analyses of the nuclear family and the operation of the principle of conjugality in determining kin relations. In other words, the emphasis derives from an attempt to analyze kinship in other societies from the viewpoint of and with paradigms appropriate to Western kin groups.[15] African *extended* families, which are the normal coresidential form of family in indigenous precolonial African societies, are *built around* consanguineal relationships; failure to recognize this has led to misrepresentation of many aspects of African kinship. One consequence of the focus on conjugal families and the concern with breaking down polygynous families into "constituent nuclear families" is the distortion of an understanding of the roles of women as wives, cowives, and mothers.[16]

Women as *wives* generally exhibit overt signals of deference to their husbands in patrilineal African societies. In matrilineal societies, the patterns may not be as pronounced, but wives still defer to their husbands. In other kinship roles, especially those of mother and senior consanguineal kinswoman, women are the recipients of deference and the wielders of power and authority.

Western students of African societies have not only focused unduly on the husband-wife relationship in describing African kinship, they have also sought to define that conjugal relationship in terms of parameters found in Western societies. This has led to a misrepresentation of the essence and implications of what is generally called "woman-to-woman" marriage. This complex institution cannot be described at length here, but I would make the following observations: First, the institution of "woman marriage" signifies most of all that gender is not the sole basis for recruitment to the "husband" role in Africa; hence, the authority that attaches to that role is not gender-specific. Second, the institution must be understood in the context of the meaning of concepts of husband and wife in African societies, not in Western societies. Third, in African societies, the term *wife* has two basic referents: female married to a given male (or female) and female married into a given compound or lineage. Thus, for example, among the Yoruba, a husband refers to his spouse as "wife"; a woman refers to her cowife as "wife" or "mate," and as noted earlier, female, as well as male, members of the lineage refer to the in-marrying spouses as their "wives." The term *husband* refers specifically to a woman's spouse but also generally to the males (and females) in her husband's lineage. Again, among the Yoruba, a woman refers to her own spouse, and in certain contexts, to his lineage members, including her own children, as "husband."

Given these usages, it is important to recognize that the terms *husband* and *wife* connote certain clusters of affinal relations, and in woman marriage the principles concerned emphasize certain *jural* relations. (They do not, as all writers point out, imply a sexual component to the relationship as in heterosexual conjugal unions.)

If the concept of conjugal relations in Africa were not

circumscribed to those common in the West, it would be appreciated that the unifying factor in the various kinds of woman-to-woman marriage is that everywhere it serves a procreative function, either on behalf of the female husband herself, or on behalf of her male spouse or male kinsmen. Because marriage is the institution and the idiom through which procreation is legitimated in Africa, it must be entered into by women (as by men) who want to acquire rights over a woman's childbearing capacity.[17] The existence of woman-to-woman marriage in Africa is consistent with a general deemphasis on gender and an emphasis on seniority and personal standing (usually but not always determined by wealth) in recruitment to positions of authority.

This brief discussion of African families and kin groups is intended to suggest that male gender predictably calls forth deferential behavior only within the conjugal relationship. The case of woman-to-woman marriage demonstrates, however, that male gender does not exclusively determine entry into the husband role, which is the more authoritative of the two conjugal roles. But even though patterns of deference emphasize subordination of the wife's role, the decision-making process and the control *over resources* within the conjugal relationship in many West African societies, including those of the Yoruba, Ibo, Ashanti, and Nupe, indicate parallel and complementary control by husbands and wives. In the consanguineal aspects of African kinship, as I have indicated, seniority and personal attributes (especially accumulated resources) rather than gender, serve as the primary basis of status in the hierarchical sense.

WOMEN IN THE POLITICAL PROCESS
IN INDIGENOUS AFRICAN SOCIETIES

Any investigation of women in the political process in precolonial Africa should begin with the excellent article by Annie Lebeuf in Denise Paulme's *Women of Tropical Africa*.[18] Here I only want to highlight certain facts that might aid in addressing the question of whether the relationship of females and males within the political domain is most appropriately conceptualized as a hierarchical one.

Africa is noted for the presence of women in very high positions in the formal governmental structure.[19] Africa is also noted for having parallel chieftaincies, one line made up of males, the other of females. One way of interpreting these facts has been to dismiss the female chieftaincies as simply women controlling women (and after all, if women are subordinate anyway, of what significance is it that they have chieftaincies or sodalities among themselves?). The presence of women at the highest levels of indigenous government has been dismissed as an instance of women distinguishing themselves individually by entering the "public world of men."[20] I would suggest that a formulation that makes an *a priori judgment* that any participation of women in the public sphere represents entry into the world of men simply begs the question. For in West Africa, the "public domain" was not conceptualized as *the world of men*. Rather, the public domain was one in which both sexes were recognized as having important roles to play.[21]

Indeed, the positing of distinct public and domestic domains does not hold true for precolonial West Africa. The distinction is also not very useful for looking at the rest of the continent. As many writers on African political structure have shown, even in states in which monarchs were elevated to statuses "removed from their kin groups," the lineage (and the compound) remained important aspects of political organization in all localities where they existed.[22] Compounds were generally the courts of the first instance and the bases for mobilizing people for public works and public services; lineages were the units through which the land was allocated and were the repository of titles to offices in many African societies. Women held formal leadership roles in matrilineages and were influential in decision-making patrilineages. Their participation in the affairs of their affinal compounds, (within which women in patrilineal societies lived most of their adult lives), was channeled through an organizational structure in which women were most often ranked according to order of marriage into the group.

To answer the question of whether women's participation in the political process should be conceptualized as subordinate to that of men, I would propose that one examine the kind of political decisions and activities in which women were involved and ask from what kind they were excluded. Throughout most of West Africa, women controlled their own worlds. For example, they had trade and craft guilds, and they spoke on matters of taxation and maintenance of public facilities (such as markets, roads, wells, and streams). They also testified on their own behalf in any court or hearing. Thus, in internal political affairs, women were generally consulted and had channels through which they were represented. External affairs were largely in the hands of men, but in any crisis, such as war, women were always involved— minimally as suppliers of rations for troops but in some instances as leaders of armies and as financiers of campaigns.[23]

The question then arises, from what political processes were they excluded? They could not participate in the male secret societies that were important in the political process in some Western African states. They were also excluded from certain councils of chiefs, although this was rare. Much more common was representation on the council by one or more of the women who headed the hierarchy of women chiefs. In all cases, however, it seems that women were consulted on most governmental affairs. Their participation through their spokespersons paralleled the participation of males through theirs. And of course in cases in which the chief rulers were female and male (for example, the queen-mother and monarch-son), the complementarity of the relationship between the sexes was symbolized and codified in the highest offices of the land.

THE INVOLVEMENT OF WOMEN IN PRODUCTION AND DISTRIBUTION IN AFRICAN SOCIETIES

It is well known that African women were farmers, traders, and crafts producers in different parts of the continent. It is equally well documented that their economic roles were at once public and private. Women worked outside the home in order to meet the responsibilities placed upon them in their roles as mothers, wives, sisters, daughters, members of guilds, chiefs, or citizens.[24] In the economic sphere, more than in any other, it is easy to show that women's activities were complementary to those of men and that women producers and traders were not subordinate to men. In most African societies, as elsewhere, the division of labor among sexual lines promoted a reciprocity of effort. If men were farmers, women were food processors and traders. Where women and men were engaged in the same productive activity (such as farming or weaving), they produced different items. Among the Ibo, females and males grew different crops; among the Yoruba, the female and male weavers produced different types of cloth on different types of looms. Where both females and males traded, there was usually a sexual bifurcation along commodity lines. Normally, too, men predominated in long-distance trade, and women were predominant in local markets. I have never heard of an indigenous African society in which differential value was attached to the labor of women and men working in the same line or in which women and men were differentially rewarded for the products of their labor.

In the management and disposal of their incomes, the activities of African women and men also were separate but coordinated. Within the conjugal family unit, women and men had different responsibilities that were met from the proceeds of their separate economic pursuits. A husband might be primarily responsible for the construction and upkeep of the home and the provision of staple foods, while the wife (or more probably the wives) assumed responsibility for nonstaple foods and the daily needs of her children.

> The separate management of "the family purse" definitely appeared to be a response to a situation in which the members of conjugal units had independent obligations to persons outside these groups. However, it was also a way of minimizing the risks involved in the expenditure (of resources) by disbursing [them] among potentially beneficial investment options, as perceived from the vantage point of the different persons concerned.[25]

Implications for Future Research on African/ African-American Women

I have tried to show that a "neutral" complementarity, rather than subordination/superordination, more accurately describes the relationship between certain female and male roles in various pre-colonial African societies. In the process, I have argued that the preconceived notion of a unitary status for female and male, respectively, is probably what led many students of African societies to paint such misleading pictures of *the* status of African women.

The data presented in this brief discussion are only an indication of those that must be considered in any serious research into the issues raised here. I have always been intrigued by what appear to be linguistic clues into the "neutrality" of gender in many African societies. The absence of gender in the pronouns of many African languages and the interchangeability of first names among females and males strike me as possibly related to a societal deemphasis on gender as a designation for behavior. Many other areas of traditional culture, including personal dress and adornment, religious ceremonials, and intragender patterns of comportment, suggest that Africans often deemphasize gender in relation to seniority and other insignia of status.

Only brief mention can be made of the fact that in contemporary Africa, the relationship between women and men has moved decidedly in the direction of a hierarchical one. In understanding the change in the nature of these relationships from the precolonial, preindustrial context to the present, it is important that we not presume the movement from an egalitarian relationship to a nonegalitarian one. Rather, it has been suggested that the domains of women and men in many indigenous African societies should not be conceptualized in terms of ranking at all (which is implied in the concept of egalitarianism because each concept entails its opposite). It is suggested that the changes that occurred with the onset of colonialism (and capitalism, its economic correlate) were ones that created heirarchical relations between the sexes. It is therefore appropriate in the modern context to investigate causes and characteristics of the status of women in Africa.

This effort to recast the study of the statuses and roles of women in indigenous precolonial African societies has important implications for the study of the roles that the descendants of these women came to play in the American context. Over the past two decades, most historians of blacks in America have come to accept the premise that in order to understand that history, one must understand the implications of saying it was "enslaved Africans," rather than "slaves," who came to these shores in chains. This implies that these Africans brought with them their beliefs and values; varying degrees of knowledge of their political, economic, technological, religious, artistic, recreational and familial organization; and codes governing interpersonal behavior between such societal groupings as chiefs and citizenry, old and young, and female and male.

Given this context, to understand the roles that black women came to play in America, it is necessary to understand the tradition of female independence and responsibility within the family and wider kin groups in Africa, and the tradition of female productivity and leadership in the extra-domestic, or public, domain in African societies. It is understood, of course, that the context of slavery did not permit the exact replication of African patterns, but the forms of behavior that did emerge had their roots in those patterns.

A brief reference to black American women's roles in three spheres will suffice to indicate the directions in which research into the linkage with Africa might take. I refer to women's activities as leaders on the plantations and in their communities at later periods; as workers helping to provide economic support for their families; and as key figures in the intergenerational kinship units that formed (and still form) the core of many black families.

Much has been written about the heroism of women such as Harriet Tubman and Sojourner Truth. Precisely because of their extraordinary deeds, they are portrayed as being unique among black women. It would seem, however, that these are but the most famous of the black female leaders whose assumption of their roles came out of a tradition where women were always among the leaders in a community. A reassessment of the roles of the so-called Mammies in the Big House; of the elderly women who looked after children on the plantation while younger people worked in the fields; of women who planned escapes and insurrections; and of female religious leaders should reveal that there was a complementarity and parallelism in the historical roles of male and female leaders among black Americans that bore clear relationship to what existed in Africa.

The roles of black women in the economic sphere have long been remarked upon, but most of the analyses have presumed that these women worked outside the home because of economic necessity, rather than because of choice or tradition. In other words, the presumption of the literature seems to be that where possible, the black woman, like her white counterpart before the era of "women's liberation," would choose the role of housewife and mother over that of working wife and mother.

The present analysis suggests that we should take another look at the phenomenon of black women in the world of work, with a view to examining the continuities that this represents with African traditions wherein women were farmers, craftswomen, and entrepreneurs par excellence. It is noteworthy that in Africa, unlike Europe, women of privileged statuses (such as the kings' or chiefs' wives, daughters, sisters, and mothers) were not removed from the world of work. On the contrary, their rank in society often conferred special access to certain economic activities. For example, among the Yoruba, the kings' wives were the premier long-distance traders among the women, as was remarked upon by some of the first European visitors to Yoruba kingdoms in the nineteenth century. Given these traditions, one might expect, therefore, that middle- or upper-class status would not necessarily incline black women in America to prefer a life of relative leisure to that of the workaday world. In other words, it would not incline middle- or upper-class black women to choose the relative confinement of the domestic domain over the public world of work. What we know about black women entrepreneurs and professionals in the nineteenth and early twentieth centuries suggests that regardless of socioeconomic status, Afro-American women were more likely to be employed outside the home than were their Euro-American counterparts.

Finally, I would suggest that a reexamination of the statuses and roles of women and men in African kin groups can help to unravel the antecedents of a number of patterns of African-American kinship that emerged in the context of slavery and evolved into the forms of family organization we see today. The importance of age and seniority in conferring authority on African females, as well as males, for example, helps to explain the authoritative roles of elderly women, as well as elderly men, in black American families. The African emphasis on consanguinity, as opposed to conjugality, helps to explain much of black American kinship, including, for example, the formation of households around two- or three-generational clusters of "blood relatives" (such as a woman and her adult daughters and their children); the transresidential extended family networks that characterized black family organization in the past and still remain in some areas today; the special obligations for mutual assistance and support that characterized relationships between sisters, regardless of their marital statuses; and the tendency, until recently, for unmarried black women with children to reside with their "blood" relatives, rather than in households of their own.[26]

Much work remains before we can confidently trace the multifaceted connections between African and African-American behavioral patterns, including those concerning the roles and statuses of women and their relationships to the men in their families and communities. The intention of this brief review of some of the possible linkages is to point to areas where research might be fruitfully pursued. I have suggested that many of the activities and attributes that have been taken to be characteristic of black women in America have their roots in Africa. These characteristics—leadership in the community, as well as in the home; prominence in the world of work; independence and pride in womanhood—are usually pointed to as evidence of the strength of black American women. What I have tried to show in this paper is that this strength had its roots in African societies where women were literally expected to "shoulder their own burdens," and where, in many contexts, respect and responsibility, as well as rights and privileges, were accorded without reference to gender.

NOTES

1. M. Perlman and M.P. Moal, in *Women of Tropical Africa,* ed. Denise Paulme, trans. H.M. Wright (Berkeley : University of California Press, 1963), 231–93.
2. Paulme, *Women of Tropical Africa,* Introduction, 1–16.
3. Ralph Linton, *The Study of Man,* (New York: Appleton-Century, 1936), 113–31.
4. Martin K. Whyte, *The Status of Women in Preindustrial Societies* (Princeton, N.J.: Princeton University Press, 1978), 170.
5. Ibid., 176, 179–80.

6. Karen Sacks, "Engels Revisited: Women, the Organization of Production, and Private Property," in *Woman, Culture, and Society,* ed. Michelle Z. Rosaldo and Louise Lamphere (Stanford: Stanford University Press, 1974), 207–22.

7. Here the term *precolonial* refers to the period before the mid- and late-nineteenth century from which European colonization is conventionally dated. Some information concerning African social life in precolonial times is gleaned from contemporaneous written sources, but most information comes from anthropological constructions of "traditional life," using oral history and ethnographic techniques. Due allowance must be made for possible distortions in these ethnographies, but, for the most part, they are all we have to rely on for descriptions of Africa's sociocultural past.

8. Gloria Marshall (Niara Sudarkasa), "In a World of Women: Field Work in a Yoruba Community," in *Women in the Field,* ed. Peggy Golde (Chicago: Aldine Publishing Co., 1970); and Niara Sudarkasa, *Where Women Work: A Study of Yoruba Women in the Market Place and in the Home* (Ann Arbor, Museum of Anthropology, University of Michigan, 1973).

9. Niara Sudarkasa, "Female Employment and Family Organization in West Africa," in *The Black Woman Cross-Culturally,* ed. Filomina C. Steady (Cambridge, Mass.: Schenkman Publishing Co., 1981), 49–64.

10. Ester Boserup, *Women's Role in Economic Development* (London: Allen & Unwin, 1970).

11. Annie M.D. Lebeuf, "The Role of Women in the Political Organization of African Societies," in Paulme, *Women of Tropical Africa.*

12. Marjorie Mbilinyi, "The 'New Woman' and Traditional Norms in Tanzania," *Journal of Modern African Studies* 10 (January 1972): 57–72; Judith Van Allen, "Women in Africa: Modernization Means More Dependency," *Center Magazine* 7 (March 1974): 60–67; Audrey Smock, "The Impact of Modernization on Women's Position in the Family in Ghana," in *Sexual Stratification: A Cross-Cultural View,* ed. Alice Schlegel (New York: Columbia University Press, 1977), 192–214; Niara Sudarkasa, "The Effects of Twentieth-Century Social Change, Especially of Migration, on Women of West Africa," in *Proceedings of the West Africa Conference,* ed. Patricia Paylore and Richard Haney (Tucson: Office of Arid Lands Studies, University of Arizona, 1976), 102–10; and Niara Sudarkasa, "Sex Roles, Education, and Development in Africa," *Anthropology and Education Quarterly* 13 (Fall 1982): 279–89.

13. Niara Sudarkasa, "African and Afro-American Family Organization," in *Anthropology for the Eighties: Introductory Readings,* ed. Johnetta B. Cole (New York: Free Press, 1982), 132–60; and Sudarkasa, "Female Employment and Family Organization in West Africa," 49–64. See these authors on Asante: K.A. Busia, *The Position of the Chief in the Modern Political System of the Ashanti* (London: Oxford University Press, 1951); Meyer Fortes and E.E. Evans-Pritchard, eds. *African Political*

Systems (Oxford: Oxford University Press, 1980); and R.S. Rattray, *Ashanti Law and Constitution* (Oxford: Clarendon Press, 1929).

14. Niara Sudarkasa, "An Exposition on the Value Premise Underlying Black Family Studies," *Journal of the National Medical Association* 67 (March 1975): 235–39; and Niara Sudarkasa, "African and Afro-American Family Organization," *Anthropology for the Eighties*, 132–60.

15. Sudarkasa, "An Exposition on the Value Premise Underlying Black Family Studies"; "Female Employment and Family Organization in West Africa"; and "African and Afro-American Family Organization."

16. Bamidele Agbasegbe, "Is There Marriage between Women in Africa?" in *Sociological Research Symposium V*, ed. J.S. Williams et al. (Richmond: Virginia Commonwealth University, Department of Sociology, 1975); and Denise O'Brien, "Female Husbands in Southern Bantu Societies," in Schlegel, *Sexual Stratification: A Cross-Cultural View.*

17. See Lebeuf.

18. Ibid.

19. Michele Z. Rosaldo, "Woman, Culture, and Society: A Theoretical Overview," in Rosaldo and Lamphere, *Woman, Culture, and Society.*

20. Sudarkasa, "Female Employment and Family Organization in West Africa."

21. See Fortes and Evans-Pritchard.

22. Paulme, *Women of Tropical Africa;* Sudarkasa, *Where Women Work;* Victor Uchendu, *The Igbo [Ibo] of Southeast Nigeria* (New York: Holt, Rinehart, & Winston, 1965); and Bolanle Awe, "The Iyalode in the Traditional Yoruba Political System" in Schlegel, *Sexual Stratification: A Cross-Cultural View.*

23. Sudarkasa, *Where Women Work;* and "Female Employment and Family Organization in West Africa."

24. Sudarkasa, "Female Employment and Family Organization in West Africa," 60.

25. Ibid.

26. Niara Sudarkasa, "Interpreting the African Heritage in Afro-American Family Organization," in *Black Families*, ed. Harriette P. McAdoo (Beverly Hills: Sage Publishing Co., 1981): 37–53.

African Feminism:
A Theoretical Approach to
the History of Women in
the African Diaspora

Rosalyn Terborg-Penn

To develop a historical theory for the study of women in Africa and the African diaspora entails the surmounting of obstacles erected by traditional historiography cross-culturally, but also poses the challenge of exploring new concepts in women's, African-American, African, Caribbean, and Latin American histories. The methodology, by necessity, is often unorthodox to traditional historians, because the concept, African diaspora women's history, requires nontraditional methods and sources. In addition, traditional sources, those recorded in manuscripts or in official documents, often failed to include the female presence other than in passing. More important, historians of the past often failed to include a female perspective when analyzing the data collected. It is now up to scholars reconstructing African diaspora women's history to reexamine some of the old documents and secondary sources to find the female perspective and to include traditionally neglected sources.

For historians, developing theories for the study of women in the diaspora is crucial at a time when taking an advocacy approach to black women's history has left scholars under attack. It is crucial because during the past few years, criticism has ranged from total rejection of the idea that black women have a history of their own to acknowledgment that we must, to some extent, have a history but that our experiences could not vary that much from that of blacks as a group or of women in general. Among those who at least feel that black women should be discussed historically, questions about why they should be separated from black history or from women's history arise. In both cases, critics assume that black women have always had a history of being victimized, like the stereotyped slave woman, or of being victimizers, like the stereotyped black matriarch. Hence, our experiences are generalized erroneously to fit into Western concepts of the masses of either blacks or women, as being oppressed while passively looking to others for liberation, or as black women pathologically abusing their own. Such theorists look askance at the idea that there have been black women leaders revered by their own people, especially their women, and black women who actively resisted oppression using their own networks. Furthermore, a historical theory that couches these ideas within a time perspective, which can be exemplified throughout areas of Africa and the diaspora, seems heretical to some.

To the advocates, however, one of the most exciting issues about the emerging field of African diaspora women's history is that it involves interdisciplinary methods, as well as cross-cultural perspectives. Because historians cannot rely upon traditional, written historical sources in order to reconstruct black women's past totally, they turn to the works of other social scientists and humanists. It is not surprising that Filomina Steady, although she is an anthropologist, includes in her book *The Black Woman Cross-Culturally* essays from a variety of disciplines, several of which provided insights for historians.[1] With this in mind, scholars searching for alternative sources on women in the African diaspora may want to examine works about black women written by sociologists, anthropologists, ethnomusicologists, and others.

Whether to use interdisciplinary approaches to historical analysis or not is a debate that reemerges periodically among historians. In the early 1960s historians of American history debated this methodology as American studies programs began to develop across the nation. Similarly, in the early 1970s historians of Afro-American history debated the virtues of black studies programs. In the early 1980s that debate surfaced again among historians of African history, as well as American history. A theory for African diaspora women's history that includes the use of interdisciplinary methods will stimulate this debate even further.

Nonetheless, such an approach seems quite viable, and Steady's concept of African feminism lends itself to a historically based theoretical framework. In essence, the theory is used to approach the study of black women's lives through an analysis of their own networks. Beginning with an examination of the values that foster the customs of women in traditional African societies, historians can plot how these customs have changed, even though the values remained somewhat the same as women of African descent were forcibly transported throughout the world, especially to the Western Hemisphere. Perhaps the two most dominant values in the African feminist theory, which can be traced through a time perspective into the New World, are developing survival strategies and encouraging self-reliance through female networks. Historically, this combination has not been present among females of Western, i.e., European origins, but can be traced among women of African descent in New World societies, as well as in Africa.[2]

Although historians have not confronted the issues of African feminism directly, at least two of them have approached the study of black women in such a way that applies well to this theoretical path. Historian Lucille Mathurin has written several works on enslaved women in the British West Indies, especially in Jamaica, which exemplify issues found in the African feminist theory. In addition, historian Bernice Johnson Reagon's work on the culture of traditional black southern women in the United States reflects this approach. Both historians identify black women leaders who provide strength, both physically and spiritually, to their communities. These women are revered in their societies as a whole, but especially by the women. In the case of enslaved women in the British West Indies, Mathurin finds that their rebellious exploits against the slave system are celebrated in song and in oral tradition. In her essay, "My Black Mothers and Sisters or on Beginning a Cultural Autobiography," Reagon finds black southern women to be the "major cultural carriers and passers-on of the traditions of our people." In this case, the culture has been influenced by African survivals. Thus, in both diaspora societies, women, often within networks, provide significant avenues for community survival—past, present, and future. This analytical approach to black women's history clearly reflects the African feminist tradition.[3]

HISTORICAL APPROACHES

African feminism as a theory differs from the other conceptual approaches used to study black women's history from the early 1960s to the early 1980s. A review of these approaches is imperative here. The first stems from the integrationist theory, which fosters a traditional approach by utilizing what historian Okon Uya calls a "white filter."[4] In using this filter, scholars evaluate African or African-American societies in terms of European or Euro-American culture, or from the outside in, rather than from the inside out. The integrationist approach seeks to identify what contributions black women have made to Western culture or looks at how black women have been passively victimized by the mainstream society. This historical approach is perhaps the oldest and most commonly used.

An example of this integrationist approach is Sylvia Dannett's *Profiles of Negro Womanhood,* which was published in the mid-1960s.[5] It reflects the integrationist theory in that most of the women selected for discussion attempted to break the barriers of racism in order to integrate into the mainstream. Although this collection of biographical sketches gives much-needed data about black women long forgotten in United States history, their lives are celebrated by Dannett more because of their contributions to America, rather than their contributions to black life.

Other examples of the integrationist approach are Gerda Lerner's documentary collection, *Black Women in White America* and Loewenberg and Bogin's documentary collection, *Black Women in Nineteenth Century American Life,*[6] both of which were published in the 1970s. Although the voices of assertive black women are heard when reading the documents, more often than not the editors' analysis deals with the plight of victimized black women, who are viewed through a "white filter." It is not surprising that the limited historical works to come out about black women in the United States from the 1960s through the mid-1970s would have an integrationist thrust, since much of the early 1960s black freedom movement espoused integration. To some extent, these works were either stimulated or influenced by the movement.

Historical works that analyzed the lives of black women in the United States and that were written by black women themselves began to emerge with a nationalist approach in the late 1970s, again reflecting the changing black mood of the times. *The Afro-American Woman: Struggles and Images,* edited by Harley and Terborg-Penn, was the first of this type.[7] All the essays were written by black scholars who used historical methods and who took a nationalist theoretical stance. Nationalist theory revised the integrationist framework by eliminating the "white filter" and by seeking to find what black women have done in their own communities or organizations to help themselves and others. The nationalist approach deals with victimization fostered by racism but rejects the thesis that black women passively accepted it or looked to others for their liberation. Although racism is seen as the major barrier to black women's self-determination, gender and class oppression are also discussed as obstacles to black female progress.

Similarly, Jeanne Nobles's, *Beautiful, Also, Are the Souls of My Black Sisters* takes a nationalist position. Although the subtitle of Nobles's work is *A History of the Black Woman in America,* she is not a historian, and her book reveals this in its inaccuracies and shortcomings in historical analysis.[8] Nonetheless, her perceptions about black women, especially in contemporary matters, reflect a nationalist view of self-determination and identity with Africa. This can be observed in her quoting of an African proverb: "'You are beautiful, but you cannot eat your looks; you must learn to work,' American black sisters will have to work for what they get."[9]

In addition to the nationalist approach, a Marxist feminist theory has been used in the last few years to assess black women's history. In this analysis, class, race, and gender are the variables discussed in the dynamics of black women's oppression. However, the class struggle is considered to be the major variable. This theory, by its nature, imposes a "white filter," in that the standards of Western feminism, as well as Marxism, are often used to evaluate culture, values, and oppression. Black women are then compared with other oppressed workers, usually nonblacks, who are struggling against capitalism.

Journalist Stephanie Urdang's work on women of the revolutionary struggle in Guinea-Bissau reflects this approach.[10] Although her writings do not include historical analysis, her perceptions about West African women formerly colonized by the Portuguese have been noted by historians of the Marxist theoretical persuasion. However, her work, like much of the work written from a Marxist feminist perspective about African-American women's history, does not include a cross-cultural perspective.

Perhaps the best historical work about African-American women that uses Marxist theory was published in 1982 by Bettina Aptheker. In her book *Women's Legacy: Essays on Race, Sex and Class in American History,* Aptheker focuses her analysis on the experiences of black women.[11] Interestingly, her book includes autobiographical statements that link her analytical development to political changes in the United States during the 1960s and 1970s. As a result, one can see how the nationalist phase of the black freedom movement replaced the integrationist phase of the movement, of which she was a part. By the late 1960s, when this transformation occurred, the women's movement had been revitalized, mainly among middle-class white women. Within this context, white women in the black freedom movement revolted, feeling rejected because of their race and their sex. Aptheker's long relationship with Marxist ideology, however, remains steadfast in her feminist theoretical development. Thus, it is not surprising that she adopted a Marxist feminist approach. Her political activities during the late 1960s intertwined with those of Angela Davis. However, as a black Marxist, Davis flirted briefly with nationalism before taking a feminist posture, and in 1981, she published a collection of essays, *Women, Race and Class,* similar in approach to Aptheker's work. Davis admitted that she was a lay person when she called for a reexamination of black women's history. This is evident. As a result, the ideas she puts forth in the book lack the theoretical, as well as the historical, continuity found in Aptheker's work. Hence, the ideologies in Davis's thirteen essays range from Marxist feminist to nationalist to radical feminist, all reflecting the secondary sources she used, as well as changes in her own political development. Despite the inconsistencies in theory, Davis's essay "Racism, Birth Control and Reproduction Rights" reflects the next step in the theoretical development process—radical feminism.[12]

Although a radical feminist theory has been applied to black women's experiences in books such as *Some of Us Are Brave,* edited by Hull, Scott, and Smith, no historical works have been published in book form.[13] Nonetheless, some attention should be given to this theory. The radical feminist approach may or may not use a "white filter." It seeks to find ways for black women to develop a political female consciousness or to fight gender, for the most part, as well as race and class oppression. The term *radicals* has been interpreted by recent scholars to mean historians who see society ruled by bourgeois liberal apologists using reform as a means to preserve their privileged places.[14] In this sense, then, radical feminist historians reject women's history that omits analytical discussions of women oppressed by male-dominated society or patriarchy.[15] Hence, a radical feminist approach to black women's history would view victimization as the major theme, with patriarchy, whether white or black, as the basis for oppression. An example of this type of analysis can be seen in an essay written by a group of black feminists, The Combahee River Collective, named for the successful campaign led by Harriet Tubman during the Civil War. The essay combines historical materials with autobiographical narrative to present the group's point of view. In describing the origins of the collective, the authors' state, "A combined antiracist and antisexist position drew us together initially, and as we developed politically we addressed ourselves to heterosexism and economic oppression under capitalism."[16]

All of these theories have their merits because they represent various stages in the development of black women's history during the twenty years from the early 1960s to the early 1980s. The African feminist theory, however, seems to be the most viable for the study of African diaspora women's history because it provides three points which the other theories have not. First, it begins with the cosmology common to traditional African women who lived during the era of the slave trade. Because the African heritage of most women indigenous to New World societies originated then, this cosmology provides a common source for historical analysis. Second, the theory eliminates the "white filter" in that it looks to black standards for interpreting culture, values, initiatives, activities, and organizations. In so doing, the theory is uniquely a black women's theory. Third, the theory can be applied cross-culturally through time in order to assess women's roles and activities during and after slavery, as well as women's struggle against human oppression. Here the variables in the liberation struggle are more diverse than in any other theory, because they include race, gender, sexuality, class, religion, and culture, all areas of human activity in which black women have achieved in spite of discrimination.

THE USE OF THE TERM *BLACK*

Before applying the African feminist theory to black women's past, it is important to look at the term *black,* because not all women of African descent identify with this term. In the United States, for example, by law, people with any measurable degree of African ancestry are considered black. As a result, since slavery, women of African descent, regardless of skin color, have been identified, and often have identified themselves, as black. In this sense, *black* symbolizes a cultural milieu, more than it does a color. On the other hand, in many Caribbean and South American societies, women of African descent vary in colors that determine legal status, as well as cultural association. Hence, a mulatto woman in the British West Indies, for example, does not identify herself as black, whereas the same woman born in the United States may choose to or be forced to do so by society. Differences in legal and cultural identification by race cause barriers to reconstructing the past, especially for researchers studying countries like Argentina and Brazil, where blacks have not been counted in the population census for several generations. The key to historical reconstruction, then, must rest first upon how women identify themselves and second on how they are identified by the society in which they live. A mulatto woman from South America may emigrate to the United States perceiving her status to be nonblack, but after years of experiencing social and economic proscription based upon race, she will begin to identify with blacks because of her need for a survival network. The necessity for this change in racial orientation may well vary among immigrants due to time of immigration. Hence, in applying the African feminist approach to historical reconstruction of black women's lives, color and cultural perception should be taken into consideration.

RESISTING OPPRESSION

African feminism can be applied cross-culturally to black women resisting oppression during the postslavery eras in the United States and in the former Danish Virgin Islands. In both of these cases, the way in which the heroines have been revered and remembered by later generations is important to understanding women's roles in carrying on the culture of black people. In addition, the women leaders in these resistance efforts were over forty years of age and were among groups of women who shared similar oppressive experiences. Hence, age appears to be an important variable among black women leaders. How female leaders were chosen is an important question; however, the historical sources and the oral testimonies that survive rarely deal with this process. Nonetheless, we can assume that women in the African diaspora believed that with age came wisdom and maturity, as did women in traditional African societies. Women who demonstrated leadership ability, then, earned leadership positions because of these qualities. Leadership, nevertheless, appeared to be a practical status for the women discussed in the remainder of this paper, for their daily lives appeared to be much like those of other women with similar status in their communities. Working-class women worked outside of the home to survive. Women of professional or higher economic status often did so, as well. Hence, work, for the most part, was an essential ingredient in the lives of black women leaders. As a result, networking among women was as important a survival strategy as establishing self-reliance imperatives.

In the United States, Harriet Tubman's name has been celebrated since the 1840s. Some conveyed the title "Moses" upon her because of her leadership in the Underground Railroad freedom movement. Although the title is a biblical, male term, Tubman functioned in much the same way as this historical figure, who was said to have delivered his people from slavery via powers divine in source. Likewise, Tubman, a victim of the mysterious disease somnolence, miraculously overcame her handicap to deliver over three hundred people from slavery to freedom. Her accomplishment of this feat was believed by many to have been divinely directed. Over the years, women, especially, have named organizations, schools, homes, and other community institutions in her honor. For example, The Combahee River Collective was named in honor of Tubman's successful military campaign against the Confederates during the Civil War. It is this rarely noted of Tubman's many accomplishments that merits discussion here.

During the Civil War, Tubman took leave from her role as a conductor on the Underground Railroad to assist in the Union Army effort. In 1862 she went to the Sea Islands and attached herself to the forces under Major General David Hunter's command in Beaufort, South Carolina. There Tubman won the respect of the newly freed slaves who had joined the Union Army after Emancipation. In various roles, she brought freedmen's problems to the attention of the military authorities, nursed the sick, and taught the women how to care for themselves, independent of their former masters. Tubman's relationship with these women was one of mutual assistance. Because she received no pay for her work, Tubman found ways to support herself. One was to spend the evenings baking root beer pies, which women in her network sold for her during the day. Tubman also acquired a special reputation for curing dysentery with roots, a remedy surely borrowed from African foreparents via slaves in her native Dorchester County, Maryland.[17]

The roles of nurse, teacher, intermediary, and entrepreneur were not unique to Tubman in comparison with other southern black folks in the United States during these revolutionary times. Other former slave women, many of whom remain anonymous, assumed similar roles during the Civil War. Among these were Susie King Taylor of South Carolina and Sojourner Truth of New York. Their recollections reveal the strong sense of networking among black women, as well as the development of survival skills among black women and others whose lives were disrupted by the war. Although Taylor was a young woman when she nursed black soldiers and taught them to read, Truth was in her sixties when she provided services to black refugees at the Freedmen's Hospital in Arlington, Virginia.[18]

Tubman's unique quality was her skill as a military strategist. Consequently, Union Army officers prevailed upon her knowledge of guerilla warfare and espionage, notably in the Combahee River campaign against the Confederate camp in July 1863. Although in January 1863, the Emancipation Proclamation had freed the enslaved in rebelling states such as South Carolina, plantation owners continued to enslave black people in areas held by the Confederacy. Breaking the Confederate control of the Combahee River was assigned to Colonel James Montgomery. Tubman biographer Earl Conrad noted that she selected Montgomery, the leader of three hundred black soldiers, to command this expedition, which in reality Tubman planned and executed. The result was the destruction of millions of dollars worth of Confederate supplies and the liberation of nearly eight hundred slaves, most of whom were women and children. A news dispatch noted that these Union Army forces were "guided" by a black woman, who remained anonymous to readers. Nonetheless, oral traditions and Tubman's recollections of the battle remained. At the time, Tubman was over forty years of age, a significant age among black women chosen to resist oppression.[19]

In her late years, Tubman described the hundreds of freed women fleeing the Confederate lines with their children, their animals, and often with their provisions still cooking in the pots. Although they escaped undaunted, many of them were whipped by plantation overseers. Tubman's description of the scene reveals self-reliant women of African descent creating their own means for survival during and after slavery.[20]

From the extant data we can conclude that Harriet Tubman assumed leadership positions and that the people she led accepted her direction and assisted her in daily survival activities, such as the root beer pie enterprise Tubman established. In short, the women in the camp became part of Tubman's practical network as they exchanged services for survival.

In the Danish Virgin Islands, slavery ended in 1848 as a result of a massive slave revolt on the island of St. Croix. The revolt was precipitated by a gradual emancipation decree the year before. It is believed that the governor of the Virgin Islands was persuaded by his free mulatto mistress, Anne Heegaard, to lobby the Danish king at least for gradual emancipation. However, slaves wanted immediate liberation and took action to achieve it. Soon after their revolt, peonage replaced the slave labor system on the sugar plantations, which dominated the island's economy. By 1878, a generation later, peons realized that the restrictions of the labor regulations legislation virtually bound them to the plantations through yearly contracts. Like the soon-to-be-developed sharecropping system in the United States, peonage in the Virgin Islands was quasislavery. As a result, on October 1, 1878, the day new contracts were to be signed, a labor revolt exploded in Frederiksted, one of two cities on the island. Laborers burned and looted the city. From the town the rebels headed for the sugar plantations between Frederiksted and Christiansted, the island's other city, burning nearly all the fields and the plantation estates. Men, women, and children took part in the war that ensued, with several women taking leadership roles. Mary Thomas, known among her people as Queen Mary, led the band of women and children, aided by her lieutenants Queen Agnes and Queen Matilda. In addition, two other women were implicated in the rebellion, Rebecca Frederik and Axelline Salomon, known as "the black Amazon." Their efforts were responsible for the rum and kerosene fires that destroyed most of Frederiksted, including the rum factory that exploded, killing fourteen women. According to accounts of the battles that ensued in the countryside, women led the burning of the sugar estates, or Great Houses, but not the livestock. Some accounts say that this was a labor riot that erupted spontaneously, with no particular leadership, while others discuss a well-organized rebellion of discontented peasants. Nonetheless, in the oral tradition, renditions of the rebellion survive, extolling the efforts of Queen Mary. One such, a Carasou folk song, reads:

> Queen Mary away ya go burn.
> Don't ask me nothin' tall.
> Just give me match and oil.
> Bassin Jailhouse ata we go burn.[21]

The three queens were all imprisoned in the Bassin jail for their rebellious acts. Subsequently, they were sent to Denmark for trial, imprisoned, but later returned to St. Croix. Of the sixty-four persons convicted of criminal acts, twelve men were executed. The others included four women, the only native-born of the conspirators. It is the women's exploits that continue to be celebrated and revered by the common folk of St. Croix.[22]

Significantly, the women leaders of this military campaign had long before earned the title "queen," suggesting their status in their own communities. Such status came with age and ability, as was the case among similar types of women in traditional West African societies. Their roles as the leaders of black women warriors reflected African roots as well, generations after the arrival of their last African foremothers. Thus, the tradition of warrior queens remained in this African-Caribbean society, as one characteristic of a system that encouraged self-reliant women developing survival mechanisms that challenged economic oppression.

All of the women leaders involved in the St. Croix labor revolt worked either in the rum factory or on the sugar plantations. Labor in either circumstance was strenuous, requiring long hours. The fact that the masses of these women brought their children with them into their struggle reveals the close bond between black women and their children. Both on the South Carolina plantations and on the St. Croix plantations women carried their children into the battle and carefully tended the livestock needed for future survival.

A comparison of the armed struggles black women waged during the mid-nineteenth century in the United States and in the Danish Virgin Islands reveals similarities in experiences, resistance strategies, and cultural frameworks. In both societies, plantation slavery had been a way of life that dominated the legal, as well as the economic, status of black women and their ancestors. Despite the attempts to foster docile behavior by the plantation system, women often looked to themselves for survival networks and openly resisted the system. In times of crisis, they selected their own leaders, often older women known for their strength and military prowess. Afterward, the oral traditions of women in the community carried the memory of these heroines on for future generations to revere. Cultural heroines are especially important in societies such as these, because the victories were short-lived. Peonage returned to St. Croix within less than a generation, although in a less oppressive way, and the sharecropping system replaced the plantation slavery system in the southern region of the United States. Survival strategies designed and executed by women remained a major imperative, and women sought various ways to maintain it. Here the African feminist approach to historical analysis is clearly applicable.

THE STRUGGLE FOR WOMAN SUFFRAGE

The African feminist approach can be applied to the early twentieth century political struggles for woman suffrage among black women in both the United States and the Virgin Islands. The woman suffrage movement was a struggle that involved mainly white middle-class women reformists in Western societies. It is not surprising that black women who championed this cause were usually from the educated and professional class. In both the United States and the Virgin Islands, class, rather than color, determined leadership among black women suffragists. These women ranged from dark brown to light brown in skin color. However, women leaders in the struggle for suffrage championed the right of all people to vote, not just the women of their class. Organizations and networks of black women effectively mobilized both women and men, using a variety of political strategies, including petitioning legislatures, holding rallies, canvassing churches and neighborhoods, and taking cases to the courts. Many of these efforts were led by black women in black communities, with support, primarily, from black women in their networks, but also from sympathetic black men and white women suffragists.

In the United States, an example of a black women's suffrage network was the Colored Women's Civic and Political League of Rhode Island. This group of Republican party women were politically active, despite their disenfranchisement. Their leaders were professional women and women married to professional men, among them Mary E. Jackson, a Rhode Island state civil servant, Susan E. Williams, a teacher, Maria Lawton, the wife of a government official, and Bertha G. Higgins, the wife of a physician. Of this group, Higgins was the prime mover. A seamstress by training, she had given up her business after marriage to devote her time to homemaking and community service. Higgins was a founder and leader of several women's political organizations, mainly the Political League and, later, the Julia Ward Howe Republican Women's Club. In these associations she fought for woman suffrage and black women's political patronage from 1913 until 1932, when she became disillusioned with the Republican party and led many of her women supporters to the Democratic party.[23]

Before this break, Higgins and women like her saw the hope for black women, both politically and economically, in the right to vote. Like many politically active blacks of the times, Higgins felt that the Republican party could best facilitate this goal. Nonetheless, these women joined a variety of political and civic organizations to foster the networking they felt was necessary for survival. In 1916, for example, Higgins persuaded the Twentieth Century Art and Literary Club, a group of black Providence women, to sponsor a suffrage minstrel show. The funds raised from this event benefitted the Providence Woman Suffrage party, a racially integrated association. Subsequent rallies and church affairs were designed not only to support the movement financially but to recruit black women into the cause.[24]

Drawn into the woman suffrage movement for a variety of reasons, Higgins first saw political patronage as a major means to racial uplift for her people. Voting citizens, of course, have greater access to patronage than do others. In addition to patronage as a goal of woman suffrage, votes for women could help reform society through several steps, including prohibiting the use of alcohol, Higgins believed, and she was convinced that "the colored ballot of our mothers, sisters and sweethearts, will purify."[25]

Black women had significant roles not only in helping to pass the Nineteenth Amendment, which enfranchised American women in 1920, but in helping to elect Warren G. Harding to the presidency that year. A black woman went on record as the second member of her gender to register to vote in Rhode Island. In addition, Mary Church Terrell, a leading black suffragist on the national scene, wrote Higgins from Washington shortly before the presidential election calling for black Republican women to reach every woman in the state. The goal was to have them register and vote for the Harding ticket. Terrell noted, "By a miracle the 19th Amendment has been ratified. Colored women all over the country have a weapon of defense which they have never possessed before."[26] The success of this effort was apparent in Rhode Island, where in June 1920, the growing number of black women Republicans organized their own club—The Julia Ward Howe Republican Women's Club—with Bertha Higgins as president. At the time, Higgins was forty-eight years of age. After the November elections, Warren G. Harding sent a message to Higgins, thanking the club members for their efforts in the campaign.[27]

Shortly after the women of the United States received the right to vote, women in the Virgin Islands began lobbying for woman suffrage. The Danish Virgin Islands had been purchased by the United States in 1917, and a decade later Congress passed a law making Virgin Islanders American citizens. From that point on, black women teachers, in particular, took the lead, arguing that as American women they, too, should be enfranchised. Numerous women became active in this campaign, but Edith Williams is the one whose name frequently is associated with the movement. In the 1980s, when Virgin Islanders talk about woman suffrage, they refer to Williams, who was living and ninety-nine years of age in 1986. One of the early black women school teachers on St. Thomas, Williams has been revered as one of the "mothers" of public education on the island. A single woman, Williams worked for nearly fifty years as a teacher. In the Virgin Islands, teachers' salaries were low; however, Williams struggled until she acquired enough money to purchase her own property. In addition, she introduced the school lunch program in St. Thomas, by developing a vegetable garden at her school, where the children grew their own food, prepared some of it for lunches, and sold the rest. Mothers and other teachers participated in this program, revealing the connection between educational and economic goals as priorities in the daily lives of St. Thomas women. The first inductee into the *Virgin Island Education Review* Hall of Fame, Williams was saluted further in 1982, when an elementary school was named in her honor.[28]

In addition to Williams, Mildred V. Anduze was amid the black school teachers esteemed by the people of St. Thomas. Among the few women listed in *Profiles of Outstanding Virgin Islanders,* Anduze was noted as an active civic affairs leader, notably cited for her efforts in the woman suffrage campaign. Unlike

Williams, Anduze was a married teacher, who raised several children. She reflected the reality of daily life among many African diaspora women, who not only divided their daily activities among their students and families, but included time for civic and political campaigns, as well.[29]

Like Williams and other women leaders in this struggle, Anduze was an older woman during the final victory of the suffrage battle, revealing again the significant role that women over forty maintained not only in African, but in African-American and African-Caribbean communities. In 1935, when the St. Thomas courts ruled that eligible women should not be restricted from the voter rolls, Williams was forty-eight, and Anduze was forty-four.

The 1935 victory involved a long process, with petitions and court battles, led by a network of teachers, mainly women in the St. Thomas Teachers Association. By November of that year, association president Amadeo Francis had successfully won a legal suit wherein the question was raised about women's right to vote under the United States Constitution. The court ruled that the Danish code, under which local St. Thomas affairs were regulated, never intended to limit the franchise specially to men. As a result of this ruling, women in the St. Thomas Teachers Association decided to test the court decision. Interestingly, the Virgin Islands electoral laws restricted the franchise to literate, property-owning men. A growing movement among the educated Virgin Islanders of African descent questioned this restriction against 90 percent of the population, who were disqualified because they were women, or had no property, or were not literate.[30]

Within a month after the court ruling, Edith Williams applied to vote in the 1936 elections. She had hoped that the Colonial Council, or local legislative body, would take the initiative to inform the Electoral Board of women's right to vote, but the council refused. Hence, the decision to accept her application would be left to the board. Shortly thereafter, twenty-three other St. Thomas and St. John school teachers filed with the board to vote in the next election. When the election officials refused to accept their applications, three of the women, Edith Williams, Anna M. Vessup, and Eulalie Stevens, petitioned the court successfully to open the election process to qualified women. Why were these women selected by their peers to test the system? First, all three were self-reliant, self-supporting women and members of the teachers association. Second, they were residents of the Virgin Islands, property owners, and they were significantly past the required voting age of twenty-five. Hence, aside from gender, they met the restricted qualifications for voters. In addition, they were respected members of their communities whose reputations were beyond reproach. As a result of their struggle, plus a United States congressional law the following year, all literate citizens of the Virgin Islands were enfranchised.[31]

In both the United States and the Virgin Islands, networks of professional women led the way to political reform that eventually brought black women the right to vote. Some of these women were homemakers. Others were single women, whose survival was determined by their personal ability to make a living. Suffrage, then, was not just a right that they sought so that women could be merely politically equal to men. On the other hand, the fight for the ballot was motivated by social and economic reasons—the desire to use political means to improve the quality of life in black communities where, historically, women had been at the bottom of the economic strata.

In a political sense, these women did not hold prestigious positions in government, nor in the economy. However, as leaders they were revered in their own communities because of years of service. With time, the memory of these women has remained in the communities through oral testimonies and institutional landmarks that have kept many of their names alive. It seems that the Virgin Islands women received considerable male support in their networks; however, whenever the legal process toward suffrage broke down, the women mobilized and chose another strategy until victory was theirs.

In comparing the suffrage activities of U.S. and Virgin Islands women of African descent, once again networks of women seeking to reform not only their status but the conditions of others in black communities is apparent. In addition, these women leaders were older, established women with a tradition of community service behind them that commanded respect. Undoubtedly, the Virgin Islands women were influenced by the woman suffrage activities and strategies of black women in the United States. By the mid-1920s, many black women's organizations were extending their networks to include women from the Caribbean and Africa. Among such groups were the National Association of Colored Women and the International Council of Women of the Darker Races.[32] In this case the cross-cultural exchange was reversing as African-American women shared their strategies and goals for survival with their sisters in Africa and the diaspora.

IMPLICATIONS FOR FUTURE RESEARCH

Within a broad historical framework, African feminist values and imperatives can be applied to women of African descent cross-culturally—as female networking to assure the survival of human rights. In this essay we have observed the use of networking among black women and the application of survival strategies among formerly enslaved women in two settings—the United States and the Virgin Islands—and in two time periods for each—the late nineteenth and the early twentieth centuries. In all cases, African feminist imperatives were operative in the historical analysis used.

Using African feminism as a theoretical method for analyzing contemporary as well as past events that focus upon women of African descent has many other possibilities. Cross-cultural studies about slavery, colonialism, gender exploitation and women's resistance against these forces are just a few themes for which African feminist analysis can apply.[33] Hopefully, scholars researching past experiences of women in the African diaspora will be challenged to consider the African feminist approach to historical reconstruction.

NOTES

1. See Filomina Chioma Steady, "The Black Woman Cross-Culturally: An Overview," in *The Black Woman Cross-Culturally,* ed. Filomina Chioma Steady (Cambridge, Mass.: Schenkman Publishing Co., Inc. 1981), 7–36.
2. Ibid.
3. See Lucille Mathurin, *The Rebel Woman in the British West Indies During Slavery* (Kingston: African-Caribbean Institute of Jamaica, 1975); Lucille Mathurin, "The Arrivals of Black Women," *Jamaica Journal* 9, nos 2 & 3 (1975): 2–7; Lucille Mathurin, "Reluctant Matriarchs," *Sava-*

cou 13 (Gemini 1977): 1–6; and Bernice Johnson Reagon, "My Black Mothers and Sisters or on Beginning a Cultural Autobiography," *Feminist Studies* 8 (Spring 1982): 81–96.

4. Okon Edet Uya, "The Mind of Slaves as Revealed in their Songs: An Interpretative Essay," *A Current Bibliography on African Affairs* 5, series 2 (1972): 3–4.

5. Sylvia Dannett, *Profiles of Negro Womanhood,* 2 vols. (Yonkers, N. Y.: Educational Heritage, Inc., 1964).

6. Gerda Lerner, ed., *Black Women in White America: A Documentary History* (New York: Random House, 1972); and Bert James Loewenberg and Ruth Bogin, eds., *Black Women in Nineteenth Century American Life* (University Park: The Pennsylvania State University Press, 1976).

7. Sharon Harley and Rosalyn Terborg-Penn, eds., *The Afro-American Woman: Struggles and Images* (Port Washington, N. Y.: The Kennikat Press, 1978).

8. Jeanne Noble, *Beautiful, Also, Are the Souls of My Black Sisters: A History of the Black Woman in America* (Englewood Cliffs, N.J.: Prentice-Hall, Inc., 1978), 17, 19.

9. Ibid., 109.

10. Stephanie Urdang, *Fighting Two Colonialisms: Women in Guinea-Bissau* (New York: Monthly Review Press, 1979).

11. Bettina Aptheker, *Woman's Legacy: Essays on Race, Sex, and Class in America History* (Amherst: University of Massachusetts Press, 1982), 7.

12. Angela Y. Davis, *Women, Race and Class* (New York: Random House, 1981).

13. Gloria T. Hull, Patricia Bell Scott, and Barbara Smith, eds., *All the Women Are White, All the Blacks Are Men, But Some of Us Are Brave* (Old Westbury, N. Y.: The Feminist Press, 1981).

14. Robert F. Berkhofer, Jr., "The Two New Histories: Competing Paradigms for Interpreting the American Past," *OAH Newsletter* 2 (May 1983): 9–11.

15. Hilda Smith, "Women's History and the Humanities," *OAH Newsletter* 2 (May 1983): 12–14.

16. The Combahee River Collective, "A Black Feminist Statement," in *Capitalist Patriarchy and the Case for Socialist Feminism,* ed. Zillah R. Eisenstein (New York: Monthly Review Press, 1979), 364, 392.

17. Earl Conrad, *Harriet Tubman* (New York: Paul S. Eriksson Inc., 1943 and 1969), 160–64.

18. See Susie King Taylor, *Reminiscences of My Life in Camp* (New York: Arno Press and The New York Times, 1968); and Sojourner Truth, *Narrative and Book of Life* (Chicago: Johnson Publishing Co., Inc., 1970), 139–44.

19. Conrad, *Harriet Tubman,* 169–72.

20. Ibid., 174–75.

21. Florence Lewisohn, *The Romantic History of St. Croix: From the Time of Columbus Until Today* (St. Croix: St. Croix Landmarks Society,

1964), 50–51, 55–57; and Isaac Dookhan, *A History of the Virgin Islands of the United States* (St. Thomas: Caribbean Universities Press, 1974), 227–31.

22. Lewisohn, *Romantic History,* 54; and Dookhan, *History of the Virgin Islands,* 231.

23. "Report to Members of the Rhode Island Suffrage Party, and League of Women," November 1919, Bertha Higgins Papers, Rhode Island Black Heritage Society, Providence, R.I.

24. Newsclipping, "Minstrel Show," *The Providence Sunday Journal,* 14 May 1916, Scrapbook, Bertha Higgins Papers.

25. Bertha Higgins to "My Dear Madam," n.d., draft, Bertha Higgins Papers.

26. Mary Church Terrell to Bertha Higgins, October 1920, Bertha Higgins Papers.

27. Newsclipping, *The Providence Sunday Journal,* 12 June 1920, Scrapbook; and Charles E. Harding to Bertha Higgins, 21 February 1921, Bertha Higgins Papers.

28. *The Virgin Islands Education Review* 1 (August 1982): 5; and June Lindqvist, interview with author, Virginia Islands Bureau of Libraries and Museums, St. Thomas, V.I., 12 January 1983.

29. Department of Education, U.S. Virgin Islands, *Profiles of Outstanding Virgin Islanders* (St. Thomas: Government of the U.S. Virgin Islands, 1976), 4.

30. *The (St. Thomas) Daily News,* 27 March 1935; and 11 November 1935.

31. *The (St. Thomas) Daily News,* 14 December 1935; and 28 December 1935.

32. Cynthia Neverdon-Morton, "The Black Woman's Struggle for Equality in the South, 1895–1925," in Harley and Terborg-Penn, *The Afro-American Woman: Struggles and Images,* 512–52; and Monroe N. Work, *Negro Year Book, 1925–1926* (Tuskegee, Ala.: Negro Year Book Publishing Co., 1925), 37.

33. For further information about contemporary issues, see Josef Gugler, "The Second Sex in Town," in Steady, *The Black Woman Cross-Culturally,* 169–84; Richard E. Lapchick, "The Role of Women in the Struggle Against Apartheid in South Africa," in Steady, *The Black Woman Cross-Culturally,* 231–61; Margaret Randall, "The Story of Monica Baltodana and Zulema," *Black Scholar* 14 (March/April 1983): 48–57; Elizabeth V. Murrell, "Our Children—Their Future: The International Year of the Child—1979," *Freedomways* 19 (First Quarter, 1979): 7–12; and The Women's Committee, International Defense and Aid Fund for Southern Africa, *To Honour Women's Day* (Cambridge, Mass.: The Women's Committee, International Defense and Aid Fund for Southern Africa, 1981).

Anthropological Research Methods for the Study of Women in the Caribbean

A. Lynn Bolles

Historically, the methods of anthropological research have tended to separate that discipline from the other social sciences. First, in anthropological research one usually incorporates the technique of participant observation. Second, in anthropological field work one participates and observes. More often than not, the inquiring anthropologist is not the social equal of his subjects. In addition, "the field," more than likely, is located in the Third World, or among poor peoples of color. The relationships between the anthropologist and the folk "of the field," during the research period and afterwards, when the investigator has returned to his or her home, has been the topic of concern for many, but not for all. Those who question the traditional model of inquiry have created alternative research methods in anthropology based primarily on notions of equality. Equal emphasis is placed on both the kind of relationship established between the researcher and the folk, and the nature of the results derived from that field work experience. My purpose is to discuss one of those nontraditional methodological approaches in anthropology and to show how it has been utilized in research on working-class women in urban Jamaica.

The discipline of anthropology has had the dubious honor of being called "the child of imperialism." Established in the late nineteenth century, during the height of social Darwinism, anthropology has been used to serve the colonization efforts of the

British, to document the U.S. government's maintenance of Native American reservations, and to romanticize the exotica of black America.

Despite its less than constructive history, however, anthropology has the ability to serve as a positive social force for advancing equality among people. This capacity is based on its nature. Unlike some other disciplines, anthropology luxuriates in its eclectic manner. That is, anthropology has taken so much from the humanities, social sciences, and natural sciences that some aspect of its perspective can be attractive to all and of value for many. Anthropology's point of view is at once wholistic, comparative, particularistic, and general. Its approach is founded on a historical-evolutionary model that takes contemporary situations and attempts to view them as just one moment in the human journey. Individual anthropologists describe and analyze the scenes before them in a variety of forms based on the four classic areas of anthropological study: archeological, physical, linguistic, and social-cultural. However, the anthropologist always returns to some concept of culture, which provides *the* social arena in which all else occurs. Culture is the crux of the discipline, and the methods one employs to illustrate culture as a phenomenon are diverse.[1]

How, then, can we use an anthropological perspective to its best and avoid the perpetuation of the sort of scientific imperialism reminiscent of the colonial and neocolonial, state-interventionist past? How can we establish what anthropologist John Gwaltney calls "native anthropology," equal relations on many levels between researcher and respondent (community or culture) based on mutual respect? Further, how can we apply the tenets of "responsible, equitable" research in our study of black women? And, given the contemporary setting for the majority of women of African descent, especially in the societies of the Americas, we speak of those who are the least powerful of the powerless. Finally, to offer an additional aspect to this query, when the intruding anthropologist is a member of one black American culture, what challenges arise in her study of black women of another black culture?

My responses to these questions are organized into three sections. The first section addresses some methodological questions—

some operational, others more ethical in nature. The second describes my own work in Jamaica as an example of how one uses native anthropology, or responsible research, in praxis. And the third offers a discussion of other approaches to the study of blacks in the Caribbean for comparison and as food for thought.

METHODOLOGY

Anthropologists' training in research methods eventually leads them to choose between becoming creative by designing alternatives or remaining traditional by following the standard fare. A variety of factors influence which methodological path students follow, including their educational situation, i.e., their graduate school and the faculty under whom they study. Regardless of these variables, for the most part, anthropologists learn research methods by reading and analyzing "classic" ethnographic literature, the descriptive account of a specific people's or group's way of life, focused primarily on preliterate folk of color during the first half of the twentieth century. Of course, it was that body of "classic" ethnography that provided the basis for anthropology's tag "child of imperialism." Gwaltney reminds us that

> traditional Euro-American anthropology has failed to produce ethnographers who are capable of assessing black American culture in terms other than romantic. . . . We have traditionally been misrepresented by standard social science.[2]

But during the period of social upheaval in the 1960s, a series of articles called for the reassessment of anthropology as a discipline, a review of its methods of inquiry, and its relations among folk in the field.[3] Many of these energies focused on black cultures in the Americas, since it was at home that the obvious harm had been done by anthropology under the rubric "culture of poverty." Also included under that heading were studies such as *Soulside* and similar examples of street-corner exotica, which owing to the misguided perceptions of their various authors, effectively obfuscated the totality of U.S. black culture.[4] Delmos Jones, Charles Valentine, and Charles and Betty Lou Valentine called for the rectification of this misportrayal of black American culture, in perspective, method, and practice.[5]

Valentine argues that "special care must be taken that studies [of Afro-America] not be used by the establishment to perpetuate the status quo."[6] Any research on black people, carried out by blacks or whites, even of the highest quality and with the best intentions, might be used as a tool to oppress and control the people being studied with better efficiency and to an even greater extent than previously possible. He also reminded us that anthropologists' responsibilities must encompass the method of data collection, publication, and the researchers' attitude. In addition, they must be concerned about who will use the information.

Various conditions necessitate that anthropologists or researchers exercise this principled responsibility in their work. Policy decisions were promoted by inappropriate techniques and a specific ideological set of baggage, whereby abused women were contributors to the salvation of their families, men and children. The price of irresponsibility becomes obvious when we acknowledge, for example, that the culture of poverty concept abused black people, particularly black women. Studies that embraced this concept overwhelmingly attributed the decay, deprivation, and composite social ills associated with urban ghetto life to these women. Their men were depicted as emasculated, their children as latch-key offspring running in the streets—their sons were dope addicts, their daughters sexually indiscriminate—and their households as pathologically organized. Finally, such studies concluded that the culture of poverty was transmitted transgenerationally; that is, it was passed on from mother to children, and so on. Thus, the effect was that the victims were ultimately blamed for their own situation, although they were scarcely in any position to refute the allegations of the culture-of-poverty enthusiasts, since they happened to be the least powerful among the powerless—impoverished black women.[7] These women could only *wish* to be able to earn fifty-nine cents for every dollar a man earned. The low-paying, dead-end jobs that most U. S. black women held did not exemplify the "work of liberation" envisioned by the 1960s and 1970s activists of the women's movement, whose goals were self-awareness and financial independence.

In the Caribbean, specifically in Jamaica, the situation was somewhat similar, with studies on household organization of poor and working-class families receiving the bulk of attention from social scientists.[8] The major concern of these studies was to explain why there were so many variations in Jamaican household structure and why there was such a high incidence of female-headed households. Considerably less attention was devoted to the various roles that women played in those societies, aside from their fertility patterns and mating habits. The rate of illegitimacy and the high number of female-headed households were seen as problematic; that factors like these revealed the resourcefulness of women, which enabled them, as well as men and children, to function, somehow, under adverse social and economic circumstances, seems to have been lost on these researchers. Therefore, the underlying difficulties associated with the poor black mothers, poor black fathers, and poor black children depicted in these studies were attributed, to a great extent, to systems of inequality based on color and class, rather than to other interconnected factors.

Sensitivity to the forms of publication and the kinds of persons and organizations given access to the materials gathered must be considered an important aspect of conducting responsible social research. The importance of how and where to make the material accessible should be underscored, and these features must be built into the research agenda. In particular, there should be a sense of accountability toward communities, groups, and individuals of the study. When anthropologists achieve this sense, they implant a certain degree of safeguard, so that situations that give rise to statements like those of Gwaltney's respondents can be avoided:

> Since I don't see myself or most people I know in most things I read about black people, I can't be bothered with that.
> —"Harriet Jones"

> I think this anthropology is just another way to call me a nigger.
> —"Othman Sullivan"[9]

Finally, researchers should not shield themselves behind the veil of "scientific objectivity" in reneging on their responsibilities toward the folk under study. "Establishment anthropologists," as Valentine calls them, tend to play "treacherous verbal games with stereotypes," and they rely on the humanist issues they address to shield them from the effects of their lack of an ethical stance.[10] However, irresponsibility may invite more than the moral indignation of the group under study. Researchers are beginning to learn that nowadays, not only can the people of the field read and write, they also can take legal action. We find that the Navajo Indians, for instance, now screen prospective researchers' proposals and will not grant entry into communities when they find that the work being proposed has already been done. The Navajo even provide bibliographies to support their denial of entry decisions.

Anthropologists must exercise particular care in conducting research among "native" folk—using Gwaltney's translation of Fanon—the subordinate, dark, and poor. And this especially should be observed when the folk are female. Formerly, the intruding imperialist, powerful stranger (social scientist) expected simply to draw from a data bank of giving, powerless people. Now, the guidelines of native anthropology, or responsible research, provide opportunity for exchange, increased accuracy, mutual respect, and the sharing of civic responsibility between the researcher and the folk under study. Not only will anthropologists' cross-cultural comparisons of the role and status of women of the diaspora be beneficial but the kinds of material generated will more likely be significant to black women and their activities. This is the kind of perspective which formed the basis of my research activities in Jamaica.

FEMALE INDUSTRIAL WORKERS
IN KINGSTON, JAMAICA

There were three underlying premises for my work in Jamaica: 1) the material would be useful to appropriate policy makers; 2) the research would involve areas already on the agendas of appropriate organizations; and 3) the outcome of the research would in some manner positively affect those under study.[11] Elsewhere, I have documented the pluses and minuses of being a black American woman carrying out research among folk similar to but distinct from her own people. Issues of nationality, ethnicity, education, and class came into play during the field work. The manner in which these biases and stereotypes were overcome had much to do with my method of inquiry—native anthropology. Moreover, since native anthropology has much in common with many aspects of core black American culture, I intensely acted out my own cultural perspective to gain that of another. Tenets of core black culture include, for those not familiar with the concept, a notion of setting the story straight, common courtesy, reciprocity, intracommunal style and status (which had to be learned Jamaican style), and a sense of nationhood, which I expanded to a sense of common ancestry and the diaspora.

The most important set of relations were found among those with whom I shared the most, and whose instructions I hold in high esteem. These individuals included, first, the personal friends who schooled me in Jamaican customs and manners prior to my entry into working-class neighborhoods; and second, those urban working-class women and their household members whose lives formed the basis for my research, and some of whose friendships I earned and still value. The following discussion will illustrate how native anthropology worked for me in the field.

My research focused on female factory workers who were employed in typical "female industries"—garment, food processing, and canning manufacturing. The goal was to see how industrial employment affected these women's productive and reproductive (in the broadest sense) activities and their household organization. To gain more information from various industrial subsectors, I visited different factories, contacted those who might be interested in helping me out, and then worked out topics for further discussion.

I entered an underwear factory in downtown Kingston. The firm is owned by a local Chinese-Jamaican family. The working conditions were the poorest I ever had seen—hot, and full of lint and overworked women. I was introduced by the trade union officer as a "lady from the States who is doing a study for her doctorate." I knew I was in serious trouble as the glares of disgust nearly paralyzed me. I began to explain what I was doing and why, that in our efforts (mine and the trade union's, in this instance) to gain maternity leave with pay and better wages for women workers, their help in the study could be directly beneficial to them. I explained that they would have to help by answering sets of questions that would show how their wages were spread too thin and that would reveal the magnitude of their responsibilities. Since men generally did not recognize or care to know these facts, and it was they, especially "big men" (members of Parliament) who made policy, males needed to be provided with all the facts to support what we already knew to be true about working mothers.

Some women walked away, while others started talking among themselves. I started speaking louder and faster. Finally, one woman began to deride me—how could I, a fine American woman with everything, come to tell them anything—I didn't know what work was. I was a soft, American so-and-so! This assessment received much applause, and soon others joined in, telling me where I should go and what I could do with myself once I got there. I realized that if I didn't respond in kind all would be lost.

To begin with, I gave a fiery rebuke (in my best Jamaican patois) to the woman who had spoken first. Then I pointed out to all of them that here I stood, a black American woman, where no Jamaican woman from campus (meaning University of the West Indies—read: Jamaican middle class) would dare come. I said to them, "Listen, there is a way to try to gain what you have been struggling for, and you cuss me off because you think all Americans are stupid. Well, if this is how Jamaican women act, then I could say the same about you. You think all Americans are soft—well, the white man tells us all what to do, and hard work has never been absent from any black woman's life, here or in the States." I concluded my soliloquy, now with a captive audience, by saying, "You are black women, and so am I. I was lucky enough to get an education to do something to help others. You try to send your children to school—would you want them to get such a hard time if they were in my shoes? You are who you are, and I am who I am. But, together, we can do one thing which might help us all." After a response of a series of begrudging "alright's" and a more positive "she alright, da Yankee gal," I left the factory floor, promising to return the next day to talk only with those interested. And I did.

The point being made here is that it was hard work to gain the respect of these black working women. They had become accustomed to having their opinions abused under similar research situations. Reciprocity also was crucial in that I had much to learn from them, and I gave of myself by showing interest, by supplying information, and by offering gratuities which they could appreciate personally—such as, for example, laundry detergent, which was scarce in the supermarkets. Our mutual plight of being black women struck a chord, and when I admitted my own vulnerability, it became another way to reach a commonality across class lines.

When the research was finished and copies of the promised material were made available to designated agencies and organizations, the women studied and other interested parties were shocked. No one could remember the last time a researcher from abroad had ever followed through with his or her promises. The working-class women most actively involved in the study particularly appreciated my description of their working conditions on the job and at home. One woman commented that she had not realized how much she did in one day, and she felt more tired than she had before, after reading about her own daily routine, but her work had to be done.

The data I collected on working-class women's opinions on maternity leave issues were made available to the Jamaica Women's Bureau. That branch of the government aided the successful battle that put into law maternity leave with pay. Whether or not my research was instrumental in the case presented before the Parliament is not known; however, the information was there if they needed it. Other data on rank-and-file trade union membership served as the basis of a three-year, regional project on women in labor organizations sponsored by the Trade Union Education Institute and international agencies.

Overall, my research method was not unique. But in contrast with other methods—the type that these women and agencies were all too familiar with—I placed emphasis on the individuals under study, rather than on the research itself. I did not set out with a precise research topic and set out to find it at whatever cost to anyone involved. Instead, the eclecticism of anthropology allowed me to study my general interests—black women, urban life, and economic systems—together as a cohesive unit. Additionally, the tenets of core black culture and native anthropology made it possible for me to achieve the three goals I set forth for myself and my work.

CONCLUSION

In contrast with my own, specifically focused, Caribbean field work situation, I would like to discuss some of the key points of what I consider to be one of the most exhaustive, exciting, extensive pieces of research focusing on the contemporary lives and issues of women of the African diaspora. Thus, I will show how some of the same principles we have been discussing here can be applied on a very large scale.

A significant example is the multidisciplinary Women in the Caribbean Project (WICP), which seeks to establish in the region a data base for teaching, research, and planning purposes and to develop guidelines for a cohesive social policy that recognizes the needs of women and draws on their skills and talents for program planning and execution. The results of the project's study should add significantly to our knowledge and understanding of women and the development process in the English-speaking Caribbean.

In September 1982, the organizers and principle researchers of the WICP sponsored a conference in Barbados. At that time, the preliminary results of their research in Barbados, Guyana, St. Vincent, and Antigua were made public. The project was carried out, primarily, by women scholars from the three campuses of the University of the West Indies (UWI)—Mona (Jamaica), Cave Hill (Barbados), and St. Augustine (Trinidad)—the University of Guyana, and small social-welfare agencies in the countries under investigation. The project director was Jocelyn Massiah from the Institute for Social and Economic Research (ISER), UWI, Barbados. Particular care was taken to involve local people, as the project's goal of influencing policy makers dealing with women-centered issues could be best acted upon by those very local people.

The WICP study used a multilevel method, i.e., one that integrated the standard sociological, structured survey sample and the anthropological, unstructured, in-depth interviewing techniques. In-country workshops; junior and senior women research teams; questionnaires; follow-up, in-depth studies; community social service inventories; and training of interviewers and supervisory staff were all provided for in the detailed research design implemented in the field work. In addition, special preparation was made for the interviewers initially entering the field situation, in an attempt to prevent inhospitable situations from arising. Whether or not all the research was conducted in the systematic, nonhierarchical manner indicated in the methodology is not yet known, and a final evaluation cannot be made until all the data can be processed for comparison. The point is, however, that a grand-scale research project attempted to follow such a plan.

The magnitude and importance of the WICP study cannot be elaborated upon here because the polished data have not as yet been made public. It is enough to say that when the data from the 1,526 respondents are coded and analyzed, the interviews analyzed, and the multitudinous notes taken from workshops, meetings, and discussions are all taken into account, the project's overall objectives should be accomplished. An ultimate goal of the research is to increase female participation in economic and social development, both nationally and regionally. Regardless of the appearance of the final document, the WICP made history on two counts. Because of it, a major contribution will be made to cross-cultural research efforts on women and specifically on women of African descent. Second, in its research design, the WICP attempted to combine a statistical profile on the lives of Caribbean women with a commonsense understanding of their day-to-day lives. To conclude, I propose that similar projects be carried out in various regions of Africa, in the United States, in Brazil, and in other parts of the African diaspora.

NOTES

1. In this paper, the term *culture* is employed in accord with Sidney Mintz's argument on the subject. That is, culture is a historically developed form through which members of a group relate to one another. It is a resource for human action, choices, materials, behavior, self-perception, and world view. Culture is used to confirm, reinforce, maintain, change, or deny particular arrangements of status, power, and identity. See, Mintz, "Foreword," in *Afro-American Anthropology: Contemporary Perspectives,* ed. Norman E. Whitten, Jr. and John Szwed (New York: Free Press, 1970), 1–16.

2. Gwaltney's seminal work, *Drylongso,* is a collection of personal narratives gathered from a group of "core black culture" participants in north-

ern New Jersey. It stands as a prime example of creative, alternative, and equitable anthropological research. The sources of data were found as an outcome of folk seminars that were held in such varied locations as churches and taverns. "Good talk" often inspired good food, which was prepared by a participant who shared Gwaltney's aim of "setting the story straight" about most black Americans—drylongso—ordinary people. Participants also donated indispensable personal documents, life histories, and other valuable commodities, including their time, because they, too, wanted to contribute to truth-building about black American culture. Gwaltney's name is the only nonfictionalized name to appear in the volume, to protect those who gave so earnestly. The narratives appear as they were taped, with Gwaltney organizing them by theme. *Drylongso: A Self-Portrait of Black America* (New York: Random House, 1981), xxii.

3. Dell Hymes, ed., *Reinventing Anthropology* (New York: Random House, 1974).

4. Ulf Hannerz, *Soulside: Inquiries into Ghetto Life* (New York: Columbia University Press, 1969).

5. Charles A. Valentine and Betty Lou Valentine, "Making the Scene, Digging the Actions and Telling It Like It Is: Anthropologists at Work in a Dark Ghetto," in Whitten and Szwed, *Afro-American Anthropology;* Charles Valentine, *Black Studies and Anthropology: Scholarly and Political Interest in Afro-American Culture* (Addison-Wesley Modular, no. 15, 1972); and Delmos Jones, "Towards a Native Anthropology," *Human Organization* 29 (1970): 251–59.

6. Valentine, *Black Studies and Anthropology,* 45.

7. Elizabeth Higginbotham, "Two Representative Issues in Contemporary Sociological Work on Black Women," in *All the Men Are Black, All the Women Are White, But Some of Us are Brave,* ed. Gloria T. Hull, Patricia Bell Scott, and Barbara Smith (Old Westbury, N.Y.: The Feminist Press, 1981), 93–98.

8. Frances Henry and Pamela Wilson, "The Status of Women in Caribbean Societies: An Overview of Their Social, Economic, and Sexual Roles," *Social and Economic Studies* 24 (1975): 165–98.

9. Gwaltney, *Drylongso,* xix.

10. Charles A. and Betty Lou Valentine, "Making the Scene," in Whitten and Szwed, *Afro-American Anthropology.*

11. Research was conducted in Jamaica, 1978–79, and funded by National Institute of Mental Health National Research Service Award (1F31MH07997–01) and a predoctoral fellowship from the Inter American Foundation. One hundred twenty-seven female factory workers and their households were the focus of the work.

I made initial contact with these women at their places of work through their trade union officers. After a degree of mutual trust was established, about a dozen women extended invitations for home visitations. Hence, only those interested enough in the project participated on a level beyond completing an interview schedule. The schedule covered household composition, domestic organization, economic responsibilities, work histories, and opinion questions on topical issues of the day, e.g., maternity leave with pay. I made observations at the factories and at the homes of those who invited me to visit.

During the eighteen-month research period, the social, economic and political situation in Jamaica was tense, and I am indebted to all of these women for their time, patience, and kindness. In addition, other social and economic materials were gathered from libraries, government ministries, and newspaper archives. Factory managers, trade unionists, and faculty from the University of the West Indies were interviewed.

Psychological Research Methods: Women in the African Diaspora

Saundra Rice Murray

Investigators interested in the psychology of women in the African diaspora have the opportunity to map unknown terrain, for currently this area of inquiry is not defined. However, the psychological study of black American women is an active field and one that offers promise for understanding the psychology of black women throughout the world. This paper presents an overview of progress to date and discusses implications for future development. The first section cites milestones in growth of the field as a professional speciality. This is followed by a summary of selected findings. The third section is a discussion of approaches that may be fruitfully applied in efforts to include women beyond the United States. The conclusion recapitulates key points.

PROFESSIONAL MILESTONES

Before the mid-1960s, when the civil rights and women's movements stimulated new scholarship on race and sex, black women were virtually invisible in psychology. The data base consisted of a small amalgam of studies, position papers, critiques, and clinical observations. To identify even that tiny base required extensive digging into the literature of sociology, anthropology, medicine, and education. Occasionally one could find a study that was sound in conception and method. Most often one found that the researcher had strayed far beyond the data in the interpretation presented or failed to collect any data at all. Theoretical efforts were nonexistent.

Today, we can point to signs of a continuing effort to measure and understand aspects of the psychological life of African-American women. For example, there is a section on black women's concerns in Division 35 of the American Psychological Association. This group has held symposia at its annual convention, published a bibliography on psychological research on black women, and compiled a directory of psychologists interested in research on black women. The anthology, *The Black Woman,*[1] features many social psychological studies, and Myer's study of self-esteem in four hundred black women presents survey data that may be useful in the development of hypotheses.[2] Two major journals, *The Psychology of Women Quarterly* and *The Journal of Social Issues,* have each devoted an entire issue to original work on black women.[3] The compilation, entitled "*The Psychology and Mental Health of African American Women: A Selected Bibliography,* lists over seven hundred entries, including books, articles, and dissertations.[4]

Although visibility within the profession is important, sustained, rather than episodic, interest in black women's psychology will depend ultimately on the quality and scope of contributions to the empirical data base. The next section presents an overview of progress toward this objective.

FINDINGS

Bodies of evidence are being generated in a handful of substantive areas, three of which are briefly reviewed here. Studies of sex roles and gender identity constitute one category. This includes investigations concerning beliefs about what men or women should be like or do and perceptions of oneself as feminine, masculine, or androgynous in relation to behavior or attitude. Overall, the findings indicate that black women hold traditional views of what woman's role ideally should be. This has been found in American and Nigerian samples.[5] However, as Scanzoni's study indicated, black American women rate themselves as both instrumental (i.e., as independent, competitive, and self-confident, traits usually associated with masculinity) and expressive (i.e., as considerate, understanding, helpful, and warm to others, traits usually associated with femininity).[6] Recent studies have explored the extent to which sex-role attitudes and gender identity are related to specific types of behaviors and to women's expectations.[7] For example, Biraimak used a multi-method approach (including such methods as observations of teacher interaction and analysis of documents) to examine the source and nature of gender-based messages transmitted in a Togolese secondary school.[8] The findings indicated that Western notions of gender roles were transmitted through aspects of the school experience, such as textbooks and teacher expectations.

Self-esteem and other concepts about the self are topics of studies in the second category. The evidence indicates that black American women, despite the negative images of them portrayed in society, regard themselves in positive ways.[9] When differences among black women are examined, however, the picture becomes complex. Findings from studies of black women's perception of personal efficacy (or locus of control) illustrate the complexity that is introduced when various populations of black women are examined.

Personal efficacy refers to the extent to which individuals perceive that their own actions control the reinforcements they receive. Individuals who believe in their own efficacy are said to be internally controlled, whereas persons who feel that forces beyond their control influence reinforcement are said to be externally controlled. Personal control in black college women has been associated with low fear of success and prestige of occupational aspirations, grades, and aspirations for graduate and professional school.[10] In Bould's study of personal control in female heads of household, black women who had little money and who depended on uncontrollable, stigmatizing, or unreliable income felt little personal control.[11] Involvement in political activities also has been found to be positively related to personal efficacy, particularly among women.[12] Personal efficacy, however, is unrelated to family planning.[13]

In a final example, Jones and Zoppel compared personality differences among black women in Jamaica and the United States.[14] One of their key findings was that these groups viewed their personal social worlds quite differently. Young Jamaican women tended to generate constructs that suggested "a highly interpersonal view of the world, one in which the social nexus is a primary determinant of an individual's perspective on life."[15] In contrast, the outlook of young black American women tended to be expressed in terms of power and personal competence.

The third category of research includes studies of career- and work-related factors. Career choice and its correlates have been widely examined. The findings indicate that black women aspire to careers in which women are predominant. Thus, Allen, in his comparison of the occupational aspirations of black and white high school males and females, found that 37 percent of the black females aspired to professional jobs,[16] but as Allen noted, a detailed analysis would probably indicate that the professional occupations selected by these women are sex-typed.

Explanations as to why black women restrict their options to fields considered traditional for women have been sought in studies of achievement motivation.[17] However, the data are inconclusive, perhaps, as Gump and Rivers suggest, because an extrinsic factor—sense of responsibility—may be more important in explaining black women's strivings than are achievement motivation and related personal preferences.[18] This has not been examined empirically, but recent efforts have been directed toward understanding the roles of other situational or external variables. For example, Long found that black women with higher incomes and nontraditional role models tended to choose nontraditional careers. Similar work has been conducted by Burlew.[19] Extremely rare, however, are studies that examine the barriers black women face when they attempt to enter the labor force and, if successful, participate.

DEFINING THE FIELD

The foregoing sketch indicates that the foundation exists for the psychological study of diasporan women. However, the promising signs of growth are tempered by three conditions I find disturbing. One is that the literature, with a few exceptions such as those noted previously, is fragmented. Bits and pieces exist on topics ranging from depression to nonverbal behavior in job interviews, but replications or extensions of studies are rare.[20] When several studies on a single topic are located, one finds little consistency in the methods used.

The second of the conditions, briefly noted earlier, is the focus on black women in the United States. Research on other diasporan women constitutes a tiny fraction of the literature. To put this material into perspective, it is useful to consider that, in the bibliography by Young and Sims-Wood, less than 1 percent of the entries refer to women in Africa or the Caribbean. In contrast, 1.4 percent of the entries refer to studies comparing Mexican American or Native American and black women.

The third condition is the absence of efforts to define the boundaries of the field. Although there is merit in allowing the field to be mapped according to what emerges from various inquiries, the lack of frameworks presents the possibility that psychological studies will continue to focus on black American populations. More serious is the likelihood that important concerns simply will not be addressed, particularly if they are of peripheral interest to black Americans. To advance us toward a consideration of definitional issues, I will outline three of the approaches that I have discerned in the literature: 1) debunking myths, 2) developing new constructs, and 3) understanding relationships.

Debunking Myths

Under the heading "Debunking Myths" can be placed the first wave of studies and essays on black women. The authors explicitly identify some of the stereotypes about black women which often are negative in tone, and then discuss data that present an accurate portrayal. Illustrations are Jackson's excellent paper entitled "Black Women in a Racist Society," which addresses the myths of black women's superiority vis-à-vis black men in education and in employment in professional occupations.[21] Similarly, Puryear, in the essay from the compilation entitled *Comparative Perspectives of Third World Women: The Impact of Race, Sex and Class,* considers the popular depictions of black women as matriarchs and emasculators of black men.[22] On one aspect of the psychological consequences of these stereotypes, Puryear writes:

Although the rhetoric has been reduced, the effects on the Black woman have persisted. These ideas have caused many Black women, especially those involved in the Black Liberation movement, to reassess their roles and have engendered a great deal of conflict. One area in which this conflict is evident is that of fear of success. Puryear and Mednick found that women who ascribed to a militant philosophy exhibited more fear of success than nonmilitant women. *Militancy* was defined as degree of concern with the struggle for Black liberation. This finding indicated that achievement in intellectually competitive situations is associated with the anticipation of negative consequences for women concerned with the struggle for Black liberation. Moreover, the findings indicate that many Black women have been seriously affected by the questions concerning their achievement—was it at the expense of the achievement of the Black man and did it have negative consequences for the maintenance of the Black family?

The Black woman indeed holds no favored position. Moreover, she is caught in the bind of being scorned for the role she has had to play for her survival and that of her family. She has been made to feel guilty and conflict-ridden for her limited achievements because of myths saying her progress was made at the expense of the progress of Black men.[23]

Distorted images of particular interest to psychologists are those associated with psychiatric observations. In *The Mark of Oppression,* for example, Kardiner and Ovesey make statements such as: "The female now has some of the social value attributes of the male, and the male those of the female. . . . Their roles are reversed."[24] While such statements may have accurately portrayed women observed in the authors' clinical practice, generalizations to the entire population from a small, nonrandom sample are extremely suspect. As indicated in the previously cited literature and in other studies,[25] data from studies using standard research designs tell a vastly different story.

Although stereotypes of black women persist in many disciplines, psychological researchers have made considerable strides in presenting evidence about realistic characteristics and behaviors. My sense is that the research has drifted away from this territory, perhaps because the exposure of myths is most useful in the earliest stages of a field's development. In later stages we strive for a more comprehensive understanding of psychological and social psychological phenomena than that obtained from the perspective of myth.

Developing New Constructs

As we set out to study neglected populations, it is extremely tempting to apply existing concepts. This happened in early efforts to study blacks and, later, women. The costs of using available tools, however, outweigh the benefits (e.g., dispensing with developing and testing new instruments; the ease of collecting comparative data and integrating new findings into the literature). Such costs pivot on the mismatches between theory and results when psychological constructs developed from the experience of one group (historically that of Euro-American men) are applied to those of a radically different one. Hence, a familiar call is for new concepts to reflect the experiences of previously invisible populations in psychological research.

In the psychology of black women, Gump was among the first investigators to attempt the derivation of new concepts.[26] She speaks eloquently of the need for new formulations and the difficulties she encountered in developing them:

> My attempt to understand something of sex-role expectations, strains, and satisfactions for black women has necessitated a sort of mental stripping. I have had to attempt a kind of anthropological naivete, to assume I knew nothing of the women I was to discuss. At the same time, I had to be subjective, as my own experience and intuitive understanding were the only guides available to me. I believe it particularly important for psychologists, when attempting to understand molar human behavior, to explore literary, historical, and sociological resources. Our disciplinary strength (i.e., our capacity to validate our hunches) has too often been our disciplinary weakness; our hypotheses about complex behavior are too often prematurely formulated.[27]

On the basis of her informal observations, data on labor-force participation, and on analysis of historical and traditional gender roles, Gump identifies one variable—the sense of responsibility—that captures a sense of the uniqueness of black women. She defines this construct as follows:

> I suggest that the sense of responsibility is deeply ingrained in black female sex-role ideology, a responsibility that includes economic provision for the family as well as provision of the more traditional functions. Further, this sense of responsibility has often become detached from economic necessity. There is no question but that most black women who work—and many who do not—need to work in order to ensure the survival of the family. But even when the need in an absolute sense is no longer present, the sense of responsibility, of having to give in this manner, remains. This sense of responsibility has, I believe, become autonomous.[28]

Alternatives exist for ways of developing appropriate constructs or making decisions about the relevance of existing ones. One alternative comes from the area of cross-cultural psychology, a field that has been addressing since the 1950s such problems as the cultural bias of tests based on the Western model, cross-cultural equivalence of instruments, and the problem of locating representative samples. The *Journal of Cross-Cultural Psychology* is useful for locating descriptions of recent methodological advances.

In our efforts to define new constructs of relevance to diasporan women's lives, I think that we must grapple with experiences that unite black women of Africa, the Caribbean, the Americas, and other places around the world. Clues toward isolating specific unitive constructs will come, I believe, from analyses of significant relationships between diasporan women and others in the environment. Social psychological studies are one vehicle for such analysis.

Understanding Relationships

Not only did the earliest empirical work on black women focus on dispelling myths, it also focused on what happened to individual women—their aspirations, their behaviors, and their attitudes. When the influence of the social context was studied, it was done, primarily, by way of comparisons, typically with white women or black men (although not both in the same study). The operation of contextual conditions, such as racism and sexism, were often inferred or presumed from the differences in the responses of various groups. Thus, in studies of fear of success in black and white college women, the relatively low level of imagery displayed by black women vis-à-vis their white counterparts was interpreted as a function of the roles black women were forced to assume in a racist society.[29] Elements of racism were not manipulated or examined directly in the studies; the emphasis was on individual and not on contextual differences.

Recently, Smith and Stewart have called for studies of racism and sexism that use the contextual interactive perspective.[30] According to these investigators, in the interactive part of the model ". . . we would shift from a research paradigm in which we look for two main effects (for race and sex) to one in which we look at the experiences of four gender-race groups."[31] The contextual aspect addresses the fact that ". . . many aspects of each group's experience of sexism or racism are entirely context-dependent."[32] In terms of research design, this indicates the need for data to be collected from different social contexts and for evaluation or control of factors (e.g., power hierarchies) that mask or increase the impact of race or sex cues.

The influence of social context has been explored in several studies.[33] Of particular relevance to the search for unitive concepts in the psychology of diasporan women is Judith Rollins's dissertation on the relationship between black female domestics and their white female employers.[34] Through literature review, participant observation, and interviews she examined the social psychology of deference, invisibility, maternalism, and related processes. This study, which won second prize in the 1984 dissertation competition of the Society for the Psychological Study of Social Issues, is extremely important in that it addresses a crucial fact of diasporan women's lives, namely, their position of servitude in relation to others of greater power and affluence.

Further study of diasporan women in their social environments might be enhanced by the application of conceptual frameworks. Two promising ones come from the disciplines of the psychology of women and black psychology.

Sherif's Formulation. The first was presented by the late Carolyn Sherif in a paper entitled, "Needed Concepts in the Study of Gender Identity."[35] I believe Sherif's approach deserves serious consideration for our field of inquiry because she has identified and specified the linkages among concepts embracing three essential concerns of a psychology of diasporan women: sexism, racism, and classism.

Sherif began with the need for a concept of *gender,* which she defined as a "scheme for social categorization of individuals." [36] The categories may be defined according to biological differences (e.g., male and female) or socially determined classifications (e.g., transsexual) and norms of behavior. Gender identity is defined as "the individual's knowledge of the categorical scheme for gender and that individual's psychological relationships to that scheme, whatever they may be and whether they involve acceptance or rejection."[37] The study of gender identity would embrace such issues as the derogation of a category; the norms and expectations pertinent to one category or another; the types of connections, such as dependency and power, between members of the varied categories; and the person's appraisal of self in relation to a category.

To link the individual to the social environment, Sherif asserts that additional concepts are needed. One is the concept of *self-system,* defined as "a constellation of attitudinal schemata, formed during development through interaction with physical and social realities."[38] The concept of self-system enables us to understand problems such as the relationship of involvement of self in a situation (such as a liberation movement); change in attitudes (for example, toward the role of women in the society); and the different ways in which gender influences behavior for women socialized in similar ways.

Other concepts that link the individual to the social context include reference persons, reference groups, and reference categories (e.g., ethnic group, social class). As Sherif notes, "Each indicates actual individuals, groups, or social categories, but the concepts refer to the individual's psychological relationship to such units. The person may actually belong with them, e.g., be an actual member of the social unit, interacting with the person or the others frequently, or may aspire to belong or be a member."[39]

Finally, Sherif asserts that the two definitions of *social power* (1. the control of resources and institutions and 2. social influence) need to be brought together as an integrative conception. She notes that "the relative power positions of interacting individuals need to be specified first in terms congruent with the social science definition, namely their relative control of resources and access to core institutions (such as the economy or law) and their use in initiating actions, decisions, policy, and effective sanctions."[40] Including this concept in studies of women would permit studies of the relative status of different social groups, the nature of the relationships between them, and group differences in the use of influence.

In her presentation of needed concepts, Sherif did not discuss specific methods. Presumably, those would be selected in accordance with the questions to be addressed in a given study. I think that before attempts are made to apply aspects of Sherif's formulation in empirical efforts, it may be useful to detail some of the issues this approach may address in work on diasporan women.

Analysis is also required regarding the approach suggested by the late Edward J. Barnes.[41] Like Sherif, Barnes calls for the need to link the psychological, or individual, level to the social context.

Barnes's Formulation. Barnes's approach is specifically directed toward the study of self-concept in black children, although I believe that the approach is generalizable to investigations of other constructs, in other populations. In brief, Barnes specifies that self-concept must be examined in relation to social systems in which it is developed and subsequently modified. Of immediate relevance is the family, which is, in turn, embedded in the black community and its structual components, such as social class and residence. This approach contrasts with those that view the self-concept of blacks as a reflection of the white community's devaluation of black people.

Barnes defines a social system as "an aggregation of social roles or persons bound together by a pattern of mutual interaction and interdependence."[42] This definition implies that the *communication process* is a central concept. To study it, Barnes outlined three levels of analysis and methods associated with each one. The first is action and the communication process, which at this level is oriented toward the content of a message and the consistency of behavior in the participants. The associated methods are observation and categorization of the content and enumeration of the behaviors.

Transaction is the second level of analysis. It involves "a unidirectional channel of communication between two systems. For example, A's output is accepted as input by B, but B's output is not accepted by A or any other system as input. The focus at this level is on the isolation of cause and effect or antecedent and consequent sequences."[43]

The third level is interaction, which focuses on the "nonlinear patterns that characterized human behavior."[44] Such patterns may unfold in interactions between two or more parties. As Barnes and others have noted, psychologists are just beginning to develop methods for capturing and analyzing interactional processes. Barnes suggested that such processes be recorded in writing, in films, or on tapes so that essential qualities are not lost. Subsequently, such records would be used to develop categories that embrace features of the recorded exchanges.

Of further note in Barnes's formulation are the practical implications of his approach. The focus on the social system permits the exploration of processes that occur in institutions, such as schools. Thus research can be directed toward the development of communication processes that enhance, rather than debilitate, the individual. Moreover, in its emphasis on the social system of the black community, the approach provides for the study of such concepts as group unity and identity.

To use Barnes's approach in studies of diasporan women, I think it is necessary first to identify and to define psychological constructs of interest. The self-concept of black women is an obvious choice, and we might wish to reassess our current knowledge about this in the light of Barnes's approach. Similar analysis might be directed at concepts involving career choice, which has previously been examined in terms of personal characteristics and motivation, and self-perceptions of involvement in militant activity. As I noted earlier, there have been efforts toward the study of situational characteristics that may determine individual attitudes and behaviors in these domains. Consideration of Barnes's suggestions may force us to examine such situations not as static forces impinging on the individual, but as circumstances that may be changed through the subject's participation.

CONCLUSION

This overview of current research on black women suggests approaches that may be used in our efforts to develop a psychology of women in the African diaspora. As often happens when we are trying to map the main features of a new field of inquiry, we find that there are more issues to be addressed than there are answers to our questions. Moreover, decisions about next steps are, in large measure, based upon the investigator's training, previous work, personal interests, and knowledge of current issues pertaining to given theoretical or methodological approaches.

However, the examination of individual experience in a social context has been cited in many places as an urgent need in psychological inquiry. Critics claim that, too often, we have studied specific behaviors and attitudes as if they were unconnected to other aspects of the person's life, such as history and group norms and values. Thus, the application of psychological tests and measures has been premature.

Investigators interested in the psychology of diasporan women have a unique opportunity to develop the field in ways that consider both the person and the social context. As previously suggested, a first step may be the reexamination of existing research using perspectives such as those of Sherif and Barnes. The analysis can be enhanced by study of the work from other disciplines, such as anthropology, sociology, and history. Because relatively little psychological research exists on diasporan women, the analysis will be one to suggest the major theoretical issues, rather than one to formulate testable hypotheses and to identify particular methods. An important issue to consider at the outset is whether we should approach the study of diasporan women from a cross-cultural perspective, guided by a set of common concepts (such as those pertaining to class), or from one that explores the unique concerns of a particular group.

Providing answers through the research enterprise is a long-term, incremental endeavor. When we address black women's issues, the task becomes extremely formidable, because we must assess the appropriateness of existing constructs or develop new ones. We can advance the field, however, by a long-overdue theoretical analysis. As this takes shape, we can begin to apply psychological research methods to the study of concepts based on the experiences of black women.

NOTES

1. L. Rodgers-Rose, *The Black Woman* (Beverly Hills, Calif.: Sage Publications, 1980).
2. L.W. Myers, *Black Women: Do They Cope Better?* (Englewood Cliffs, N.J.: Prentice-Hall, 1980).
3. See *Psychology of Women Quarterly* 6 (1982); and *Journal of Social Issues* 39 (1983).
4. G.S. Young and J. Sims-Wood, *The Psychology and Mental Health of Afro-American Women: A Selected Bibliography* (Temple Hills, MD.: Resources on Afro-American Women, 1984).
5. F. Barnes, "Black Women and White Women: A Comparative Analysis of Perceptions of Sex Roles for Self, Ideal-Self, and the Ideal Male," in *Perspectives on Afro-American Women,* ed. W.D. Johnson and T.L. Green (Washington, D.C.: ECCA Publications, 1975); J.P. Gump, "Comparative Analysis of Black Women's and White Women's Sex-role Attitude," *Journal of Consulting and Clinical Psychology* 43 (1975): 858–63; J. Scanzoni, "Sex Roles, Economic Factors, and Marital Solidarity in Black and White Marriages," *Journal of Marriage and the Family* 37 (1975): 130–44; and R.A. Essien, "Perceptions of Nigerian College Students Toward the Role of Women in Nigerian Development," *Dissertation Abstracts International* 42 (1982): 4272–A.
6. See Scanzoni, "Sex Roles."
7. F.G. Brown, "The Effect of Autonomy on the Daydreams and Sex Role Autonomy of Black College Women, *Dissertation Abstracts International* 43 (1982): 242B; and V.R. Long, "Situation and Person Variables Influencing Professional Career Aspirations of Black College Women, *Dissertation Abstracts International* 43 (1982): 2041B.
8. K.C. Biraimak, "The Impact of Gender—Differentiated Education on Third World Women's Expectations: A Togolese Case Study," *Dissertation Abstracts International* 43 (1982): 21A.
9. See A.O. Harrison, "Black Women," in *Toward Understanding Women,* ed. V.E. O'Leary (Monterey, Calif.: Brooks/Cole, 1977); P. Gurin and E. Epps, *Black Consciousness, Identity and Achievement* (New York: Wiley, 1975); S. Owens, "Self-esteem of Black Women in a Comparative Perspective," in Johnson and Green, *Perspectives on Afro-American*

Women; and E.J. Smith, "The Black Female Adolescent: A Review of the Educational, Career, and Psychological Literature," *Psychology of Women Quarterly* 6 (1982): 261–88.

10. J.E. Savage, A.D. Stearns, and P. Friedman, "Relationship of Internal-External Locus of Control, Self-Concept, and Masculinity-Feminity to Fear of Success in Black Freshman and Senior College Women," *Sex Roles* 5 (1979): 373–83; and Gurin and Epps, *Black Consciousness.*

11. S. Bould. "Female-headed Families: Personal Fate Control and the Provider Role," *Journal of Marriage and the Family* 39 (1977): 339–49.

12. Gurin and Epps, *Black Consciousness.*

13. C.M. Cochran, C.E. Vincent, C.A. Haney, and R. Michielatte, "Motivational Determinants of Family Planning Clinic Attendance," *Journal of Psychology* 84 (1973): 33–43; M. Fisch, "Internal versus External Ego Orientation and Family Planning Effectiveness Among Poor Black Women, *Dissertation Abstracts International* 35 (1974): 1045B–1046B; N.M. Morris and B.S. Sison, "Correlates of Female Powerlessness: Parity/Methods of Birth Control, Pregnancy," *Journal of Marriage and the Family* 36 (1974): 708–12.

14. F.F. Jones and C.A. Zoppel, "Personality Differences Among Blacks in Jamaica and the United States," *Journal of Cross-Cultural Psychology* 10 (1979): 435–56.

15. Ibid., 451.

16. W.R. Allen, "Family Roles, Occupational Statuses, and Achievement Orientations Among Black Women in the United States," *Signs* 4 (1979): 670–86.

17. J. Fleming, "Fear of Success, Achievement-Related Motives and Behavior in Black College Women," *Journal of Personality* 46 (1978): 694–716; Gurin and Epps, *Black Consciousness*; M.T.S. Mednick, *Motivational and Personality Factors Related to Career Goals of Black College Women* (Washington, D.C.: Manpower Administration, U.S. Department of Labor, 1973); M. Mednick and G.R. Puryear, "Motivational and Personality Factors Related to Career Goals of Black College Women," *Journal of Social and Behavioral Sciences* 21 (1975): 1–30; and P. A. Okediji, "The Occupational Aspirations of Black and White College Females and Their Personality Correlates," (M.A. thesis, Howard University, 1971).

18. J.P. Gump and L.W. Rivers, "A Consideration of Race in Efforts to End Sex Bias," *Issues of Sex Bias and Sex Fairness in Career Interest Measurement,* ed. E.E. Diamond (Washington, D.C.: U.S. Department of Health, Education and Welfare, National Institute of Education, 1975).

19. V.R. Long, "Situation and Person Variables Influencing Professional Career Aspirations of Black College Women," *Dissertation Abstracts International* 43 (1982): 2041B; and A.K. Burlew, "The Experiences of Black Females in Traditional and Nontraditional Professions," *Psychology of Women Quarterly* 6 (1982): 312–26.

20. C.H. Carrington, "Depression in Black Women: A Theoretical Appraisal," in Rodgers-Rose, *The Black Woman;* and S. Fugita, K.N. Wexley, and J.M. Hillery, "Black-White Differences in Nonverbal Behavior in an Interview Setting," *Journal of Applied Social Psychology* 4 (1974): 343–50.

21. J. Jackson, "Black Women in a Racist Society," *Racism and Mental Health,* ed. C.V. Willie, B.M. Kramer, and B.S. Brown (Pittsburgh: University of Pittsburgh Press, 1973).

22. G.R. Puryear, "The Black Woman: Liberated or Oppressed?" in *Comparative Perspectives of Third World Women: The Impact of Race, Sex, and Class,* ed. B. Lindsay (New York: Praeger, 1980).

23. Ibid., 265–66.

24. A. Kardiner and L. Ovesey, *The Mark of Oppression* (New York: Norton, 1951): 348–49.

25. See Harrison, "Black Women"; S.R. Murray, "Images and Roles of Black Women," in *Female Psychology: The Emerging Self,* ed. S. Cox (New York: St. Martin's Press, 1981); and E.J. Smith, "The Black Female Adolescent: A Review of the Educational, Career, and Psychological Literature," *Psychology of Women Quarterly* 6 (1982): 261–88.

26. J.P. Gump, "Reality and Myth: Employment and Sex Role Ideology in Black Women," in *The Psychology of Women: Future Directions of Research,* ed. J.A. Sherman and F.L. Denmark (New York: Psychological Dimensions, 1978).

27. Ibid., 352.

28. Ibid., 376.

29. See P. Weston and M. Mednick, "Race, Social Class, and the Motive to Avoid Success in Women," *Journal of Cross-Cultural Psychology* 1 (1970): 284–91; G.R. Puryear and M.S. Mednick, "Black Militancy, Affective Attachment and Fear of Success," *Journal of Consulting and Clinical Psychology* 42 (1974): 263–66; M.T.S. Mednick and G.R. Puryear, "Race and Fear of Success in College Women: 1968 and 1972," *Journal of Consulting and Clinical Psychology* 44 (1976): 787–89; and Fleming, "Fear of Success."

30. A. Smith and A.J. Stewart, "Approaches to Studying Racism and Sexism in Black Women's Lives," *Journal of Social Issues* 39 (1983): 1–15.

31. Ibid., 7.

32. Ibid., 8.

33. See J. Fleming, "Black Women in Black and White College Environments: The Making of a Matriarch," *Journal of Social Issues* 39 (1983): 41–54; Gurin and Epps, *Black Consciousness;* and C.T. Gilkes, "Holding Back the Ocean With a Broom: Black Women and Their Community Work," in Rodgers-Rose, *The Black Woman.*

34. J. Rollins, "The Social Psychology of the Relationship Between Black Female Domestic Servants and Their White Female Employers" (Ph.D. diss., Brandeis University, 1983).

35. C.W. Sherif, "Needed Concepts in the Study of Gender Identity," *Psychology of Women Quarterly* 6 (1982): 375-98.
36. Ibid., 376.
37. Ibid.
38. Ibid., 381.
39. Ibid., 385.
40. Ibid., 389.
41. E.J. Barnes, "The Black Community as the Source of Positive Self-Concept for Black Children: A Theoretical Perspective," in *Black Psychology,* ed. Reginald L. Jones (New York: Harper & Row, 1980).
42. Ibid., 112.
43. Ibid., 119.
44. Ibid., 121.

Part II

Women and New Roles
in African Societies

Privilege Without Power: Women in African Cults and Churches

Bennetta Jules-Rosette

Social science seldom proves to have the predictive value that its practitioners would like to claim. Instead, it is possible to watch the unfolding of patterns that repeat themselves and appear to establish a realm of "truth."[1] In the study of the role of women in Africa's new cults and churches, two such patterns emerge. First is the overwhelming failure of women who have founded new religious movements to designate female successors. Indeed, leadership succession is a difficult problem in all new religious movements, but it is particularly extreme in the case of movements established or led by women. The second pattern is the predominant association of women with healing and nurturing images and activities in these movements. While there is a general tendency to associate women with nurturing, one may wonder why this association persists in movements that appear to engender protest and change in both Africa and the New World.

In this paper, I shall examine these patterns by reviewing a cross-section of ethnographic and historical data on women in new African churches. After summarizing the evolution of several movements in which women have figured prominently, I shall evaluate women's leadership roles with respect to the dynamics and growth of Africa's new religions. Beginning with the premise that these groups engender movements of symbolic protest, I shall examine the ways in which they have shaped and redefined the status of women. I shall analyze the limitations that these movements place on the development of new symbolic and organizational possibilities for women in terms of the concepts of

99

privilege and power. I have presented some of this material in my previous publications.[2] Here I shall analyze the data on women in African churches with respect to the particular limitations placed upon their leadership roles. Parallel developments have arisen in black cults and churches in the New World. Although the institutional conditions of colonialism in Africa and slavery in the New World were quite different, the processes of domination and control were similar. As a result, comparable cultural and religious responses have taken place on both continents.

Africa's new religious movements have often situated women in positions of privilege without power. For the most part, although there have been some exceptions, women have not been the founders of Africa's new religions. They have, however, played decisive organizational and leadership roles. When describing women's roles in Africa's new churches, a crucial distinction must be made between leadership and adepthood, or ordinary membership.[3] In addition, it is possible to differentiate between those religious organizations that give women political leadership positions and those that stress the influence of women without officially recognizing them. Ceremonial leadership offers women the opportunity to rise to power in African churches without holding an official leadership status.[4] It holds forth possibilities for women to exercise virtual power in ritual interactions. Ceremonial leadership is generally limited to specific social contexts. Such leadership is essentially symbolic and does not imply the exercise of legitimate authority within a group. Similarly, in New World movements, such as the spirit cults of Haiti and Brazil, women hold ceremonial leadership positions as spirit mediums.[5]

WOMEN IN AFRICAN CULTS
AND CHURCHES: AN OVERVIEW

New African religious movements differ in terms of their history, organizational structure, and doctrinal base. Women have held positions of privilege and positions of limited power in indigenous churches, separatist groups, and neotraditional movements. As early as the eighteenth century, women appeared as leaders of the prophetic sects and cults that preceded the contemporary indigenous churches in Central Africa. These groups emphasized themes that apparently appealed to women, including spiritual purification, healing, and the denunciation of witchcraft.

Among the earliest women leaders in the eighteenth century groups were Fumaria, reportedly a charismatic seer, and Dona Beatrice-Anthony, a visionary who claimed to be the incarnation of St. Anthony.[6] Little is known about Fumaria apart from her claim to have direct revelations from the Virgin Mary through which she claimed to detect and punish sins. Dona Beatrice also appeared in the Kongo Kingdom of San Salvador during the early 1700s. Her following grew large enough to be labeled a heretical break from the Catholic church. The prophetess challenged the Portuguese Capuchin missionaries, urging followers to return to polygamy and traditional family units, to abandon the symbols of the Catholic church, to purify themselves with rain water, and to oust priests from the kingdom.[7] Dona Beatrice assured her followers of the messianic coming of princes who would restore the line of Kongo kingship. Ultimately, she was burned at the stake by the Catholic church and gained immortality in the legends that survived her.

There is a considerable gap in the historical research on African religious movements that appeared during the eighteenth and the early nineteenth centuries. However, some of the religious movements arising from the 1880s to the present throughout Africa have contained themes similar to those of the earlier religious movements, with respect to the role of women. The tradition of spirit mediumship became a resource for women who were founders of contemporary indigenous churches. A handful can be named: Mai (Mother) Chaza in Zimbabwe, Alice Lenshina Mulenga in Zambia, Marie Lalou in the Ivory Coast, and Gaudencia Aoko in Kenya. Mai Chaza was an extraordinarily charismatic figure whose claims to spiritual power largely paralleled those of male leaders in the Shona churches. She was a former Methodist, and she was inspired by spiritual revelations to begin her healing ministry. In 1954, Mai Chaza allegedly died and was resurrected. During her "death," according to Mai Chaza's account, she had communicated with God and had been given the gift of healing. She received further spiritual inspiration on a mountain, afterward dubbed *Sinai,* and was commanded to abstain from alcohol, sexual activities, and traditional medicines. Mai Chaza then pursued her mission to heal women who were barren, those possessed by alien spirits, and the blind. Her success drew large numbers of followers, estimated at seventy thousand by the late 1950s. She established holy villages called *Guta ra Jehovah* (Cities of God), where she cared for the sick—first at Seke, then at Zumunya, Zuimba, Harare, and Bulawayo in Zimbabwe. At the healing centers, members were urged to confess publicly and were then cared for through special healing ceremonies and exorcisms.

To establish her unique position, Mai Chaza built on the prominence of the ritual women in Shona tradition. Drawing on the methods of a spirit medium and traditional doctor, she used her charismatic talents to win support in a position of power and self-expression already legitimately available to women. In terms of supernatural powers, the ritual woman is perceived as equal to the man. Mai Chaza, however, made no provision for female succession in her movement, and her own children did not follow her in leadership positions.

Shortly after her death in 1960, Mai Chaza was succeeded by a male Malawian, Mapaulos, who began to perform extraordinary healings in her name. He assumed the title of *Vamutenga* (he who is sent from heaven) and continued his mission at Mai Chaza's healing centers. Mapaulos claimed not only to have prophetic and healing powers but also to be an incarnation of God. These vast claims were perhaps necessary to equal the status of Mai Chaza, who was viewed as a black messiah, equated by her followers with both Moses and Jesus.[8]

In the same year that Mai Chaza received her spiritual calling, Alice Lenshina Mulenga allegedly died and came back to life with a religious mission. Naming her new church *Lumpa* (Bemba for highest or supreme), Lenshina promised her followers health and a new life if they abandoned traditional magic and witchcraft to follow her. She established a holy village at Kasomo in northern Zambia and proclaimed the political and religious autonomy of her followers in the "New Zion." Reputed to have become aligned with the African National Congress, a former Zambian political party, Lenshina's followers refused to pay their taxes, and in 1964 they defended their village through armed opposition to the newly independent Zambian government. These activities eventually led to the expulsion of Lenshina's followers from Zambia in 1970. The cohesiveness of the Lumpa movement was ultimately broken through political struggles. Although Lenshina's group began as a prophetic, anticolonialist movement, it failed to integrate itself into the new nation-state. Like Mai Chaza, Lenshina was unable to name a female successor to lead her church.[9]

While they came into being in similar ways, Lenshina's and Mai Chaza's holy communities relied on different idioms and concepts of leadership. However, Lenshina could draw upon the precedent of institutionalized power and authority granted to women as chiefs and leaders among the Bemba. Although her activities in healing and antisorcery added a new element, Lenshina's regulation of the community and the apparent secular ties and support that she developed indicate that the Lumpa church was a significant means of access to power in the larger political arena. Women who are not priestesses or preachers tend to concentrate on supportive positions at a lower level by participating through ceremony. However, ritual influence, as exemplified by Lenshina's case, may be extended to interactions in other settings and to the group's overall recognition of women's exclusive control of certain types of organizational activities.[10]

The Deima cult was an offshoot of the prophetic movement founded by the Liberian William Wade Harris in 1913.[11] Established in 1940 by Marie Dahonon Lalou, a Godie woman from the Ivory Coast, the Deima movement emphasized healing through the use of a special form of holy water said to have been obtained from serpents. Like some of the traditional mediums and diviners in her area, Marie Lalou renounced marriage and sexual contact. She virtually became a "ritual man," no longer subject to the traditional roles of other Godie women. Four aspects of the Deima cult are crucial to the discussion of women's status: (1) that Lalou, its founder, was a woman; (2) that some of the activities of women were conceived of as ritually exclusive to them, even though male adepthood was involved; (3) that ceremonial leadership required celibacy; and (4) that healing, often related to the nurturing role of women, was one of the cult's major concerns. Several leaders made abortive attempts to succeed Marie Lalou. One of them was a woman who was unable to maintain group support for her leadership.

The preceding examples have all been drawn from indigenous churches, which are independent of mission organizations, rather than from separatist movements. Since separatist movements involve a direct break from mission control, one might conclude that they, too, would emphasize influential roles for women. To a certain extent, this is the case as exemplified by Gaudencia Aoko, who had joined the Legion of Mary *(Legio Maria)*, which began as an offshoot of the Catholic lay organization by the same name. Its origin in East Africa dates from 1963. By the early 1970s, the group was estimated to have a membership of over ninety thousand, primarily within the Luo ethnic group in Kenya and Tanzania. In 1963, two of Aoko's children fell seriously ill following an accident that she attributed to sorcery. As a result of this incident, Aoko began a religious crusade and established her own anti-witchcraft movement that ultimately broke away from the Legio. She sought the assistance of a self-styled prophet, Marcellanius Orongo, a Luo from Tanzania, and was baptized by him.

Crucifix and rosary in hand, Aoko healed the sick, burned amulets, and battled against alien spirits.[12] Aoko's group offered women curing and release from sorcery. Her example inspired Luo women by introducing the possibility of freedom from the domination of their husbands' families. In encouraging these reforms, Aoko's movement opposed the political structure of the Catholic church by developing a lay clergy with married priests and priestesses. Nonetheless, her appeal was short-lived. As her following began to decline, Aoko was unable to establish a stable church community, and her influence did not spread to the outlying Tanzanian branches of the Legio. Again, the problem of female leadership appears to have been the inability to institutionalize a ceremonial role into an official position of full-time leadership. Similar patterns of ceremonial leadership characterize the new religious movements of the Apostolic type in Africa. Further research may reveal parallels in leadership succession within New World religious movements.

Women's Ceremonial Leadership: The Apostolic Case

Movements of the Apostolic type emphasize the importance of spiritual inspiration as a healing force. Women, in this case, hold the ceremonial roles of healers and prophetesses, without direct political authority. In two churches of this type, the Apostles of John Maranke and the Apostles of John Masowe, both founded in 1932 in eastern Zimbabwe, women are not allowed to preach or to participate in major decision-making processes.[13] However, as prophetesses, women may exercise ceremonial and spiritual control over high church leaders. The subtleties of women's influence within the Apostolic groups may be seen by examining the ceremonial roles that they hold in these groups and the relationship between leadership and adepthood.

Women in the Maranke and Masowe churches are not taught the skills of public oratory, argumentation, or collective decision making. Although the concept of Christian equality—the expectation that men and women will enter heaven side by side—is basic to the doctrine of both Apostolic groups, women were denied equal access to political leadership. The domains of leadership and church participation are defined by contrasting gender-based expectations for men and women.

The weekly Sabbath ceremony, or *kerek,* is the major ritual occasion in which most Maranke Apostolic women participate. Through song, women exercise a form of ceremonial leadership and are able to voice their opinions on moral and biblical themes. Women may intervene during sermons with songs that modify and redirect discourse. In such cases, they chastise men and suggest alternative topics and perspectives for their sermons. A relationship of mild ritual competition arises through the vehicle of song interruptions and responses. If women do not interrupt enough, male leaders chide them for being too passive and withdrawn from worship. When the women interrupt a speaker too frequently, however, he may override their songs with continued preaching, stating, in effect, that hearing the gospel directly from the Bible is more important than song. Insofar as women actually alter the direction of discourse, they exercise a restricted form of ceremonial leadership. Didactic songs are regarded as their form of preaching. The following excerpt from a sermon illustrates how a topic may be modified through a woman's song:

Kananga, Zaire, 1969:

Speaker: Do you think that this baptism is a simple matter? Jesus himself said it. He stands in a harsh condition until his baptism is accomplished. You see this baptism can bring division among people who were once dear to each other. We—We are in a hard situation—

Woman Singer: The baptism of John is difficult. Jesus is on one side and Satan on the other. They fight and the whole earth needs the Holy Spirit. Light shown on those who believed. All the commandments are in the Bible.

Speaker: Life to you Apostles. You heard how Mama did the gospel. She lets you know that the baptism of John is a difficult problem. How easy would it be to believe in Jesus if he is engaged in a fight with Satan? Before you believe and get saved, you experience a fight within your consciousness, but once you join you will see what Spirit you get.

The woman interrupts using the speaker's topic but shifting the emphasis. While the evangelist stresses the divisions and conflicts created by baptism, the woman emphasizes that the baptism introduces difficult individual problems arising from the battle between God and Satan. Though maintaining the theme of the sermon in her song interruptions, the woman simultaneously presents her own message and causes the speaker to alter his for the remainder of the sermon.

While men use the ritual aspects of preaching to assert political and moral leadership, women operate more indirectly to control and to reshape discourse. Women's reading and singing groups formed outside of kerek increase and direct their influence during the ceremony. The women use their associations to enhance ceremonial leadership. When one woman initiates a song in kerek the others join immediately, assuring the song's survival and making it difficult for the speaker to regain the floor until the women decide to terminate.

Women who distinguish themselves as a group of performers are able to coordinate their ceremonial interventions through song. They often plan a repertoire of songs to be introduced within the kerek. This activity highlights the distinction between formally recognized (or institutionalized) leadership found in the case of male preachers and some women prophetesses, on the one hand, and expressive participation exemplified by women singing in kerek on the other. Through ceremony, women are able to devise a variety of leadership strategies but are able to sustain this leadership only in a restricted manner within a particular setting.

Some Maranke Apostolic women are confirmed as gifted or master singers *(maharikros)*.[14] These women often, although by no means always, are the wives of elders and have a large repertoire of songs they employ not only to supplant sermons but to interrupt or to extend songs already initiated by men. The maharikros are among the first to lead off songs in kerek, and through their frequent interjections, they teach members new song versions, verses, and harmonies. On occasion, contests take place between male and female maharikros to initiate and to continue special songs.

Another form of ceremonial leadership is exercised by Maranke prophetesses. They examine each member before the main ceremony to determine sins and transgressions of church laws. All members are subject to the prophetesses' evaluations. Women granted this power may control decisions made by the male hierarchy by presenting spiritually based modifications or suggestions. In one instance, a prophetess and wife of an important leader criticized her husband's policy toward the church's leaders and called upon him to confess past errors and to change his stand. Although such confrontations are rare, prophecy is one arena in which a woman's charismatic, spiritual leadership can challenge political leadership.

Spiritual healing, or *burapi,* is an important realm of participation for women in the Maranke church and is the focus of most of their expressive activities. Because healing is associated with nurturing, women in the African churches commonly participate in healing activities as a form of religious expression. While healing is defined as an inspired spiritual activity for which one must be especially gifted, it is also the most basic of all spiritual concerns for the Maranke Apostles. Maranke members often refer to their organization as a church of healing and prophecy. All other forms of spiritual exercise, including baptism and evangelism, are considered to contain an element of healing. In the absence of an official healer, other members routinely perform these duties. When women in one congregation protested against this overlap in functions, they were informed that the most competent and spiritually powerful members of a congregation could heal. Thus, while healing is chiefly reserved for women, it is considered to be within the domain of expertise of all members.

There are several types of women healers among the Maranke Apostles: healer-prophetesses *(baprofiti mapipi),* regular healers *(marapi),* and midwives (also referred to as marapi). All operate with the basic assumption that there are no "natural" illnesses. Evil actions and demons are believed to cause sickness. Spiritual laxity, such as anger or transgression of food taboos, allows demon possession to occur. The possibility of possession is always present. Baptism, which cleanses the new members and makes a spiritual redefinition possible, is accompanied by a comparable vulnerability. Healers and exorcists help to protect the member. The mapipi specialize in diagnosing illnesses and often develop a reputation for their proposed cures. Similarly, the activities of the midwives are charismatic, involving hearing the mother's confessions, diagnosis, and delivering of the child. The regular healers, on the other hand, are instructed in a standard healing ceremony that is performed after kerek or when requested. The majority of these healers confine their activities to the domestic arena. In fact, women are encouraged to begin to practice their healing activities within their own families, particularly in caring for their young children.

This discussion of ceremonial and expressive participation among the Maranke Apostles emphasizes that women's strongest impact as ceremonial leaders derives from the status of prophetess. Often, only one or two women per congregation attain this position. They are frequently the wives of important elders who are able to present the case for their ordination at the church's annual Passover ceremony, where official spiritual gifts and ranks are bestowed.[15] Each potential prophetess must pass a spiritual test to determine the extent of her charismatic powers before ordination. Evidence of visionary abilities alone does not provide sufficient grounds for the official prophetic rank (which has political as well as spiritual implications) to be granted.

Seclusion of Women Among the Masowe Apostles

John Masowe was an African prophet who began to preach in the Rusape district of eastern Zimbabwe (then Southern Rhodesia) in 1932. He promised his followers spiritual healing and a golden age of freedom, opportunity, and self-sufficiency for the future. Like the Maranke Apostles, Masowe's followers hold a weekly Sabbath ceremony in which male elders preach and women function as song leaders and healers. The ceremonial roles of women among the Masowe Apostles are similar to those of the Maranke churchwomen, and their political influence, also, is similarly indirect. However, early on, Masowe established a special group of "Sisters," young women exclusively dedicated to serving him through spiritual work. These women are particularly worthy of discussion because of the symbolic role of their ritual seclusion.

The young girls whom John Masowe had acquired as devoted disciples were referred to as his spiritual "wives."[16] Their duty was to sing at weekly ceremonies and baptisms. During his lifetime, Masowe allowed some of the Sisters to marry under special conditions. However, before his death, he decreed that those Sisters who had been with him as spiritual devotees should not marry again. Today, the major congregations of the Masowe movement have secluded, living quarters for Sisters. New young women continue to be given over to the spiritual cause. Their movements and activities are watched closely, although some of the women eventually are allowed to marry. The Sisters symbolize the spiritual purity of the Masowe church. The restrictions placed on their lives are used to reinforce a group ideal of perfection. Most other women in the Masowe group are not subject to these regulations and do not have to demonstrate the same degree of religious commitment that the Sisters do. I am unaware of similar arrangements in New World religious groups.

Conversion Experiences and Women's Participation

The participation of women in the new African religions is intricately tied to the conversion experience. However, it is not possible to establish a simple cause-effect relationship between reasons for conversion and the extent of eventual participation by women. Women in both Apostolic groups often join as a result of their husbands' involvement. The regulation of exogamy is an essential mechanism for maintaining group identity among the Maranke Apostles. This reinforces the religious community as an insulated group that can only be entered through conversion. Women whose husbands are not members of the group are instructed to make every effort to convince their husbands to join. Young unmarried women are urged not to marry "pagans," including both traditional religionists and members of mission churches. Voluntary polygyny is permitted among the Maranke Apostles, and it serves as a means of assuring group endogamy in a situation where women outnumber men demographically.

Virginity is expected at the time of marriage, and young Maranke girls are examined to see whether they meet this requirement. Those girls found to be virgins are, in theory, allowed free choice of a mate. Those who fail the test are given away in arranged polygynous marriages to church elders.

As a result of these marriage practices, some women describe their conversion to membership with respect to domestic circumstances. Joining the church, in this instance, does not appear to be an independent personal choice but is instead related to women's marital commitments. Thus, the women who join as a result of coercion by husbands and other relatives may be clearly distinguished from those who initially become involved through a visionary or other religious experience. Women in the first category tend to remain more passive after membership, while those of the latter group become more directly involved in ceremonial leadership.

My investigations revealed that regardless of the avowed motivations for joining, the explanation for conversion given by the Maranke women differed substantially from the benefits of membership that they perceived. Some women who admitted joining to follow suit with their husbands or parents stated that they remained members "to receive the hidden life of Christ" and the Holy Spirit's blessings. When these women described their responsibilities in the church, only routine healing was mentioned. Many of these women stated that they neither questioned their conversion nor their spiritual gifts of healing but merely expected them to be confirmed *because* they were women.

Three accounts, in particular, demonstrate the differing conversion experiences of Maranke women. In the first case, the woman felt pressured to join through her husband's affiliation. For seven years, she resisted membership until a final confrontation occurred. She described this experience as follows:

> While we were in the village, my husband became very ill with a stomach disease. The prophet said that he could be cured only if I were baptized. I agreed that the Apostles could baptize my body but they could not have my soul. When I approached the water and reluctantly entered it, a snake appeared out of nowhere. The baptist hit the snake and broke it in two pieces with his staff. I then said go ahead. Baptize both my soul and my body.[17]

This woman, subsequently confirmed as a healer, remained committed, though not active, as a member of the church. Although her husband was a leading evangelist and a special church judge, she did not attend women's subgroup and song sessions. Her attendance at kerek was also sporadic. Nevertheless, she was considered a member in good standing and a competent healer.

The second respondent was a prophetess. She described illness as the motivation for joining and stated emphatically that she had not joined through her husband's influence. She met regularly with a woman's subgroup and, as its only prophetess, was considered its leader. Her participation in kerek and in individual wilderness retreats in quest of visions was regular and active.

The third respondent, a healer, stressed the connection between a spiritual quest and physical healing. She stated that she had joined the group to seek a hidden life in Christ and to receive help in childbirth. She found relief from birth disorders through the church and proclaimed that as a result of joining she had given birth to six children, without complications.

Many women gave pregnancy problems and childbirth as reasons for joining. One woman stated that she joined after losing her child in the seventh month of pregnancy. Another woman said that she had joined in order to cure a menstrual disorder that had caused continual bleeding. The latter informant recalled that for several years she had resisted her parents' request that she join the church, viewing it as incompatible with her high school education and secretarial training. However, complications resulting from the birth of her first child drew her to the church, although her husband remained a nonmember. She stated that her faith had increased through the "miracles" of healing that she had witnessed, and she found an active outlet for church life in her parents' family. In this case, the parents' family and church activities provided some escape from the duties of her own home.

A critical element leading to increased commitment seems to be active participation in either familial or women's prayer and social groupings supportive of the Sabbath worship services. Those women involved in associational subgroupings seem to be more active in both worship and leadership. Similar observations may be made about the role of women's associations in New World cults and in black sects and churches in the United States. However, it is difficult to generalize about the transition from passivity to active membership of women who were forced to join the African churches.[18] The extent of a family's participation in the church also seems to be an important aspect of a woman's conversion and membership experience. My observations suggest that the wives of elders are more assertive and directly involved in church activities than those women who participated neither in leadership through their husbands' nor in women's associational subgroupings. The wives of elders, however, are unable to function as co-owners of their husbands' positions in the absence of a grouping of women ready to respond to the wives' leadership. They cannot develop an independent power base for their activities alone.

Rites of Power and Roles of Power

As discussed, women in the Apostolic groups exercise most of their influence and leadership through ceremonial activities.

Through singing in the weekly ceremony, they compete with men
to present public moral messages. Healing is a religious activity
in which most Maranke Apostolic women engage and which may
eventually lead to ceremonial authority. The virginity examination
(mushecho), midwifery, and certain types of healing also exist as
separate activities for women. In these cases, women derive their
influence on the basis of rites of power, independent of men's
activities.

In the Maranke Apostolic group, prophetesses hold roles of
ceremonial leadership that transcend the domain of women's
ritual activities. Even in this case, they are able only to comment
upon and veto men's activities. The influence of the prophetess is
based on her charismatic appeal and spiritually derived skills and
does not involve the direct exercise of political decision making.
For the Maranke Apostles, it is possible to distinguish between
ceremonial leadership and expressive participation by contrasting
the following activities:

Ceremonial Leadership	Expressive Participation
Prophecy	Healing (includes formal rank)
(includes formal rank)	Routine healing
Midwifery	Songs of exorcism and healing
Morality songs	Free choice of mate
(women's sermons)	Song and prayer
Virginity examination	
Decision making for	
women's issues	

Expressive participation in ceremonies, including rites of power
for women, may translate into ceremonial leadership roles.
However, healing and midwifery are directed toward other women
or domestic activities. The position of the prophetess is broader
but is based on a charismatic source. While this portion of
the analysis is based largely on the Maranke Apostolic data,
it also applies to the new religious groups discussed earlier in
which women like Mai Chaza and Lenshina achieved a status
of prophetic leadership but were unable to transfer their roles
to future generations or to institutionalize the leadership roles of
women in religious groups.

[handwritten marginalia: this does occur for women in leadership in So. America.]

RESEARCH NEEDS AND NEW DIRECTIONS

The new African religions in which women have played significant roles are by-products of processes of rapid social change and development. Uprooted, rural-urban migrants have found in these movements new networks for association and support. This has particularly been the case for women who, deprived of their previous productive economic roles in the countryside, have experienced drift and underemployment in the city.

The new religious groups founded by women have emphasized the formation of utopian communities in which former, productive domestic roles held by women could be reestablished or strengthened. A parallel development may be noted in the appearance of neotraditional women's initiation rites in African urban areas.[19] These rites include the virginity examination in the Maranke church, as well as modified forms of traditional initiation. Initiation rites have served to reinforce the domestic roles of women but have not increased their political influence outside of the home. Movements of religious protest have seldom developed into voluntary associations that directly influence the economic lives of women in the city.[20] They have, instead, reemphasized the integrity of conventional roles for women.[21]

Ceremonial leadership for women has, however, emerged as an important contribution of Africa's new religions, both as an extension and a reinterpretation of traditional forms of spirit mediumship and women's influence. In some cases, this form of leadership is accompanied by rights of office or is supplemented by political leadership. In other cases, it is replaced by expressive participation through which women exercise some influence over a ritual occasion. Present ethnographic and historical data indicate that the record of women as leaders of indigenous churches has been precarious and short-lived. However, case-study materials drawn from the Maranke Apostles suggest that participation in their own subgrouping leads women to have a sense of efficacy and to use collective interactions to redefine their positions in the religious community. The next step in such research is to begin to compare information about household structure, the economic autonomy of women, and child-rearing practices with information about traditional ideals. This comparative information could become the basis for assessing the sources of women's leadership and self-assertiveness in other contexts.

The data that I have presented suggest that women in Africa's contemporary religious movements have difficulties in redefining family structure and collective action to meet their new ideals. These problems have contributed to the marked contrast between ceremonial leadership, which often remains ephemeral or limited to a particular ritual context, and the pervasive experience of masses of women as rank-and-file members of Africa's new religious movements. As prophetesses and symbols of ritual purity, some of these women are recipients of positions of symbolic privilege without political power. The study of women in Africa's new religions is still in its early stages and has not been the focus of much of the previous research on African independent churches. Both additional data and new avenues of inquiry are needed in the following areas:

1. Data on the interaction between men and women in Africa's new churches is necessary to document their strategies for gaining access to the influence and authority in these movements. These materials should contain life history and family profiles, as well as detailed ethnographic documentation.
2. Comparisons of Africa's new religions with popular religious movements in other areas of the Third World and in the West, including black religious movements in the New World, will help to illuminate the causes and structural conditions for the rise of such movements and the position of women as leaders and agents of change within them. Little reliable cross-cultural material of this sort is currently available.
3. More complete data on the life options of women who join Africa's new religious movements is a critical need. In particular, stronger links should be established between the social backgrounds and economic situations of these women and the strategies of religious participation that they select.
4. Further research by scholars of Afro-American and African studies should be conducted on the relationship of New World movements and Pan-Africanist groups to local African

religious movements. There are several areas of parallel development and direct linkage that may be profitably explored by historians and cultural anthropologists.

The masses of women who join the new African religious movements remain underemployed and marginal in the urban setting. If the new religions are responses to a colonial legacy of psychological dependency, the position of women in these groups evidences a double oppression. Although the new religions purport to offer women members hope for change, the social and cultural impact of these movements upon the actual predicament of women in the African city remains to be seen. Unless the cycle of women's adepthood and participation in the new religions alters considerably, the pattern of short-lived leadership, most recently exemplified by the demise of Lenshina's movements, will undoubtedly be repeated in the future before a significant change occurs in the balance between privilege and power in Africa's new religions.

NOTES

1. This approach has been presented by Karl Mannheim in his discussion of the documentary method: *Essays on the Sociology of Knowledge* (London: Routledge and Kegan Paul, 1952), 51–52.
2. I have analyzed the role of women in African churches in the following publications: Bennetta Jules-Rosette, "Women as Ceremonial Leaders in an African Church: The Apostles of John Maranke," in *The New Religions of Africa,* ed. Bennetta Jules-Rosette (Norwood, N.J.: Ablex Publishing Co., 1979), 127–44; and Bennetta Jules-Rosette, "Women in Indigenous African Cults and Churches," in *The Black Woman Cross-Culturally,* ed. Filomina Chioma Steady (Cambridge, Mass.: Schenkman Publishing Co., 1981), 185–207.
3. A similar distinction between leadership and adepthood, or ordinary membership, in new groups is made by Paul Breidenbach in his analysis of women in the Twelve Apostles movement in Ghana, an offshoot of the Harrist Church. *Adepthood* is defined as rank-and-file participation in a group, as opposed to ceremonial or political leadership. "The Woman on the Beach and the Man in the Bush: Leadership and Adepthood in the Twelve Apostles Movement of Ghana," in Jules-Rosette, *The New Religions of Africa,* 99–115.

4. The contrast between ceremonial leadership and political decision-making may be compared with Max Weber's categories of charismatic and rational legal authority. Cf. Max Weber, *The Theory of Social and Economic Organization,* trans. A.M. Henderson and Talcott Parsons (New York, The Free Press, 1947), 328 and 358–69.

5. For a comparison of forms of spirit possession in Africa and the New World, see Sheila S. Walker, *Ceremonial Spirit Possession in Africa and Afro-America* (Leiden: E.J. Brill, 1972), 84–88.

6. Several sources present accounts of the early prophetic movements in the Kongo Kingdom of San Salvador. These accounts emphasize the similarities between the Antonians (followers of Dona Beatrice) and contemporary African indigenous churches. Sources include: Jan Vansina, *Kingdoms of the Savanna* (Madison, Wis.: University of Wisconsin Press, 1968), 154; Andre Doutreloux, "Prophetisme et Culture," in *African Systems of Thought,* ed. Meyer Fortes and Germaine Dieterlin (London: International African Institute, 1965), 255; and Efraim Andersson, *Messianic Popular Movements in the Lower Congo* (Uppsala, Sweden: Almqvist and Wiksells, 1958), 244–55.

7. These descriptions are suggested by Andersson in *Messianic Popular Movements,* 244.

8. Little has been published on Mai Chaza's movement. The most definitive account is probably the brief essay by Marie-Louise Martin, describing the origins, ritual, and social organization of the group. "The Mai Chaza Church in Rhodesia," in *African Initiatives in Religion,* ed. David B. Barrett (Nairobi, Kenya: East African Publishing House, 1971), 109–21.

9. In 1974 I analyzed the direction that Lenshina's movement appeared to be taking in the early 1970s. My predictions concerning Lenshina's ability to pass on leadership to a woman successor have since then proven to be the case. See Bennetta Jules-Rosette, "Ceremony and Leadership: The Influence of Women in African Independent Churches" (Paper presented at the UCLA African Studies Center Colloquium, "Women and Change in Africa, 1870–1970," Los Angeles, April 1974).

10. Both Sister Mary Aquina and Marie-France Perrin Jassy argue that positions of ceremonial leadership for women may ultimately imply political subordination, rather than increasing access to positions of political power. Mary Aquina, "The People of the Spirit: An Independent Church in Rhodesia," *Africa* 37 (London, 1967): 206; and Marie-France Perrin Jassy, "Women in the African Independent Churches," *Risk* 7 (1971): 46–49.

11. William Wade Harris, a Grebo from Liberia, converted large numbers of people in the Ivory Coast, Ghana, and Liberia in 1913 and 1914. Subsequently, a number of Harris's converts established offshoot movements espousing the original founder's doctrines, including the Deima cult described here. The practices of some of these offshoot movements were mixed with local traditional religions, especially in the rural areas. The Deima movement has been described briefly in the

following: Denise Paulme, "Une Religion Syncretique en Côte D'Ivoire: Le Culte Deima," *Cahiers d'Études Africaines* 1 (1962): 5–90; and Sheila S. Walker, "Women in the Harrist Movement," in Jules-Rosette, *The New Religions of Africa,* 87–97.

12. This group has been analyzed in the context of local communities and everyday religious practices appearing in the new religious movements among the Luo of Tanzania. Cf. Marie-France Perrin Jassy, *La Communauté de Base dans les Églises Africaines.* Centre des Etudes Ethnologiques, series 2, vol. 3 (Bandundu, Zaire, 1970), 80–82.

13. Both of these Apostolic movements emphasize spiritual healing and the charismatic roles of their founders. A definitive history of both groups in the context of eastern Zimbabwe is provided by Marthinus L. Daneel in *Old and New in Southern Shona Independent Churches, Background and Rise of the Major Movements,* Vol. 1 (The Hague: Mouton, 1971), 319–44. A more focused study of the origins and doctrine of the Masowe movement is presented by Clive M. Dillon-Malone in *The Korsten Basketmakers: A Study of the Masowe Apostles, an Indigenous African Religious Movement* (Lusaka, Zambia: Institute for African Studies, 1978). I have studied the Maranke Apostles, with a particular emphasis on their outlying branches in Zaire and Zambia. See Bennetta Jules-Rosette, *African Apostles: Ritual and Conversion in the Church of John Maranke* (Ithaca, N.Y.: Cornell University Press, 1975); and Jules-Rosette, *Symbols of Change: Urban Transition in a Zambian Community* (Norwood, N.J.: Ablex Publishing Corporation, 1981).

14. These singers are considered to be particularly gifted, and their services are sought for baptisms and exorcisms, as well as for weekly church gatherings. The origins of the term *harikros* seem unclear. Marshall W. Murphree, in his *Christianity and the Shona* (New York: Athlone Press, 1969), 95 and 99, argues that the term may be derived from the Greek for *hilltop.* Most Maranke Apostles use the English *high cross* as a translation of the term. To my knowledge, similar singing groups do not exist in New World religious movements.

15. Each year, the Maranke Apostles hold a Passover ceremony, which is a combination of the Last Supper and a eucharist. At this time, church members confess sins that they have committed during the past year. John Maranke also designated the Passover as the occasion on which he would bestow official grades and ranks for church members. Since Maranke's death in 1963, these responsibilities have been assumed by his two eldest sons. Cf. Daneel, *Background and Rise,* 329–30; and Jules Rosette, *African Apostles,* 225–30.

16. These women were given to John Masowe by their families at an early age. Eventually, some of these women were allowed to marry other church elders upon John Masowe's approval. Cf. Dillon-Malone, *Korsten Basketmakers,* 62–63.

17. Jules-Rosette, *African Apostles,* 66.

18. Jules-Rosette, *Symbols of Change,* 31–54. Here I discuss the role of women's domestic groups among the Maranke and Masowe Apostles in reinforcing a sense of commitment to and identification with the group. Particularly within polygynous families, such identification appears to be strengthened within the household unit.

19. Elsewhere, I have noted that new forms of women's initiation rites seem to be increasing in the urban areas of southern Africa. These rites include combined ceremonies performed together by members of diverse ethnic groups (e.g., the Bemba, Ngoni, and Cewa women in Lusaka, Zambia) as well as modified forms of initiation incorporated into the ceremonies of Africa's indigenous churches. In both cases, these initiation rites appear to focus on the household skills and domestic roles of women in the city. These ceremonies involve a form of cultural substitution that symbolically recalls but does not entirely supplant the customary rites. Bennetta Jules-Rosette, "Changing Aspects of Women's Initiation in Southern Africa," *The Canadian Journal of African Studies* 13 (1980): 1–16.

20. Judith Van Allen describes the economic associations developed by West African market women. Such groups have a direct impact upon the economic lives of urban women. "Women in Africa: Modernization Means More Dependency," *Center Magazine* (Santa Barbara, Calif.: Center for the Study of Democratic Institutions, May/June 1974): 60–67.

21. Barbara C. Lewis has described the growth of women's marketeers' associations in West Africa in "The Limitations of Group Action among Entrepreneurs: The Market Women of Abidjan, Ivory Coast," in *Women in Africa,* ed. Nancy J. Hafkin and Edna G. Bay (Stanford, Calif.: Stanford University Press, 1976), 135–56. Her materials and my own research in urban Zambia suggest that religious and work associations do *not* tend to overlap. Although cottage industries have formed within the indigenous churches in Lusaka, Zambia, these enterprises involve men in work associations on a much larger scale than they do women.

Afro-American Women Missionaries Confront the African Way of Life

Sylvia M. Jacobs

During the nineteenth-century American Protestant missionary movement in Africa, black Americans assumed a role in the evangelization of their ancestral homeland. Most Afro-Americans accepted the idea promulgated by whites that blacks had been brought to America for slavery by "providential design," to be Christianized and "civilized" and to return to the "dark" continent with the light of "civilization." Many blacks concluded that they should assist whites in the evangelization of Africa. As one Afro-American minister declared in the early twentieth century: "Negroes of America, God calls you to duty; He calls you to service and He calls you now."[1]

Some white church leaders also voiced the opinion that black Americans, because of their African ancestry, had a greater immunity to African fevers than whites and began to perpetuate the myth that Afro-Americans were suited better than whites for African missionary work. Indeed, enough black missionaries survived to lend support to the idea that they had a special immunity to the African climate.

American blacks, endorsing the perception of Africa as a "dark" continent, supported mission work there, believing that the exposure of Africa to Western religious and cultural influences would make the continent acceptable to the world. Since Afro-Americans historically have felt that the negative Western image of Africa has affected white attitudes toward them, they saw the "redemption" of Africa as their "special duty." Thus, as whites

121

took up the "white man's burden" in Africa, black Americans volunteered to help in the "civilizing mission" there.[2]

The majority of American Protestant missionaries assigned to Africa in the nineteenth and twentieth centuries were males, although they usually were accompanied by their wives, who shared in mission duties. Church officials of American mission boards eventually became convinced that wives were indispensable to the success of mission work. Nonetheless, wives received no official recognition as missionaries. The husband was the appointed missionary, and the wife, who was seen as secondary and subordinate, was designated "assistant missionary." Most important, in the final analysis, married women missionaries were first of all wives and homemakers. Because of this perception of the role of married women, religious leaders became aware of the need for unmarried women to carry on the work. But even single women were second-class missionaries, since they rarely sent back mission reports or carried mission work into the interior, as did men. These women also were designated assistant missionaries. The first single woman (not a widow) sent overseas by an American board was Betsey Stockton, a black woman who served in Hawaii from 1822 to 1825.

Women who went to Africa, either as "missionary wives" or as commissioned missionaries, generally aided in efforts to transform the lives of African women and children, since the mores of the late nineteenth and early twentieth centuries dictated that women missionaries be employed in capacities designated as "women's work." They taught in day, Sunday, and industrial schools; maintained orphanages and boarding schools; made house-to-house visitations; did evangelistic work; conducted Bible classes; prepared vernacular literature; and dispensed medical care to women and children.[3]

The total number of American Protestant missionaries sent to Africa from 1820 to 1980 never has been computed. From an average of the published statistics for the period 1900 to 1975, combined with a rough estimate for the nineteenth century, between 350,000 and 450,000 Americans served in Africa from the 1820s to 1975. Black Americans represented an infinitesimal percentage of that figure. Between 1820 and 1980 no more than eight hundred Afro-Americans, sent out by almost thirty missionary societies, served in about a dozen sub-Saharan African countries. Of the total number, almost half were women, with about two-thirds commissioned single missionaries and one-third assistant missionaries or "missionary wives."[4]

Although missionary societies in the United States saw women missionaries as indispensable to the work, they were not always able to translate this support into steady and consistent financial subsidy. Often, women missionaries would be the first called home during a monetary crisis. Church women in the United States many times raised the money to pay the salaries of overseas women missionaries. In fact, it was the female-led missionary societies that provided an important sphere of operation for the male-dominated black American churches. There was a kind of "international networking" between Afro-American women raising money in the United States through the African Methodist Episcopal Church, the African Methodist Episcopal Zion Church, and the black Baptist conventions and Afro-American women missionaries serving overseas, as the two groups had face-to-face exchanges when the missionaries came home on visits.

The total mission movement could not have existed without women, both black and white. Women were and continue to be the most numerous and faithful supporters of missions, both in financial support and volunteerism. American women rallied to the cause of overseas missions. As leaders in the missionary societies and as missionaries, women found a status and role denied them in other areas of the church. Today, women make up about 60 percent of North American overseas missionaries.[5]

This essay will discuss ten Afro-American women missionaries who served in Africa from 1882 to 1951 (the era in which missionary fervor was at its peak). These women served in six African countries and represented seven mission societies. Their experiences and responses help to demonstrate how one segment of women in the African diaspora reacted to African women and children and to the African way of life. This group represents a sample of the total number of black American women missionaries who served in Africa and is a part of a larger research project.

Black American women missionaries expressed a special concern for African women and hoped to improve their position in African society. By working among women, girls, and younger boys, these female missionaries believed they could bring about change in African society and elevate African womanhood.

Black women's sincere religious convictions came from their reading and interpretation of the scriptures: Their interpretation of African society was separate and distinct from the negative views whites generally held about African customs. Prior to their departure, Afro-American missionaries often voiced their ideas about Africa and the role that they hoped to play in evangelizing the continent. Nancy Jones, the first unmarried black woman commissioned by the Congregationalist American Board of Commissioners for Foreign Missions, confesses before her sailing in 1888 that she had always thought that she was destined to give service to Africa. She admits:

> I have prayed to the Lord and asked Him what He would have me to do ever since I became a Christian and I believe He has given me the work of a missionary and He directs my mind and heart to Africa, the land of my Forefathers. To those who are living in darkness and sin. To those who are calling to their sons and daughters to come and help them. . . .[6]

A departing message delivered by Eliza Davis, who went out as a single missionary of the National Baptist Convention and served in Liberia from 1913 to 1915, also reveals something of the attitudes that missionaries took with them to Africa. She discloses:

> Kindred and friends I bid farewell,
>   To go on yonder's shore.
> The love of God is mine to tell.
>   The heathen is my store.[7]

Similarly, a poem written by Minnie C. Lyon, a Lott Carey Baptist Home and Foreign Mission Convention missionary in Liberia from 1921 to 1951, reflected a feeling for the continent of Africa. Lyon, unmarried, wrote the poem after she was asked by so many people why she gave up a secure life as a teacher in the United States to work in an unknown land. Her reply was the poem, "You Ask Me Why," written in 1928:

You ask me why I wish to leave
The land that gave me birth,
And journey to some distant clime
Seeking for joy and mirth?

You ask me why I wish to part
With friends and loved ones dear
A strange companionship to seek,
And why I do not fear?

You ask me why I wish to sail
The ocean far and wide,
With the angry billows tossing
The ship from side to side?

You ask why I wish to roam
O'er Africa's scorching sands,
Through jungles dense and treacherous,
Into the Hinterland?

If to these many questions
I dare to make reply,
I summon all my power
To declare the reason why.

'Tis not for land nor country, that
My journey I pursue,
Nor friends and relatives alone,
My duty I must do.

'Tis not for me to estimate
The horrors of the sea,
But only to be certain that,
His voice is calling me.

'Tis but to know that He is there
Asleep among the crew,
The voice that spoke to Galilee
Can still the ocean too.

He promised to be with me,
His promise is so true,
'Til heaven and earth shall pass away
His promise shall endure.

You ask me why He suffered
On Calvary's rugged Cross?
You ask me why He came to earth
To seek and save the lost?

It was for you, my comrades,
Dear, He left His home above,
His own beloved Father's House
To manifest His love.

For every tongue and people
The cruel cross He bore,
For every tribe and nation
The crown of thorns He wore.

They tell us He's not partial
And so, if this be true,
The story of Salvation
Is true for heathen, too.

I see them sick and dying there
Without His gentle touch
Without a knowledge of His grace,
For those He loved so much.

And that's why I am going there
This message to convey,
Through deeds of love and helpfulness,
Teach them the better way.[8]

The explicit theme in these parting messages was that Western missionaries were offering to Africans a better religion and way of life than what they already had. But the perspectives of these black female missionaries did not differ much from the views on Africa held by black male and white missionaries.

Although they traveled to Africa with many ideas about its

transformation, upon their arrival, Afro-American women missionaries, as white women missionaries, generally were concerned with the status of women in African society. Amanda Berry Smith, a widow, served as a Methodist missionary in Liberia for eight years in the 1880s. During her stay she describes African women in the following manner:

> The poor women of Africa . . . have a hard time. As a rule, they have all the hard work to do. They have to cut and carry all the wood, carry all the water on their heads, and plant all the rice. The men and boys cut and burn the bush, with the help of the women; but sowing the rice, and planting the cassava, the women have to do.

Of course, missionary work in Liberia differed from mission activities elsewhere in Africa because there already existed in that country a small but influential group of Christianized Americo-Liberians. Smith was distressed particularly by the African practice of not educating girls. Accurately perceiving the need for a system of education for Liberian girls, she emphasized: "There is so little attention paid to the education of girls; not a single high school for girls in the whole republic of Liberia. It is a great shame and a disgrace to the government."[9]

By the time missionaries came, introducing another way of life, there was already an eager readiness for change in the minds of many African girls and women. Still Afro-American women missionaries expressed sorrow that they were unsuccessful in reaching many African girls and women. One, Lulu C. Fleming, who in the late nineteenth century worked for the American Baptist Missionary Union in the Congo Free State as the first single black woman, indicated her concern about "the suffering ones of the Dark Continent." In a letter written in 1888 she states: "I feel that our success here in the midst of this darkened people is as sure as are the promises of Him in whose name we have come. All our converts thus far are men. Oh, how I long to see the women reached."[10]

Another missionary, Nancy Jones, of the American Board, who served in Mozambique from 1888 to 1893 and in southern Rhodesia from 1893 to 1897, also discussed the lives of the girls and women of Africa. She admits: "Their [girls'] chief ambition is to get married and work for their husbands, that he may be considered great by the large number of wives. The men and boy[s] sit while the women and girls do the digging. . . . I hope to be able to help them [the girls] rise from the low degraded life." She continues:

> I am very much grieved because I have not been successful in getting hold of the girls as I wish to do. They seem very fond of me and I have had two to come and stay with me a short while. . . . They do not desire much clothing, they want their forms to be seen by the men. They will not come to school unless they are expecting to be paid in some way. It is very sad to see them so low in the scale of morality and I am praying and hoping for a brighter future.

Jones's statements are somewhat reminiscent of comments made by whites in the late nineteenth and twentieth centuries about Afro-American and African morals.

Jones proposed setting up, on a small scale, a boarding school for girls and boys at the Kambini mission station. She affirms:

> I feel that if I kept house, I could get hold of the girls better. I could gather them into my home and teach them various things. Then having an oversight over them, I think I could sow the seed of higher things into their hearts. I do not know whether I shall be successful, but as it has not been tried here, I feel that the good Lord will bless the effort. Please pray for me for I am anxious to help these people out of this state of heathenism.

Unfortunately, Jones never realized her dream. Although she took many abandoned and orphaned children into her home, she never was able to persuade the American Board of the necessity and benefit of a boarding school.[11]

However, Maria Fearing, an unmarried Southern Presbyterian missionary who arrived in the Congo in 1894, was more successful than Jones. Fearing also believed that her major duty in Africa was to assist females and thought that the best way to do this was to take a few girls under her care, keeping them separate from the local population. She decided this could be done by raising orphaned and kidnapped youths, who would have no reason for returning to their villages. News spread, and Miss Fearing eventually had enough children to begin her home.

During her stay in Africa, the "Fearing family" grew to almost one hundred, as she managed the Pantops Home for Girls at Luebo until her departure from the Congo in 1915. Although Fearing reached only a small portion of the Congolese female population, her impact surely was considerable over twenty-one years. Most of the adolescents she trained married, became mothers, and eventually did some kind of civic work in the communities in which they lived. Fearing emphasized to the Presbyterian Church that these girls would grow up to be "Christian women" and that "much good may be done through them among their people in years to come."[12]

Rachel Tharps Boone, a Lott Carey Baptist missionary in Liberia in the 1920s and second wife of Clinton C. Boone, also believed that women were being used by God to perform a special task and that through them, lasting victories would be won for the Christian church. She affirms:

> In modern times, missionary women have labored incessantly, at home and abroad, to flood the world with the Gospel light of love and salvation. . . . As teachers in the schools, as nurses in the hospitals, as promulgators of the Word of God, woman has her much-deserved place in modern evangelism.[13]

Lucy Gantt Sheppard, wife of the pioneer missionary William Sheppard, served as a Southern Presbyterian missionary in the Congo from 1894 to 1910. She volunteered her home at Luebo to train girls of the Pantops Home and boasted that "the making of a Christian home was part of my missionary task and I was glad that my home could be used as a demonstration and practice center." It was at Ibanche that Sheppard formed, in 1903, the first women's society of the Congo Mission. According to her own account, this is how the society began:

> When I saw the first native woman in her strip of cloth, her hair daubed with paint, her body smeared with grease and her mind filled with sin and superstition, I could not help but wonder if she could be changed. . . . Some weeks ago, I invited a few to meet

with me at my home for a prayer service. Fifty have been coming and we have emerged into a missionary society whose aim is to care for the sick, look up indifferent members, and help others in need. We are learning to pray and sing together.

The women met once a week, every sixth day. She pointed out that the gatherings were simple, and "the one great object in these meetings is to get these women, interest them, and by God's help keep them." Sheppard expressed a recurrent theme among women missionaries when she announced that there was much work to be done among African women which was sadly neglected because of lack of workers.[14]

Fanny Jackson Coppin followed Sheppard's example. During her stay in South Africa from 1902 to 1904, Coppin, second wife of Levi Jenkins Coppin, the first African Methodist Episcopal bishop in South Africa, concentrated her efforts in Cape Town on organizing black South African women into Women's Christian Temperance Union societies and Women's Mite Missionary societies. She was less successful in establishing these clubs in Cape Town than she was in inaugurating strong societies at several nearby towns. In the South African interior, Coppin held religious and other meetings for women and formed small missionary groups among wives of black South African ministers.[15]

Finally, Emma Delany, an 1894 graduate of Spelman Seminary, served as an unmarried missionary of the National Baptist Convention in Nyasaland from 1902 to 1906 and in Liberia from 1912 to 1920. She was the second Afro-American missionary to enter Nyasaland. Delany taught in the schools of Chiradzulu. Moreover, she was influential in establishing at the mission station a women's society and a weekly sewing class for girls. After her arrival in Liberia in 1912 Delany selected a spot near Monrovia to establish a school for the uplift of African womanhood, the Suehn Industrial Mission. She certainly was responsible for arousing interest among Afro-American church women for African redemption.[16]

Afro-American women missionaries who traveled to Africa went with the idea of aiding in the "civilizing mission" there. Each was active in efforts involving the women and children on the continent. The accomplishments of these women have been underestimated and overlooked, although, obviously, their work among the women and children of Africa had far-reaching results.

In assessing the comments of these few Afro-American women missionaries of the late nineteenth and twentieth centuries, it is apparent that many went to Africa with preconceived Western notions of what a woman's work should and should not be and of the nature of African society. When they reached the continent, black American missionaries found that some white missionaries and white officials viewed both Afro-American and African society as depraved. Most black missionaries faced the same prejudice and discrimination in Africa they had confronted in America. Those Afro-American missionaries sent out by black churches worked at segregated stations, as did many blacks who were commissioned by white churches, but there was a greater latitude of activities for black missionaries sent out by black churches than for those working for white churches. The duties and responsibilities of black missionaries in general were limited, and in some African countries they were denied entrance to certain regions.[17]

Black women missionaries, like their male counterparts, had mixed feelings about their ancestral homeland. While acknowledging Africa's historical greatness, they also were forced to deal with negative stereotypes perpetuated by whites about the continent. Upon their arrival in Africa, Afro-American women missionaries held out great hope for the work that could be done among African girls and women. However, political and financial realities often squashed their lofty dreams.

In the final analysis, these women missionaries often sacrificed comfortable lives in America to travel to an unknown land, where they would confront a culture with features both admired and despised. Nevertheless, they remained committed and dedicated workers and left Africa probably having made a more positive, albeit limited, contribution than a negative one to African society through their contact with African girls and women.

NOTES

1. L.G. Jordan, "The Responsibility of the American Negro for the Evangelization of Africa," in *The United Negro: His Problems and Progress,* ed. I. Garland Penn and J.W.E. Bowen (Atlanta: D.E. Luther Publishing Co., 1902), 310.

2. Sylvia M. Jacobs, "The Historical Role of Afro-Americans in the American Protestant Mission in Africa," in *Black Americans and the Missionary Movement in Africa,* ed. Sylvia M. Jacobs (Westport, Conn.: Greenwood Press, 1982), 16–18.

3. R. Pierce Beaver, *American Protestant Women in World Mission: History of the First Feminist Movement in North America* (Grand Rapids: William B. Eerdmans Publishing Company, 1980), 49, 53–54, 59, 62, 67, 117–18.

4. Edward R. Dayton, ed., *Mission Handbook: North American Protestant Ministries Overseas,* 11th ed. (Monrovia, Calif.: Missions Advanced Research and Communication Center, 1976), 36.

5. Beaver, *Women in World Missions,* 48, 216–18.

6. Nannie Jones to E.M. Cravath (Fisk University), 20 March 1887, no. 610, American Board of Commissioners for Foreign Missions Papers (hereafter cited as ABCFM Papers), Houghton Library, Harvard University (Cambridge, Massachusetts), 6, v. 35, Candidate File, Nancy Jones.

7. L.G. Jordan, comp., *In Our Stead* (Philadelphia: Foreign Mission Board, National Baptist Convention, c. 1913), 39.

8. Florence Matilda Read, *The Story of Spelman College* (Atlanta, 1961), 359–60; and Minnie C. Lyon, interview with author, 16 November 1981, Durham, North Carolina. The poem is in my possession.

9. Amanda Berry Smith, *The Story of the Lord's Dealings with Mrs. Amanda Smith . . . An Autobiography* (Chicago: Meyer & Brothers, 1893), 342, 378, 384, 389, 393, 437, 453.

10. Lulu C. Fleming to Dr. J.W. Murdoch, 12 October 1888, no. 4, American Baptist Historical Society, Archives of the American Baptist Missionary Union (Rochester, New York), Lulu C. Fleming Letters.

11. Nancy Jones to Dr. Judson Smith, 2 May 1888, no. 70; 29 May 1888, no. 71; and 20 September 1888, no. 72, ABCFM Papers, 15.4, v. 12, East Central Africa File.

12. Sylvia M. Jacobs, "Their 'Special Mission': Afro-American Women as Missionaries to the Congo, 1894–1937," in *Black Americans and the Missionary Movement in Africa,* 157–59.

13. Clinton C. Boone, *Liberia As I Know It* (Richmond, n. p., 1929), 100, 112–14, 119.

14. Jacobs, "Their 'Special Mission,'" 163–64.

15. Sylvia M. Jacobs, "Three Afro-American Women: Missionaries in Africa, 1882–1904," in *Women in New Worlds* 2, ed. Rosemary Skinner Keller, Louise L. Queen, and Hilah F. Thomas (Nashville: Abingdon Press, 1982), 277.

16. Read, *The Story of Spelman College,* 352–53, 357–58; Jordan, *In Our Stead,* 17–18; Emma B. Delany, "Why I Go as a Foreign Missionary," *Spelman Messenger,* (February 1902): 5; and "Spelman Women in Africa," *Spelman Messenger* (February 1945): 2, 7–8.

17. Walter L. Williams, *Black Americans and the Evangelization of Africa, 1877–1900* (Madison: University of Wisconsin Press, 1982), 112.

Extended Family Involvement of Urban Kenyan Professional Women

Harriette McAdoo and Miriam Were

In Kenya the status of women is changing socially and economically. The traditional roles of the Kenyan woman as mother, wife, and farmer are taking on new forms and meanings, especially for the upwardly mobile woman. Women are experiencing advancements in education, politics, professional and nonprofessional employment and as independent business and property owners. These gains have come about because of modernization drives and the current women's movement in Kenya. For women directly involved in the modern workplace sector, substantial changes in the traditional roles and lifestyles are occurring in a variety of forms. This study examines the impact of urbanization and upward mobility on Kenyan women and their families.

While the majority of Kenyan women are in rural surroundings, there is increasing diversity in the roles women now play, especially in the urban centers. To augment the stereotypical view that all African, or Kenyan, or even Nairobi women are a monolithic group, a small group of professional women were selected from the group of professional women in Nairobi. These women are indeed an elite group, for they have become the leaders in their fields of education, business, government, and the professions. Participants' experiences as professional women, as mothers, as wives, and as members of traditional extended families, will be told as a group. Their experiences will, in turn, be compared with those of Afro-American middle-class women, who are employed, mothers, and members of smaller extended family networks. Both groups of women are functioning in several demanding roles simultaneously, while effectively coping with their family responsibilities.

URBANIZATION

A review of the literature revealed very little empirical research on upwardly mobile females in Kenya. Safa indicates that white-collar jobs created by industrialization did not cause lower-strata women to move up but caused a horizontal move into the labor force of women who may already have had a privileged position.[1] The little that has been written on this subject shows that urbanization and changes in women's economic status have a profound impact on family life.[2]

The majority (65 percent) of rural-to-urban migrants have been men. However, in recent years the proportion of males to females in urban areas has been relatively equal, particularly among young age groups and the highly educated. Also, in many cases the males are unmarried or have left their wives in the villages.

Monsted and Walji found that men and women are migrating to urban areas in large numbers for a variety of reasons. The most common ones are: 1) the attainment of higher education (Monsted indicates that women with any formal education have a tendency to move to the city in order to "free" themselves of the traditional roles); 2) the perception of better job opportunities; 3) the higher incomes; 4) the contact with relatives and friends already staying in urban areas; and 5) the lack of both land and the opportunity to inherit land.[3]

Urban growth has tended to separate members from the traditional supportive networks of the extended family as they go to school, move into urban centers far away from kin, and move into homes designed by Western architects that inhibit shared dwelling. Because of urbanization, professional women in Kenya have sometimes been forced to pay for child care, rather than seek help from kin, to have limited social lives, and to have fewer children than nonprofessional women.

Van Allen found that there is a tendency for the urban woman to lose important family roles that are most powerful in the rural family network. Usually the woman has influence as both elder sister and mother of grown sons living in the same household, but urbanization has created a nuclear household that separates her from her sons and the rest of the family.[4] With the decline in polygamy and the increase in "modern" attitudes toward marriage and premarital sex, the incidence of single parenthood has increased in urban areas. More women in contemporary Kenya are deciding to forego marriage and take on a career; however, motherhood continues to provide the basic measure of self-worth for Kenyan women.[5]

Researchers have found that regardless of where women live in Kenya today, they are influenced by the processes of modernization and urbanization. Their personal and family lives have undergone some major changes, and in some cases, these changes have not been in their favor.[6] According to Van Allen and Munene, the new social framework within which changes are occurring may be directly related to a decline in the socioeconomic status of women. Some scholars argue that the existent social structure of Kenya has caused "modern" urban women to be dependent on men emotionally and economically. Also, as a result of modernization, rural women must work twice as hard to support their families because of the increased migration rates. Employed women in general tend to work longer hours than men because of their multiple roles in the home and in the marketplace.[7]

However, in spite of rapid urbanization and the influence of Westernization, the traditional character of the men and women of Kenya has not changed, for they still continue to maintain a high level of contact with their families, and marriage, as well as motherhood, are still highly valued.[8] Others have found that regardless of the migration to urban areas, kinship bonds, on a whole, remain relatively strong.

The kinship bonds are maintained in many forms of help exchange and through frequent visits. The urban dweller in Kenya is not totally committed to a life in the city. Many persons have land in rural areas or invest in land and have homes in the country. Research data also support the hypothesis that kinship ties increase when social status increases. Ross and Weisner report that kinship ties were severed or lowered only in cases of economic need, rather than out of social choice. The findings from rural-urban migration studies show that traditional culture coexists with urban culture.[9]

Studies of urban professional Afro-American women have

revealed similar findings. Women maintain extensive and intensive kinship bonds of visitation and reciprocal help exchanges with relatives even when they become economically upwardly mobile. The extended family patterns are maintained even when relatives live in separate apartments and houses.[10]

Women and Motherhood

Van Allen found that regardless of the Western influence and modernization, motherhood provides the basic self-identity of Kenyan women, and African women in general. For this cultural reason, Kenya has the highest birth rate in the continent. Children are regarded as a precious gift and represent hope for continuity in the future.[11]

With the increase in modern institutions, marriage, fertility, and family life have been modified in varying degrees. A survey conducted by the government of Kenya in 1973 reveals that the majority of women were married by age twenty-four and had had at least one child. However, the report also shows that many women with some secondary school training tended to have fewer children than those with less education. This finding characterizes both rural and urban women. Reining et al. have found in their study of Kikuyu women, in the Village of Kikuyu, that women would limit their family size in order to educate their children. These same women were also beginning to use contraceptives to limit the size of the family. They saw this method as a way of providing more freedom for themselves and creating more opportunities for their children. The surge of new attitudes, especially among the young women, has meant some changes in rituals for girls. Girls can now decide to forego initiation rites and marriage, and they can move to other areas, but motherhood is still highly valued.[12]

Women and Education

Due to the daily demands of farming activities, child care, and household supervision, rural women, in particular, lack the time to obtain a formal education, and therefore the educational status of rural women, in comparison with urban women, is comparatively low. Approximately 80 percent of rural females do not have a formal education, compared to 66 percent of rural males. Recent government figures show women's representation in education, especially at the primary level, has doubled since the 1960s. Nevertheless, while the trend in Kenya has been to upgrade the educational status of females, illiteracy rates remain very high among those twenty-five years of age and older. The illiteracy rate for females is twice that for males on a national level.[13]

The high illiteracy rate for females can be attributed to many factors. Maleche reports that the lack of adequate boarding facilities contributes to the high dropout rates after primary school. In many cases, families continue to give boys preference over girls, particularly at the high school and university levels. Another factor is that far greater daily demands are made on female children for field work, fetching water and fire wood, and caring for younger siblings.[14]

Although the disparities between males and females are reduced at all levels, educational officials find that disparities must also be reduced in the types of curricula offered to boys and girls. As in many industrialized countries, the Kenyan educational system prepares boys for technical and scientific endeavors, while girls are trained in the arts and education. This prevents many girls from attending higher institutions of learning, because more emphasis is placed on science and math. As a result of their earlier training many women end up in teaching, agriculture and home economics, nursing, and in offices as secretaries.

Women and Work

In spite of increased urbanization, the increases in migration among women have not meant any significant changes in the geographic concentration of Kenyan women in rural areas, where over 80 percent reside and work. Their most common work activity is farming. Close to 90 percent have their own small holdings, but the productivity of women farmers is often low compared to their male counterparts. Women's labor input, however, is often as much as 30 percent greater than that of men. Women are excluded from agricultural training programs and extension services. As a result, rural women continue to practice traditional methods of growing food for subsistence and cash crops. Very few (under 5 percent) of the women are engaged in other work activities. This small percentage of females are usually teachers and government employees. Rural females also constitute a small proportion of permanent wage employment. The labor activity of rural women in Kenya is one area in which fewer advances are being made.[15]

The typical urban woman is hardworking, with significant roles as mother, household supervisor, and worker. For the most part, her roles are very similar to those of the rural woman. One distinction between the urban and rural women is that urban women are more directly influenced by modern and Westernized institutions, which introduces a variety of experiences that rural women do not encounter.[16] The economic activity of urban women is somewhat varied, but a large proportion are unemployed. Women are highly represented in three occupational categories: 1) agriculture and forestry; 2) finance, insurance, real estate, and business services; and 3) community, social, and personal services. A very large proportion of women in the private sector are unskilled and casual laborers, whereas the largest number in the public sector are teachers and nurses. According to a 1976 Labor Enumeration Survey, the only occupational group where women outnumber men are secretaries (91 percent). The opportunities in wage employment are, thus, rather limited and, in some cases, patterns of professional employment are declining.[17] Women in urban areas are mostly visible at the marketplace, while men dominate the modern sector, e.g., industries and offices. The only exception for females is in schools and clinics, where they work as teachers and nurses.[18]

Social science literature and government reports on rural women, generally, show that there has been very little positive change in economic, political, or social status. The drive for modernization has essentially offered fewer opportunities for the educational advancement and wage employment for women. Although women have gained less than males, they are and have been actively involved in nation-building projects, such as water projects, tree-planting projects, and family-planning and nutrition projects.[19]

Urban women, like their rural sisters, are at a disadvantage economically, politically and educationally. Very few women in urban and rural areas have achieved a high socioeconomic status equivalent to that of men. Women, in general, are systematically denied equal access to social and economic institutions in Kenya.[20] According to Shorter, the educated professional woman is a rarity and belongs to a very small elite. Thus, most of the women in urban areas would not be classified as middle or upper class.[21]

In the past decade the number of women in Kenya who have been able to achieve advanced education has increased, thus increasing the pool of women able to achieve professional status. At the same time they have fulfilled the traditional female roles of becoming wives, mothers, and members of their husbands' families, while remaining active in their own extended families of origin. The balancing of the multiple roles played by the women in Nairobi is similar to the balancing experienced by Afro-American women.

METHOD

This study is the only empirical examination that could be found in the literature on professional Kenya women who were mothers and who had families. The purpose was to obtain descriptive data on: 1) their educational and occupational mobility patterns over three generations of their families; 2) family structural patterns over three generations; and 3) religious changes over the same period. The additional dependent variables were: 4) extended family interaction and help-exchange patterns; 5) the reciprocal obligations and kin help; 6) child-rearing attitudes; and 7) levels of stress and significant changes they had experienced in their lives.

Instrument Development

Because of sensitivity to the biases that often exist in cross-cultural comparative research, a great deal of care was taken in developing the research instrument in this study. The protocol had to accurately assess the forementioned variables, without introducing undesired or unexpected impediments to the data-collection process.

The instrument used was a variation of the McAdoo Family Profile Scale (1978, 1983), used to study middle-class Afro-Americans. Certain questions were selected from the scale that might adequately assess the impact of professional mobility on the family. All of the Kenyan students enrolled at Howard University were asked to go over the protocol individually, as a pilot test. With the assistance of these students the researcher was able to select the questions most appropriate to Kenyan culture. The students went over the protocol, made corrections, and were each interviewed about any biased, misleading questions, or culture-bound items they found. Modifications were made as indicated by these Kenyans.

Sample

All of the respondents were interviewed in Nairobi by the researcher and were selected on the basis of their employment, status, residence, and status as mothers. A total of twenty-two Kenyan women participated in the study. Although the number of actual participants is small, the Kenyan women selected were generally representative of the female Kenyan professional population. All of the women were professionals, mothers, and worked and resided in the city of Nairobi. The respondents' ages ranged from twenty-six to forty-eight years, with a mean age of 34.06 years. All but one had children under eighteen living at home. There were nine ethnic groups represented in this sample. Nine of the women were Kikuyu.

While the women all lived in Nairobi, their identification with the family's home was very great. Many indicated that they "lived and worked in Nairobi" but their "home" was in the province or the town of their extended family. This was true even if they had been in Nairobi for twenty or more years. All felt a strong need to have an actual home in their province of origin near their family. This need was great enough that they often made big sacrifices to acquire a homestead with a *shamba*, or garden area.

According to their family's homeland area, the largest proportion of women came from the western province (32 percent); 27

percent came from the eastern and Nyanza provinces (see Table 1). Over the three generations, no mobility across provinces occurred, indicating a high level of stability and strong identification with their home areas.

Education and Occupation

The women were highly educated, placing them in the educational elite of their country. Thirty-two percent had earned graduate and professional degrees, 45 percent had earned college degrees, 9 percent had received advanced training beyond high school, and 14 percent had earned a secondary degree. Almost all had received at least one degree from abroad.

Their achievements were much higher than were their parents' achievements, with 70 percent having only primary school educations. Thirty percent of their mothers and 15 percent of their fathers had traditional training, and 15 percent of their fathers had secondary educations (see Table 2). All but one of their grandfathers and grandmothers had traditional educations.

Table 1 Frequency Distribution of Sample, by Geographic Mobility Over Three Generations

Geographic Mobility	Subject		Subject's Parents		Subject's Grandparents	
	f	%	*f*	%	*f*	%
Town or Province						
Central	6	27	6	27	7	32
Coast	1	5	1	5	1	5
Eastern	2	9	2	9	2	9
Nyanza	2	9	2	9	2	9
Rift Valley	4	18	4	18	3	14
Western	7	32	7	32	7	32
Total	22	100	22	100	22	100
Type of Area						
Rural	16	73	18	82	19	86
Small town	4	18	3	14	2	9
Urban	2	9	1	5	1	5
Total	22	100	22	100	22	100

Note: The percentages may not always total 100% due to rounding error.

Table 2   Summary of Educational Achievement of Subjects and their Ancestors

Educational Level	Subject		Parents				Maternal Grandparents				Paternal Grandparents				Spouse	
			Mother		Father		Mother		Father		Mother		Father			
	f	%	f	%	f	%	f	%	f	%	f	%	f	%	f	%
Traditional	—	—	6	30	3	15	18	90	17	85	19	95	19	95	—	—
Primary	—	—	14	70	14	70	2	10	3	15	1	5	1	5	—	—
Secondary	3	14	—	—	3	15	—	—	—	—	—	—	—	—	—	—
Advanced	2	9	—	—	—	—	—	—	—	—	—	—	—	—	2	10
3 yrs. college	10	45	—	—	—	—	—	—	—	—	—	—	—	—	8	40
Grad./Prof.	7	32	—	—	—	—	—	—	—	—	—	—	—	—	10	50
Total	22	100	20	100	20	100	20	100	20	100	20	100	20	100	20	100

Note: The percentages may not always total 100% due to rounding error.

The majority of the women in this study were employed in highly demanding positions. Twenty-seven percent were executives, 14 percent were in administrative positions, and 55 percent were managers. Only one participant was employed as a clerical worker. The socioeconomic status of the sample ranged from lower-middle class to upper-middle class.

The occupational mobility patterns paralleled the educational changes (see Table 3). However, a large proportion of the grandparents were skilled draftsmen and artisans, and their status would have been similar to today's professionals. Both the grandmothers (59 percent maternal, 55 percent paternal), and the grandfathers (50 percent maternal, 55 percent paternal) were skilled. The next highest occupational group was composed of managers. Thirty-two percent of both groups of grandfathers were managerial; 23 percent of maternal and 27 percent of paternal grandmothers were managerial. Their grandparents had higher status than their parental generations, for in this generation only 23 percent of the fathers and 50 percent of the mothers were skilled, while 27 percent of the fathers and 14 percent of the mothers were managers; and administrators accounted for 32 percent of the fathers and 14 percent of the mothers. These women were the children of people with high occupational status and were the grandchildren of those who were among the elite of the traditional societies.

The urban-based occupational status-coding schema had limitations and was adapted to different cultural environments for the earlier generations. For this reason, in reviewing the grandparents' generation, the community-based status of the existing rural traditional society was used to determine status. For example, a traditional healer in the grandfather's generation would be scored the same as a physician in the subjects' generation. Another modification the author has used in previous studies with black Americans was to put a greater factor weight on education, rather than occupation. Black Americans tended not to have occupations commensurate with their education, and it was assumed that the same discrepancies would be found in Kenya, where the colonial system had left a similar differential status legacy for Kenyans.

With these modifications, the status over two generations was determined based on the combination of occupation and education. The culture-bound nature of the SES coding is shown in the

Table 3 Occupations by Percentage of Subjects and their Ancestors over Three Generations

Occupations	Subject		Parents				Maternal Grandparents				Paternal Grandparents				Spouse	
			Mother		Father		Mother		Father		Mother		Father			
	f	%	f	%	f	%	f	%	f	%	f	%	f	%	f	%
Executives	6	27	—	—	—	—	1	5	1	5	1	5	2	9	14	67
Managers	12	55	3	14	6	27	5	23	7	32	6	27	7	32	6	29
Administrators	3	14	3	14	7	32	1	5	1	5	1	5	—	—	1	5
Clerical	1	5	3	14	2	9	—	—	1	5	—	—	—	—	—	—
Skilled	—	—	11	50	5	23	13	59	11	50	12	55	12	55	—	—
Semi-skilled	—	—	1	5	1	5	1	5	1	5	1	5	1	5	—	—
Unskilled	—	—	—	—	1	5	—	—	—	—	—	—	—	—	—	—
Unemployed	—	—	1	5	—	—	1	5	—	—	1	5	—	—	—	—
Total	22	100	22	100	22	100	22	100	22	100	22	100	22	100	22	100

Note: The percentages may not always total 100% due to rounding error.

lower status of the parents' generation. It is also the generation during which the families made the transitions from traditional rural to urban lifestyles. In the present generation both subjects and their husbands had very high status (see Table 3). Seventy-three percent were middle class and 23 percent were upper class. Both groups were very high in Kenyan status.

Self-Perceived Social Status

The respondents' ratings of their own status is probably the most accurate assessment. They were asked to rate themselves within the context of their society. Their self-status ratings were almost identical with that assigned by the researcher using the modified scoring. This provided a form of accuracy or reality check upon a scoring procedure based on industrial environments. Seventy-one percent rated themselves as middle class and 19 percent as upper class (see Table 4).

The very high status of these women, which was determined both by objective and subjective assessments, reflected their unique positions in Nairobi. For the most part, their status would be higher than most Afro-American professional women and, thus, the pressures they may feel could be greater than those faced with playing multiple roles.

Religion

Almost all of their maternal grandparents (sixteen out of twenty-two, or 73 percent) practiced traditional Kenyan tribal beliefs. The impact of the missionaries could be seen in the fact that only 14 percent of their parents were traditional religious practitioners, while 23 percent were Anglican. A few increases had occurred in the other Western religious denominations (see Table 5). By the present generation the change was so complete that none identified themselves completely as traditional. Yet, during the interview, 9 percent indicated that they had combined traditional beliefs and Christianity. Several more indicated that they were strictly raised as Christians and were gradually going back and incorporating or reevaluating their group's traditional beliefs.

Table 4   Social Economic Status of Subjects, Spouses, and Ancestors using Modified Coding Based on Kenyan Culture and Self Perception of Subjects

| | Social Economic Status | | | | | | | | | | |
| | Mothers | | | | Spouses | | | | Parents | | |
Social Class	f	%	f	%	f	%	f	%	f	%	f
Upper	5	23	7	32	13	65	11	55	—	—	—
Middle	16	73	12	55	6	30	8	40	—	—	—
Working	1	5	3	14	1	5	1	5	9	41	3
Lower	—	—	—	—	—	—	—	—	11	50	11
Poor	—	—	—	—	—	—	—	—	2	9	8
Total	22	100	22	100	22	100	22	100	22	100	22

| | SES Self Ratings | | | | | | | |
| | Subjects | | Spouses | | Parents | | Grandparents | |
	f	%	f	%	f	%	f	%
Upper	4	19	4	22	8	44	9	50
Middle	15	71	13	72	9	50	6	33
Working	2	10	1	6	1	6	1	6
Lower	—	—	—	—	—	—	2	11
Total	21	100	18	100	18	100	18	100

Note: The percentages may not always total 100% due to rounding error.

Most of their present memberships were in the various Protestant denominations (77 percent), while 9 percent were Catholic, and one had no affiliation.

Family Structure

The majority (82 percent) were in two-parent homes. We wanted to know if single mothers had grown up in families that differed in structure. Of the four presently single mothers (18 percent), two were from one-parent homes without extended kin, and two were from two-parent homes with extended kin. Of the eighteen married women, only one had grown up with a single mother, and one with a single mother within an extended pattern. All of the others were in two-parent homes of one form or another (see Table 6).

Table 5 Religious Memberships Over Three Generations

| | | | | | | | Subjects' | |
| | | | | | | | | |

	Subject		Subjects' Parents		Subjects' Paternal Grandparents		Subjects' Maternal Grandparents	
Religion	f	%	f	%	f	%	f	%
Traditional (Kenyan tribal beliefs)	—	—	3	14	17	77	16	73
Methodist	2	9	2	9	1	5	—	—
Catholic	2	9	2	9	—	—	1	4
Quaker	1	5	1	5	1	5	1	4
7th Day Adventist	2	9	2	9	1	5	1	4
Protestant	5	23	2	9	—	—	—	—
Pentecostal	1	5	2	9	—	—	—	—
Anglican	2	9	5	23	—	—	1	5
Presbyterian	4	18	2	9	1	5	1	5
Combination of traditional and others	2	9	1	5	1	5	1	5
None	1	5	—	—	—	—	—	—
Total	22	100	22	100	22	100+	22	100+

Note: The percentages may not always total 100% due to rounding error.

The family structure of their families of orientation was examined and several different structures were found, with no one type existing in a majority of the homes. Nine of the women (42 percent) grew up in extended families of parent(s), children, and

Table 6 Frequency Distribution of Family Structures of the Kenyan Women and of their Families of Orientation

			Family Structure		
Women	f	%	Their Families of Orientation	f	%
Two parents	18	82	Both parents, children, nonrelatives	6	27
			Both parents, children, relatives	7	32
			Both parents, children	4	18
One parent	4	18	Mother and children alone	3	14
	22	100	Mother, children, relatives	1	5
			Mother, children, nonrelatives	1	5
				22	100

Note: The percentages may not always total 100% due to rounding error.

relatives; seven (32 percent) were in nuclear families of only parent(s) and their children; and six (27 percent) were in augmented families, of parent(s), children, and nonrelatives. This variety of forms would be common throughout Nairobi and Kenya, but it is often overlooked within the literature. With the frequent intervisitations, even children who were living only with their mothers or with both parents were able to have a high level of support from a variety of relatives in different households.

While none of the women admitted to being in a polygynous union, it was found from other sources that at least one woman was in a polygynous union as the first wife, and another made allusions to the possibility of another wife. Over the three generations the families had become Europeanized, mainly through the influence of the missions, the churches, and the present economic prohibition against multiple wives. While most were now monogamous, 31 percent of the women grew up in polygynous families, as did 72 percent of their fathers and 75 percent of their mothers (see Table 7). Both their paternal and maternal grandmothers tended to be the first wife; 73 and 92 percent, respectively, of their grandmothers and 93 percent of the mothers were ranked as first wife. Over three generations their families had gone from two-thirds polygynous among their grandparents, to one-third of their parents,' to almost none in the present generation.

RESULTS

One purpose of the study was to obtain a picture of how professional Nairobi women were functioning in their multiple roles and how they were interacting with their extended families.

Extended Family Interaction

There were frequent contacts with the extended family: 50 percent of the women saw family members several times a week, and 68 percent were in regular contact at least several times a month (see Table 8). They also were frequently in contact with their kin via the phone or by mail. In spite of long distances from their

Table 7 *Frequency Distribution of Type of Parents' and Grandparents' Marriage, Rank, and Number of Wives*

	Paternal Side				Maternal Side	
	Father		Grandfather		Grandfather	
Group	f	%	f	%	f	%
Polygynous	5	31	13	72	12	75
Monogamous	11	69	5	28	4	25
Total	16	100	18	100	16	100
Rank of wife						
1st	14	93	11	73	11	92
2nd	—	—	3	20	—	—
3rd	—	—	—	—	—	—
4th and over	1	7	1	7	1	8
Total	15	100	15	100	12	100
Number of wives						
1	11	69	5	29	4	27
2	1	6	3	18	3	20
3	3	19	2	12	4	27
4	1	6	3	18	—	—
5	—	—	2	12	1	7
6 or more	—	—	2	12	3	20
Total	16	100	17	100+	15	100+

Note: The percentages may not always total 100% due to rounding error.

home provinces and the difficulties and cost of transportation, a lot of visiting was done back and forth between households in Nairobi and in the provinces. Frequently, relatives came to stay, and children were sent on extended visits with their cousins or grandparents. The month-long school holidays that occurred every three months facilitated the visiting and their ability to maintain very intimate knowledge of the everyday goings-on in both Nairobi and the provincial households. As a group, they felt it was very easy to visit their relatives and for the relatives to visit them. They all felt contact with relatives was very close and that the amount of contact with their friends was about right. No significant social class differences were found in frequency or ease of visiting with kin. The researchers' visits to families clearly showed

Table 8 Description of the Extent of Kenyan Kin Interaction Patterns

Extent of Contact	Total *f*	%	Extent of Contract	Total *f*	%
Visits to relatives			Frequency of seeing relatives		
Very easy	14	64	Almost everyday	3	14
Somewhat difficult	5	23	1 or 2 times a week	8	36
Very difficult	3	14	1 or 2 times a month	4	18
Total	22	100+	Every other month	2	9
			Few times a year	4	18
Visits from relatives			Once a year	1	5
Very easy	12	55	Total	22	100
Somewhat difficult	7	32			
Very difficult	3	14	Frequency of phoning or writing		
Total	22	100	Almost everyday	7	33
			1 or 2 times a week	5	24
			1 or 2 times a month	3	14
			Every other month	3	14
			Few times a year	1	5
			Only in emergency	2	10
			Total	21	100

Note: The percentages may not always total 100% due to rounding error.

a pattern of frequent contact on special occasions and on a routine daily basis. The households of the women and their siblings and cousins were separate, but the interaction and visits were so frequent that they all existed as one extended family across different domestic units.

Help Exchanges

Different patterns emerged when the types of help-exchange were classified according to help given and help received. The help that the women gave to their relatives was a clear mixture of all types (91 percent), with finances being outstanding. In turn they received a combination of different types of help in most cases (57 percent), with the clear indication that help received was in the form of finances and land (14 percent). Only 14 percent indicated that they received nothing from their relatives (see Table 9).

The women indicated that they received a great deal of help

Table 9 Types of Help Given and Received from Family and Friends, by Social Economic Status of Subjects

Types of Help Exchanged	Total *f*	%	Amount of Help Received	Total *f*	%
Given to family			Most help received from		
Financial, land	2	9	Family	10	48
Combination of types	20	91	Friends	9	43
	22	100	About the same	1	5
			No help given	1	5
Received from family			Total	21	100
Financial, land	3	14			
Emotional, friendship	2	9	Amount received from family		
Clothes, furniture, food	1	5	Very great deal	11	58
Combination of types	12	57	Great deal	3	16
Nothing	3	14	Somewhat	3	16
	21	99	Very little	2	11
			Total	19	100
Given to friends					
Financial, land	3	15	Amount received from friends		
Emotional, friendship	3	15	Very great deal	5	24
Clothes, furniture, food	1	5	Great deal	10	48
Combination of types	13	65	Had no effect	2	10
	20	100	None at all	4	19
Received from friends			Total	21	100
Financial, land	1	5	Change in amount received from family		
Emotional, friendship	7	33	Increased	5	24
Clothes, furniture, food	2	9	Decreased	8	38
Combination of types	10	48	Remained the same	8	38
Nothing	1	5	Total	21	100
	21	100	Changes in amount of help given		
			Increased	11	50
			Decreased	3	14
			Remained the same	8	36
			Total	22	100

Note: The percentages may not always total 100% due to rounding error.

from their family (74 percent) and from their friends (72 percent). Only 11 percent received little help from their families, and 19 percent received little from friends. Both sources of help were important, but they saw family help as greater, for 58 percent received a very great deal of help from family and 24 percent from friends. When asked to directly compare friends and family, the women rated the family higher (48 percent), but they rated friends nearly as high (43 percent) (see Table 9).

An exploration was made of changes in the amount of help given to or received from kin over the past few years. Half of the women (50 percent) indicated that they had increased the amount of help they had given to others in the family, while one-third (36 percent) felt that they had given help at the same level. In assessing changes in the amount of help they had received from kin, most felt it had decreased (38 percent) or remained the same (38 percent) (see Table 9). While involved closely with kin they appear to be giving more than in the past but are getting about the same amount of help from kin. Again, there were no apparent class differences between the five upper class and seventeen middle-class women, either in the involvement level or the type of kin-help exchanged. Patterns were clearly evident, regardless of the women's status.

One frequent form of help the women received was child care and domestic help provided by distant kin who had left the home province and come into Nairobi to live with them. They were often the poorer family members who exchanged help for the opportunity to live in the city and earn small wages. While these kin performed service tasks for the household, they could not be treated impersonally as servants, for they were blood relatives. They were a definite help to the women, while at the same time these relatives, often adolescents, were an additional responsibility. The women were totally responsible for their helpers' health care, clothing, supervision, and possible school fees.

Harambee Efforts. The women reported that Harambee was commonly used to gather family members together to overcome a family need. A Harambee would be called on a variety of occasions, such as when an adult was ill and needed a crop harvested, or a child was going oversees to get advanced training and needed to raise tuition or living expenses. Individuals could be involved in several Harambees at one time. In order to remain in good standing with the family, participation was mandatory. Participation in the Harambee was like an insurance policy for the future, when the women might need help for their own children or family members. Additionally, the Harambees sometimes were considered to be a financial strain, especially when many cousins reached college age at the same time or when several crops had failed.

The Harambee cultural concept extended beyond the family into community-wide efforts. For example, the Harambee schools were an important aspect of the Kenyan educational system, for the local elementary schools were mostly built through Harambees. Universal elementary education became available only in 1980, and until then the shortage of school spaces excluded the majority of children. Each village had to come together to build the buildings and seek a teacher or volunteer to teach in the school. Therefore, the concept of shared help was basic to the families and institutionalized within the wider society.

Reciprocity and Obligations

There was an inherent expectation that one share with the wider family. There was a very strong obligation to help those who are less fortunate in the family (82 percent). Even those who did not feel this strongly indicated that one should usually help them, depending on the situation (see Table 10). In terms of the expectation to share, a great deal of sharing was the accepted norm (41 percent), and at least some sharing was expected. Sharing within the family was multi-directional. Reciprocity flowed from the top down, from the bottom up, and out from each family member in concentric circles.

When money was loaned to a relative, over half (59 percent) did not expect it to be returned, while some (32 percent) usually expected it to be returned by a relative. In reality, the money was a gift transmitted in the form of a loan in order that the relative could maintain "face" or save pride.

While there was a clear obligation to share, there was the clear expectation that some help would be provided if they, too, were in need, but the expectation and the extent of help that would be forthcoming were not as strong. The majority (59 percent) felt that the family was not obligated to give them anything in return, while a few (18 percent) expected help only in emergencies. Some

Table 10   Expectation of Sharing Obligations Felt Toward Family and Friends

	Total	
Expectation of Sharing	f	%
Obligations Felt		
Obligated to less fortunate		
Yes, without question	18	82
Usually, depends on situation	4	18
Total	22	100
Expectation to share with family		
Great deal expected	9	41
Some sharing expected	6	27
Very little sharing	4	18
Other	3	14
Total	22	100
Balance of Exchanges		
Amount owed family		
Nothing in return	13	59
Only in emergencies	4	18
Expect the same	3	14
Other	2	9
Total	22	100
Exchange balance in family		
Given more	11	50
Received more	3	14
Given same as received	7	32
No obligation felt	1	5
Total	22	100+
Loan of money to family		
Always expect repayment	2	9
Usually expect repayment	7	32
Rarely or never expect repayment	13	59
Total	22	100
Exchange balance in friends		
Given more	7	33
Received more	3	14
Given same as received	11	52
Total	21	99

Note: The percentages may not always total 100% due to rounding error.

(14 percent) expected the same level of assistance as they had given to kin.

There was a general feeling among the women that they had given more to their relatives than they had received (50 percent), and a third (32 percent) felt that they had received as much as they had been given. Only a small number (9 percent) had received more than they had given to relatives. There was a clearer level of balanced exchanges between the women and their friends, for most (52 percent) felt that they had given as much as they had received, and only some (33 percent) had given more than they had received.

One of the clearest obligations was in the area of school fees that must be paid for all of the children. The great emphasis that is placed on education, the lack of spaces in some of the preferred schools, and the paucity of employment among those without a school degree put entire families under the strain of paying the very expensive fees. Education was highly valued, and 41 percent of the mothers had no preference for educating boys, rather than girls, when money was limited. This meant that in cases of large families, still considered an ideal in spite of economic and housing-size difficulties often found in Nairobi, school fees become a major cost that requires wide participation.

Child Care

The continuity with the family line was important. Most of the women (89 percent) felt that they raised their children in the same way they had been raised. They also felt (89 percent) that family history was important, and they often told stories about famous Kenyans or Africans (66 percent). Many repeated family history to their children (47 percent), while others seldom did (26 percent).

These women had assumed demanding professional roles and simultaneously continued their traditional parenting and housekeeping roles. They all indicated that they were responsible for raising the children and controlling the house. Husbands were reported to be not as involved with the children. Several women mentioned that the men continued the earlier rural pattern of meeting male friends in the beer halls and bars after work and often not coming home until long after the children were asleep. Therefore, the responsibility of actual childrearing was placed upon the mothers.

The women did have servants who lived in, but since they were also distant relatives there were certain restraints imposed in terms of the amount of work demanded and greater responsibilities for their care and maintenance. Mothers, also, were sometimes burdened with relatives who, as students, were not helpful until the end of the school term.

In spite of the live-in relatives in their homes, the mothers indicated that when they worked (72 percent) or went out socially (75 percent), their children were cared for by paid babysitters. These caretakers usually also lived in the home. In a few cases it was hard to tell if the mothers were referring to their relatives, who often were also paid a small salary (see Table 11).

When asked who would raise the children if something happened to them, all of the women felt that their children would be cared for within the family, with 66 percent being care for by the paternal side and 28 percent by the maternal side. This pattern would be consistent with traditional beliefs in Kenya that children belong to the father's line, or clan. The only cases in which the mother's side would raise the children were when marriages had occurred across cultural tribal groups or when there was a great deal of hostility between the mother and her husband's people.

Some Sources of Stress

The women appeared to be very self-confident and on top of their world. Yet when we finally had deeper conversations about how they juggled all of their roles, it became apparent that they carried a *tremendous* amount of responsibility. They felt responsible for many relatives, both in Nairobi and at home. Often the most wealthy and educated family person, they were constantly called upon to help others, give advice, and make personal appeals on behalf of kin to members of the bureaucracy. Every family had one or two people overseas in school, and these

Table 11 Frequency Distribution of Child-rearing Practices

Variable	f	%
Child care while employed		
Relative	2	11
Paid babysitter	13	72
Not applicable	3	17
Total	18	100
Child care while on social occasions		
Relative	1	6
Friend	1	6
Paid babysitter	12	75
Not applicable	2	13
Total	16	100
Would raise children if parents unable to care for them		
Maternal side	5	28
Paternal side	12	66
Both equally	1	6
Total	18	100
Raise children differently from family		
Yes	2	11
No	17	89
Total	19	100
Family history important		
Yes	17	89
No	2	11
Total	19	100
Tell stories about Kenyans/Africans		
Yes	12	66
Sometimes	3	17
Other, too young	3	17
Total	18	100
Tell stories about family history		
Yes	9	47
Sometimes	3	16
Rarely	5	26
Other, too young	2	11
Total	19	100
Education preference according to sex or age		
Male	5	29
Female	4	24
No preference	7	41
Eldest	1	6
Total	17	100

Note: The percentages may not always total 100% due to rounding error.

157

arrangements for passports, travel, housing, and college admission almost always fell on those in Nairobi.

Some of these women were married to successful men, and several were required to entertain for him. This demanded organizational skills and carried additional responsibilities, over and above family obligations and their own professional obligations.

Some women indicated that, with their professional advancement, they met resistance from their husbands. Although the men wanted to marry women who were educated to help them out financially and to be able to raise their children in order to succeed, they did not want the women to go too high. Some women indicated that they had met great resistance when they attempted to get advanced degrees or if their jobs became higher in status than their husband's. Some women related stories, which could be echoed by women in all other countries, about being manipulated to allow the husband to remain dominant or about the husband's ambivalent feelings toward her success. A pregnancy occurred more than once at a crucial time in a woman's career advancement or when she was about to return to school.

The other source of stress was that of husbands' girlfriends. Many men were continuing the traditional polygynous type patterns in an informal manner. Several women mentioned this competition and their sense of powerlessness to fight it. Legally, husbands could take another wife, although financially this has become impossible. However, if women were not careful and pushed their husbands too hard, the men did not hesitate to remind their wives of the options.

The women reported that girlfriends often were an established part of their lives and were tolerated but not totally accepted. Although based on limited data, it appeared that women who had married while they were in school in America and who had lived there with their husbands were apparently able to maintain a little more control. For them a more monogamous pattern had been established early in their marriage. Others were coping as best they could. They were evolving their own separate social lives with their female kin and business associates. Gentle prodding revealed that "most other women" were not, as a group, choosing the alternative of "boyfriends." A few did go out, but they were rare. It was socially acceptable for a man but not for a woman to stray far from the marriage; the same double standard common in Western societies also existed in Kenya.

Levels of Stress

The Holmes and Radke Scale of Life Changes, based on Western standardization, has been found to be associated with physical and mental stress in Western countries. It was unknown how the women in the Kenyan sample would relate to it, but the pilot tests revealed no difficulty with it, and the women enjoyed that part of the interview. In fact, this series of questions elicited additional responses that were more enlightening than some of the responses from the pre-established questions. It was used, not so much for its relevance as an instrument but because it generated several spontaneous expressions by the women on sources of stress in their lives.

The Significiant Life Events Scale measures the number of stressful life events that have occurred in a woman's life over

Table 12   Means of Stressful Life Events of Kenyan and Afro-American Professional Women

Holmes and Radke Stressful Life Events Time Scale		M
Nairobi Women		
Stress Intensity Total	0–2 yrs.	325.86
	Last 6 months	170.52
	6 mo. to 2 yrs.	155.19
Frequency of Events	0–2 yrs.	13.05
	Last 6 months	6.91
	6 mo. to 2 yrs.	6.14
Afro-American Women		
Stress Intensity Total	0–2 yrs.	247.93
	Last 6 months	103.65
Frequency	0–2 yrs.	10.96
	Last 6 months	4.98

a stated period of time. Black and white women in Western communities under the same amount of stress experienced by the Kenyan women were found to have a great likelihood of experiencing major physical or mental illnesses within a twelve-month period. The scores of the Kenyan women reflect both the personal observations of the researcher and the responses of the Kenyan women surveyed in this study.

The most culturally unbiased scoring of this scale would be the frequency count of those events that have occurred in their lives. The women had experienced in the past two years an average of 13.05 such events that would cause them to make adjustments in their lives and, therefore, would be expected to cause strain in their lives. In the most recent six months they had experienced an average of 6.91 such events. This would be considered a high level of stress.

The stress intensity scores have not been standardized on a Kenyan sample and therefore will be used only for comparative purposes. The total score indicated that the women indeed were under a great deal of stress. Over two years the stress levels were 325.86 (SD 102.84). Stress at this level was scored as major and intense on the American clinical studies of Holmes and Radke. Over the past six months the women had experienced a stress intensity level of 170.52, which would be considered high.

In an earlier study of American upper-class and upper-middle class Afro-American women with children in Washington, D.C., the author found that these women had an average of 247.93 points on the same scale. This level of stress was considered moderately high for these professional women. Holmes and Radke found that 51 percent of the individuals in their study within this score range developed a major illness associated with this moderate continuing level of stress. The Afro-American women had experienced an average of 10.96 stress events over the past two years.[22]

The scores of the professional Afro-American women, also residents of their country's capital, were considered high, but the women in Nairobi had scores that were much higher. These scores could reflect the higher levels of stress that the Kenyan women may be experiencing because of the uniqueness at their high occupational levels. In the course of the study it was impossible to give an accurate reflection of the actual jobs that these women held, because in several cases they were the only women in the positions, and their confidentiality would be violated. Occupationally they were isolated. They felt strongly the need to remain competitive in traditionally male-dominated occupations. Their stress scores reflect the extra strains that persons experience when their countries are undergoing rapid urbanization and are establishing newer forms of government. Their stress levels also reflect the great responsibilities they were carrying for their extended family and the large numbers of persons of all ages within their households.

The Kenyan women under apparently greater stress were those in the middle range of socioeconomic status. Women at the very top jobs were in positions to obtain the services needed to support their functions. Women interviewed who were at the lowest levels had apparently accepted their positions and were not striving as hard. The most stressful appeared to be those in the middle who were moving into positions of great responsibility but were financially strapped. Their own job and family demands were marked and, therefore, they often could not meet obligations without great sacrifice. The more wealthy women also tended to come from homes with more financial security and, therefore, family members probably made fewer financial requests.

SUMMARY

The subjects of this study held positions of great leadership within their country and had skills sorely needed by Kenya during this first quarter century of independence. It is important that, somehow, these young women, in their mid- and late thirties, become aware of the fast pace they are keeping and the overload that their demands may have on them. Many of the women have young children, and as their child-care responsibilities decrease with the maturity of their children, some of the extreme stresses may be lessened.

As they have done in the past, the women will need to call upon their extended families to give them more help. They will need the in-house help provided by distant relatives and live-in servants for the foreseeable future. The extended family support systems in which they have participated will continue to be of immeasurable help in the future. However, the women will need to be fully aware that there are strong inherent reciprocal obligations that are built into any kin-help relationship. The obligation to share with the majority of family members who are less financially secure will continue and probably increase in the future, with the gradual aging of family members.

The patterns of stress and family obligations that these Nairobi women exhibit are somewhat familiar to Afro-American professional women in similar positions. The sense of occupational isolation may not be as extreme in America, but there still is the same reality that women are often entering jobs that have not been held by women before. They, therefore, do not have supportive networks within the workplace, as do men, but the increase in numbers of educated younger women may lessen the isolation of all professional women in the future.

The Kenyan women seem to face greater difficulty than the American women with obtaining the overt cooperation of the husband in the household. However, this is offset by the fact that every one of the mothers had live-in domestic help, in spite of the limitations about this help earlier noted. All of the husbands were supportive of their wives working, but several appeared ambivalent about the jobs that were becoming high-level careers. Those women who did not have this support required a high level of personal motivation in their careers.

This study of professional women who were also mothers and who lived in Nairobi points out the many similarities that exist for these Kenyan women in particular and Afro-American women in general. They were often experiencing role overloads as they tried to effectively meet the responsibilities of their multiple roles. Yet, both groups were attempting to perform well in their roles of mother, wife or lover, professional, and extended family member. A fair amount of stress was being experienced by both groups. Yet, the supports that were being provided by the extended family members of both groups enabled them to cope successfully in their family and professional lives.

Despite the pressures and role juggling, these women and professionals, in general, are very talented persons within Kenyan society who have already begun to exert their leadership ability.

They have the combined potential of having very productive lives and being able to make signficiant contributions to their country in the future.

NOTES

We extend our appreciation to the busy women who shared so much of their time and lives. Their names cannot be mentioned because of the pledge of confidentiality.

1. H. Safa, "Women and the International Division of Labor," in *Women and Work in the Third World,* ed. Nagat M. El-Sanabary and Margaret Wilkerson (Berkeley: Center for the Study, Education and Advancement of Women, University of California, 1983).

2. A. Maleche, "A New Status for Women in Kenya," *East Africa Journal* 9, 6 (1972): 28–31; P. Reining et al., *Village Women, Their Changing Lives and Fertility: Studies in Kenya, Mexico, and the Philippines* (Washington D.C.: American Association for the Advancement of Science, 1977); A. Shorter, *East African Societies* (London: Routledge and Kegan Paul, 1974); B. Whiting, "The Kenyan Career Woman: Traditional and Modern," in *Women and Success: The Anatomy of Achievement,* ed. R.B. Kundsin (New York: William Morrow and Company, Inc., 1974); B. Whiting, "Changing Lifestyles in Kenya, *Daedalus* 106, 2 (1977): 211–25; and F. Weisner and S. Abbot, "Woman, Modernity, and Stress: Three Contrasting Contexts for Change in East Africa," *Journal of Anthropological Research* 33 (1977): 421–51.

3. M. Monsted and P. Walji, *A Demographical Analysis of East Africa: A Sociological Interpretation* (Uppsala: Scandinavian Institute of African Studies, 1978).

4. J. Van Allen, "African Women, 'Modernization' and National Liberation," in *Women in the World,* ed. L.B. Iglitzin and R. Ross (Santa Barbara: Clio Books, 1976).

5. J. Zollner, "Women's Rights in Africa and the United States," *Africa Report* 22, 1 (1977): 6–9.

6. Reining, *Village Women;* Shorter, *East African Societies;* Van Allen, "African Women"; and Whiting, "Changing Lifestyles in Kenya."

7. Van Allen; "African Women"; and F. Munene, "A Kenyan Perspective," *African Report* 22, 1 (1977): 18–19.

8. M. Ross and F. Weisner, "The Rural-Urban Network in Kenya: Some General Implications," *American Ethnologist* 4 (1977): 359–75; Whiting, "The Kenyan Career Woman"; and Whiting, "Changing Lifestyles in Kenya."

9. Shorter, *East African Societies.*

10. Harriette McAdoo, "Factors Related to Stability in Upwardly Mobile Black Families," *Journal of Marriage and the Family* 40, 4 (1978):761–78;

and Harriette McAdoo, *Extended Family Support of Single Black Mothers, Final Research Report* (Department of Health and Human Services, National Institutes of Mental Health, Grant, 1983).

11. Van Allen, "African Women."
12. Reining, *Village Women.*
13. Central Bureau of Statistics, *Women of Kenya* (Ministry of Finance and Planning, Government of Kenya, 1978).
14. Maleche, "A New Status for Women in Kenya."
15. Central Bureau of Statistics, *Women in Kenya;* and G. Kitching, *Class and Economic Change in Kenya, The Making of an African Petite Bourgeoisie, 1905-1970* (New Haven: Yale University Press, 1982).
16. Weisner and Abbot, "Women, Modernity, and Stress."
17. Central Bureau of Statistics, *Women in Kenya.*
18. Van Allen, "African Women."
19. Central Bureau of Statistics, *Women in Kenya;* and A. Wipper, "Equal Rights for Women in Kenya," *Journal of Modern African Studies* (1971).
20. A.O. Pala, "Definitions of Women and Development: An African Perspective," *Signs* 3, 1 (1977): 9-13; P.A. Ododa, "History of the Development of Women's Education in Kenya," (Master's thesis, Howard University, 1966); and Wipper, "Equal Rights for Women in Kenya."
21. Shorter, *East African Societies.*
22. Harriette McAdoo, "Levels of Stress and Family Support in Black Families" in *Family Stress, Coping and Social Support,* ed. Hamilton McCubbins et al., (Springfield, IL: Charles Thomas Publishers, 1982).

Part III

Black Women in Folk Culture and Literature

African Diaspora Women: The Making of Cultural Workers

Bernice Johnson Reagon

I mark my beginnings as a cultural worker with my involvement in the civil rights movement. This was my first experience with distancing myself from the culture in which I was living and selecting things from that culture, organizing them, and using them to bring back information, positions, and political stances to the community that had created the material in the first place. All of my work—in the civil rights movement; as a student of William Lawrence James at Spelman College; as a graduate student at Howard University; as a vocal director of the DC Black Repertory Company, a theater workshop conducted by Robert Hooks and Vantile Whitfield in Washington, D.C.; and my work with the Smithsonian Institution and with Sweet Honey in the Rock—falls into this category. It was after some ten years in this kind of activity that I began to think that maybe the culture offered more than data content; that maybe the culture also offered a process, a way to get things done, a way to collect, assemble, and present material; that maybe the culture offered a methodology for these activities, a theory for use, and an analysis of the conditions of black people in the larger world.

Through reflection, I discovered that to some extent I was already operating on the premise that the culture being studied includes its own methodology for the development of archives, analysis, presentation, and practice. When I became the program coordinator of the Albany Georgia movement, what knowledge influenced my execution of my responsibilities? I already knew how a mass meeting was done. It was to be done the way all gatherings of Afro-American people were done. There was always a song before the spoken word. Always first a song. Then, a statement of definition about why we had come together. Then, another song followed by a prayer that, in some way, acknowledged the presence in the gathered group of the totality of the history of the people.

In the civil rights movement, our base was Christian, and we prayed to God, announcing our understanding of our commonness with all life in the universe, calling on that force to be with us. Then came another song and then announcements. Then came the sermon or speech or the testimonies and another song, with singing all the way through the collection to support the movement. (Some progressives put the offering before the sermon to imply that people should give money during a very conscious moment and should not be manipulated while in the higher, spiritual state which successful sermons are alleged to produce. An even newer position, opposed to the use of song as background for other activity, advocates the collection of money during the sermon or during the speech as well and maintains that songs should not be used to cull money out of people.) Once the sermon and the money collection were over, you would close, unless the police were present and you deemed it best to continue. In that case you could just start again and go on forever. Continuance or expansion of the structure has always been done with song.

My culture had already educated me to be a program coordinator. I had spent my life in gatherings, seeing people who were the masters of gathering us together to do this work. When I began to understand that I already operated out of an Afro-American cultural context, I began to look to that source for patterns of analysis and theory that I could use in my investigative research. I had the opportunity, while developing the African Diaspora Program at the Smithsonian Institution, to witness the role of women in the development of New World African diaspora societies. In this program, which brought together African and African diaspora cultural expressions, especially those traditions that had illuminating value when analyzing the Afro-American experience, we found that women were central to the continuance of many of the traditional practices.

In the following examples, the women were the heads of

their communities, the keepers of the tradition. The lives of these women were defined by their culture, the needs of their communities, and the people they served. Their lives and their work are available to us today because they accepted the responsibility when the opportunity was offered—when they were chosen. There is the element of transformation in all of their work. Building communities within societies that enslaved Africans, they and their people had to exist in, at least, dual realities. These women, however, became central to evolving the structure for resolving areas of conflict and maintaining, sometimes creating, an identity that was independent of a society organized to exploit natural resources, people, and land.

Olga Da Alaketu, translated as Olga of the Ketu Nation or, as she is called, Dona Olga Regis Alaketu, is Queen of the Ketu Nation, which existed in what is now Benin, West Africa.[1] She also is known as the mother of saints, Ialorixa. Olga lives in Bahia, Brazil. She is the highest priestess of Candomblé in Bahia and is recognized throughout Brazil and West Africa, especially Yorubaland, for her rituals and ceremonies. The descendant of a long line of queens and priests, she was trained in the priest-craft by her great aunt.

I was introduced to Olga Alaketu when she came to Washington, D.C., to participate in the Smithsonian's African Diaspora Program, as the head of a cultural delegation from Brazil.[2] The African Diaspora Program had as its goal the investigation of Afro-American culture as part of a larger family of culture rooted in Africa, extending through African-derived communities in the Caribbean and in Latin America. Olga represented Brazil as a nation, but as her name demonstrates, she represented another nation as well. Brazil was the country to which Africans were brought as slaves by the Portuguese. The story of Olga Alaketu and the culture she represents is the story of the evolution or rebirth in Brazil of a people and culture which was at once of Brazil and beyond Brazil.

Candomblé is the culture and religion evolved by slaves in Brazil, as well as a way of continuance and transformation required to survive as a people in a new place. Survival here does not simply imply staying alive but encompasses the need to survive beyond the narrow definitions afforded by the slave structure. To function simply as slaves is much too narrow to ensure that a people will prosper. There was a need to establish a structure and system with its own content that would allow an improved situation for survival beyond the confines of carrying out the required functions as slaves.

For many years, the development of Candomblé took place as a subcultural activity, for slave owners had no need for slaves to maintain or to evolve an identity beyond their slave status. The lacing, or intermingling, of the identities of Candomblé deities with the saints of Roman Catholicism was one dimension of insuring the survival of African-based culture. Today, Candomblé is widely practiced in Bahia, and its devotees transcend racial and class boundaries. In structuring presentations for sacred rituals, we encouraged our guest groups to become hosts and to reorder the presentation space according to their ceremonial and ritual needs.

When Olga began her presentation, people who entered the space were separated: men were asked to sit on one side and women on the other. When Olga entered, the audience was asked to stand because she was a high priest. When the North American audience stood, it taught us, on a physical participatory level, who she was among her people, because in our society, you stand in court rooms when judges come in, in deference to the position of the office. During the ceremony people were asked not to cross their legs and hands because to do so would block the spirits. This is reminiscent of images of old Afro-American women in the United States sitting wide-legged with their skirts looped between their legs, never crossing their legs, whether on the porch or in the church or in the streets. However, within the Afro-American community, as class enters the picture as a force, we are taught that this posture is improper for women. The correct position is to be seated with your legs closed very tightly or crossed at the ankles. Occasionally, if you are wearing a full skirt, you may cross at the knee, but that indicates a bit of daring flash.

I always have trouble with sexual delineations because of the oppressive and exploitative power of sexism in my life as an Afro-American woman. In the physical act of separating men from women, there seems to be an emphasis placed on our not being the same and on our functions within society as being different.

Dona Olga's services, however, did not convey inequality in any sense, especially since everyone stood when Olga entered and everyone sat with legs open to the spirits. Olga herself held the highest position in the house, and as a woman, took rank over the men in her group who were drummers. Also, the fact that Olga learned her craft from a great aunt indicates that within African and Brazilian religious practices there was a tradition of powerful women in leadership roles.

Olga traveled with six of her children. Her four sons were drummers, and her two daughters were dancers. There were dancing and drumming ceremonies to Obu, the hunting god; to Obawehey, the god of skin disease; to the deities of the sun and wind; to Shango and his wife Isla; to Osia, the god of leaves and medicine; to Osun, goddess of the river; to Eshu, the messenger between man and God; to Shuman, the rainbow god from Dahomey; and to Yamaniah, the mother of all gods. When they did the dances to Shango and Isla, they were dressed in the colors of the gods: red, gold, and white. On Friday, the day of Oshawa, the dancers were in white, and Olga was in blue. Oshawa is the supreme deity within Candomblé.

Olga's responsibility as a participant in the program of Candomblé culture was to share what she could with us, maintaining her own sense of cultural and sacred integrity. At the same time she was present, there were also Santería worshipers from New York City and a group from Oyotunji, the reconstructed Yoruba village in South Carolina. The Yoruba village group was always in her audience. At one point, she called on its high priest, Oba Enfuntola, to join in the dance to Shango. Near the end of that ceremony, she gave roots to each member of the Yoruba village.

What we were able to gather from our experience with Olga Alaketu was that there had evolved in Brazil a powerful culture, based in African tradition, with infusions of European culture. Candomblé is no longer submerged or oppressed by the Brazilian government. Olga actively participates in more modern areas of society. In addition to her responsibilities as head of the oldest Candomblé house in Bahia, Olga has been giving lectures at the Psychiatry Department of the University of Sao Paulo, on the subject of the religious or spiritual causes of illnesses often diagnosed as mental. If the problem is of the first category, Olga is trained to identify the problem and to resolve it through initiation. This separation between the spiritual and mental parts of the human unit is very important in Africa and African-derived communities and often is blurred and ignored in Western disciplines that deal with the nonphysical aspect of human life and behavior.

The presence of Olga Alaketu working as part of the training process for psychiatrists at the university indicates a way in which the nurturing and mothering process has to extend in order to take care of the needs of the people. Candomblé was initially submerged as a part of the subculture in slave and postslavery society. As Brazilian culture evolved and those barriers lifted, it became important for Candomblé to be an overt, valid part of the national culture, as well as the culture of the descendants of the Ketu nation. In some way, Brazil and the Ketu nation must acknowledge each other as compatible, if future generations are to be nurtured.

Another cultural worker to participate in the African Diaspora Festival was Imogene Kennedy, queen of the Kuminas from Jamaica.[3] Her people call her Queenie and state that she is an African queen. The Kumina, a Jamaican cult group, blend Christian concepts with those of West Africa, especially the Ashanti of Ghana. Their ceremonies open with Baila songs, phrases from Christian hymns and prayers including some Ashanti words. These songs, used for mourning and healing, call the spirits to the earth and, when they arrive, present them with the needs of the group. The Kumina members state that the Ashanti words were taught to them by the spirits, referring to the role of possession in the ceremony and the belief that everything that happens in that state comes from the spirits.

During the festival, each Sunday was devoted to ceremonies. The first Sunday, Imogene Kennedy chose to do a selection of songs, rather than a full ceremony. She began all songs sung by the full group in union and antiphony. The melodies were modal, with the voices spanning three octaves: low-medium to Queenie's high, piercing lead soprano, characteristic of the African soprano. This very clear, piercing tone, without vibrato, is made by sounding the note forward in the head. Drumming, which signaled the beginning of the ceremony, was from the kbandu and cast drums, the kbandu establishing the snap rhythm and the cast drum establishing the overlay rhythm.

The troupe was with the festival for two weeks. At the beginning of the second week, Queenie came to us and stated that she wanted to do a table ceremony. We had not heard of a table ceremony. It seemed that initially the Kumina group had viewed the African Diaspora Program as a part of the dominant society and had, as a way of protecting the integrity of their culture, presented a series of selections. It was not until they had lived for several days with other participants from the United States and Africa and had gotten a sense of the structure of the program and of the energy that was from the Afro-American community of the festival that they decided they were an integral part of this community and that this was a community with which they could celebrate and memorialize.

Preparations for the table ceremony were elaborate. Queenie was taken shopping to select the necessary ingredients. James Early, staff member in charge of programming, remarked that when Queenie picked up what was to him a bottle of soda pop, he knew she was picking up something that to her was part of a ritual. It was a lesson for him in how the meaning of something can be redefined when the context is changed. In this case, a bottle of grape soda became a drink of memorial and celebration.

On the day of the ceremony, a long table was spread, laden with bread, soda, watermelon, bananas, other fruit, and a large number of candles. To begin the ceremony, Queenie selected four bananas and threw one to each of the four corners of the room. This fruit was an offering to the four sources of the universe, and it was to fly freely. As she threw the fruit, North American members of the audience, who thought all was for them, tried to catch it. It took a while before it was understood that the fruit was supposed to be offered to the gods and not the audience. Queenie began the ceremony with phrases from conventional Christian hymns and the Lord's Prayer and then moved into more African lyrics. While the hymns were sung, the drums beat African rhythms. Members of the audience came up, gave a contribution, and received a blessing and a symbolic candle lit by Queenie or one of her assistants. The structure of the Kumina table ceremony was very similar to the Baptist communion. However, in the Kumina ceremony, food preparation was more elaborate, in contrast to the bland fare of bread and wine in Christian communion, and offerings seemed to be made to the deities by the participants, as well as from deities to each other.

The decisions by Queenie to do this ceremony at a festival, which had so much that was not from the Kumina culture, signaled a redefinition of the diaspora area. It became, for that period of time, a Kumina community where Queenie held the highest status as a spiritual leader. It was in her position as leader of her community and keeper of the tradition that Queenie was able to come into a new situation and, after some observation, to determine that she could practice more fully the sacred rituals and ceremonies. The experience of the Kumina at the African Diaspora Program of the Smithsonian Institution's Festival of American Folklife (FAF) might be analogous to how people of African descent move or are moved into new situations. There is the need, first, to carry out the basic requirements for our physical survival and then, slowly, to create the means through which we can continue to be who we are. The Kumina tradition in Jamaica, like so many of the African traditions—such as Candomblé in Brazil—was outlawed and had to go underground. It was always left to those like Queenie who assumed the responsibility of protecting and nurturing the community to work out ways to keep the traditions strong for the people, whether banned or in the open.

Bessie Jones was another cultural worker who participated during the festival. She was born in 1902 in Smithville, Georgia, and grew up in nearby Dawson, about twenty miles from Albany, Georgia, where I was born.[4] I met Bessie Jones for the first time at the Newport Folk Festival in 1963. I was there as a singer with the SNCC Freedom Singers. We were traveling all over the country to develop support for the movement and to raise funds for specific activities in the South. Bessie Jones was singing with the Georgia Sea Island Singers, led by John Davis. When I listened to the group, I was so excited and deeply moved to hear sounds and songs with which I had grown up. There were also songs I have never heard, seemingly of the same family but slightly different. The group did a song called "The Buzzard Lope" and another where John Davis beat a broomstick in a cross-rhythm to the song, like beating a drum. The songs were introduced by Alan Lomax, who recorded this group during the 1930s, when he was taken to the Sea Islands by Zora Neale Hurston. In his introduction, Lomax said that the Georgia Sea Island Singers spoke with such a deep Gullah dialect that it was difficult for the Newport audience to understand them.

What I remember most strongly about Bessie that first time, when we ran up to the stage after the group came off and surrounded them, was Bessie saying, "I usually speak for the group, you know, but Mr. Lomax has been so nice in bringing us here that we let him introduce us." The first statement struck me as she tried to make it clear to this group of young black singers that the Georgia Sea Island Singers were more than singers, that they were able to represent their songs and their stories to any audience. I have heard her many times since, talking about the songs and games. Bessie Jones has remained consistent in making it very clear that a song was more than a song, and a game was more than a game, and that some games that people call games were plays and, as such, carried in their content and structure a foundation piece of Afro-American culture, or a basic unit for the building of an Afro-American community. She seemed to want us to know that during slavery and afterwards we, as a people, had to take care of ourselves and, sometimes, in ways that went far beyond European or Euro-American culture or knowing.

There was a song she taught us called "Gimme the Gourd To Drink Water." This song would not be clear without the story, she said. The call is "Regular, roll in under/ Gimme the gourd to drink water." One verse reads: "Never heard the likes since I been born, bull cow kicking on the milk cow's horn." Bessie said the song was about the glass and tin dippers that white people drank from and did not want Afro-Americans, who worked in their houses or in the fields, to drink from. Black people drank from a gourd because water from a gourd was cooler than water from a glass or tin dipper. The bull cow verse is about how the bull is dependent on the milk cow in similar ways that men were dependent on women or slave owners on slaves. So why kick something that you need to survive? The insanity of abusing something that supports your life is clearly expressed in these lyrics.

Bessie Jones learned her field songs, work chants, and game songs from her grandfather, a former slave named Jed Samson, who she describes as "a natural born African who wore a braid all the way down his back." Samson, who lived to be 105 and worked as a brickmaker, also taught his granddaughter about herbs and how to make teas to deal with certain ailments. With this knowledge, she was for many years a midwife and "worked on" people. She curtailed these activities when the authorities began to license midwives and, therefore, what she was doing became illegal. Bessie Jones also grew up surrounded by music in her home, in her church, and in her school. Her mother was a fine singer and dancer, and her father played several musical instruments.

When Bessie Jones was thirty-one, she moved to her husband's home on St. Simon's Island, off the Georgia coast. The relative isolation on these islands provided an atmosphere in which the African and Afro-American cultural traditions of the predominantly Afro-American population flourished. There, Bessie Jones gained a reputation as a powerful singer and was asked by John Davis to join the Coastal Georgia Singers. This group sang indigenous island songs at the A. W. Jones plantation's hotel for the tourists, who had begun to discover the coastal island. "The singers," recalled Bessie Jones, "were paid a little but not that much" and were required to wear "a big white apron and a head-rag." The group also sang in their own community, adding to their repertoire dances and games such as "Sandy Rose," "The Horses and the Buggy," and "Step, Uncle Jesse," which Bessie Jones had brought from the mainland.

Jones states that many times she felt members of her community wanted to forget the traditions and mores of slavery, along with the oppression. "People wouldn't listen to the music and what it meant. Some people acted like they were embarrassed by what they were." But being the grandchild of a slave is nothing to be ashamed of, according to Jones. What we were doing was important. "It's like with Jesus. If nobody preached about him, how would other folks know? If we didn't teach what we're teaching, some would never learn how far we've come and how hard it was."

For me, as an Afro-American woman, singer, and cultural

scholar, Jones had been a mother, giving me content songs, stories, and traditions I needed to develop. She also taught me to witness and allowed me to be a sort of apprentice to her. Jones showed me how traditions, content, and structure are transmitted within the boundaries of Afro-American culture. Being able to walk in her shadow was very much like the experience of the womb. The relationship was a strong, nurturing one.

Many times when we think of nurturing life, we think of a healthy mother who gives birth, having eaten the food that is best for her baby. That, in fact, is an ideal. One can, however, investigate a mother's physical condition, what she consumes on a day-to-day basis, and, thus, what she can possibly feed to her children. Using mothering as a data category affords the researcher a potential method of examining mothering in its ideal form, wherein each generation is born into a situation that is very healthy and affirming for them. It is also useful in evaluating exploitative situations, where the group's experience is like a baby taking milk from the mother's breast that might really be weak or poisonous; or worse, that the mother might be in such poor shape that the next generation does not come. It might seem that in using the mothering process as a method of analyzing data, I will be eliminating the role of the father or the sisters and brothers. However, it is in the mothering process that all of these can be included. My primary examples are female. However, one can use the concept of a mothering generation to mean the way the entire community organizes itself to nurture itself and its future generations.

When I began to look at relationships between people in the community as a major way of developing models to investigate and evaluate data, I went to the same relationships in the larger, natural world, beyond and before, sometimes, the human family. Among all living things in the universe, there is a nurturing process. It is the holding of life before birth, the caring for and feeding of the young until they assume independence. This process is called mothering. When applied to the examination and analysis of cultural data, it can reveal much within the historical picture of how a culture evolves and how and why changes occur in order to maintain the existence of a people. It is important, as one reviews the data, to look for the nurturing space or ground. Look for where and how feeding takes place. Look for what is passed from the mothering generation to the younger generation.

Within the story of the African diaspora, there is the opportunity to see a process of continuance and transformation at work among women cultural workers. Their struggle to contend with a new space entails defining their people and their children in new ways. That definition disrupted and threw into severe trauma cultural practices that had been nursed in African societies. Mothering, therefore, required a kind of nourishing that would both provide food and stamina for survival within a cruel slave society and the passing on of traditions that would allow for the development of a community that was not only of but also beyond the slave society. These women had to take what they were given from their mothers and fathers and make up a few things. Nurturing was not only reconciling what was passed to them with the day-to-day reality but also sifting and transforming this experience to feed this child, unborn, this new Afro-American community, in preparation for what it would face.

Mothering and nurturing are vital forces and processes in the establishment of relationships. Exploring and analyzing the nature of all components involved in a nurturing activity puts one in touch with life's regenerative character, with the female presence and the earth as a woman. Africa is a woman. The earth holds and feeds it there. The fathering energy in the universe is the seed. It will drop from the tree, but if there is a wind, there's no telling where it may fall. Sometimes, if it falls to the earth, there is new life. When you view the earth as mother, it is also important to grapple with its capacity for violence, as in earthquakes, so that you do not overdo that overworn concept of mothering being an unending process. Mothers are not forever. Mothering within human communities requires conscious choice. A woman must come to terms with herself, her life, her sanity, and her health, as well as with the health of life around her.

My use of the term *mothering* does not refer only to biological reproduction. These women—Olga Da Alaketu, Imogene Kennedy, Bessie Jones—are nurturers and womb-like holders of a people, of a birthing community in a strange land. Through their lives, they challenge those of us who "know" the system of the larger society, as academics, to find what it is that we nurture. What do we have to transform? The lives of these three women invite us to apply their principles in our work as scholars. We, too, can choose to be mothers in the sense that I have defined this role, as nurturing and transforming.

We have the opportunity to nurture a union between the knowledge we gather of the Afro-American community and of the larger society. There is the need to create a new space larger than the space that Olga or Queenie or Bessie created, larger than the space we now occupy, large enough for our people to continue as a people, sharing a commonness of humanity with other people and a unity with all that is living. We are today looking at a reality that the space we have is no longer sufficient. Most of us cannot talk to the teenagers of today. We are afraid of them. When we get on the bus or the subways, we hope they won't attack us or steal something from us. If they wear dreadlocks, at any age, we know they have already rejected the inadequate, nonemployment status society offers them.

We can choose to do this other job, mothering for our people, even as we hold our positions as the heads of Afro-American studies departments. In fact, the blood and struggle of our people has created the positions we hold. Too many of us spend time disassociating ourselves from the protestors and the radicals. When we get our budgets cut and our tenure rejected, we don't even know how to organize a response. We can choose to know that even though we look, sound, and behave like scholars, we can also choose to be mothers, nurturing and transforming a new space for a new people in a new time.

NOTES

1. Information on Olga Da Alaketu was gathered during observations of her presentation at the 1976 Smithsonian Institution Festival of American Folklife (FAF), documented in the reports of Smithsonian field researcher, James Early, and Luisa Marquez, scholar for the Brazilian delegation, Program in Black American Culture, National Museum of American History, African Diaspora Files, Smithsonian Institution, Washington, D.C.

2. The Smithsonian Diaspora Program developed out of a series of meetings organized in 1972 by Dr. Gerald Davis, then the associate director of

Smithsonian Institution's Festival of American Folklife. It was then that I began to work in the area of African diaspora culture. In large part, through the effort of this gathering of scholars, the *African diaspora* concept began to be recognized as a legitimate and valuable term to conduct comparative crosscontinental studies in African-based communities around the world. This is a term that was in full use during the black consciousness and Pan-African movements of the mid- and late 1960s. The concept existed within the Afro-American political community. Many of us who were involved in political activism during the 1960s had consciously chosen to train ourselves within Afro-American culture and within formal, Western educational institutions. We were scholars and cultural workers. We were theoreticans, poets, and singers.

When Davis pulled together a national panel of scholars in Afro-American culture to discuss the scope and definition of an Afro-American presentation program, many of the Afro-Americans in the room came with degrees in various disciplines—folklore, cultural history, anthropology, art history—and with years of experience in radical political organizing. When the overall concept of the Bicentennial Festival was explained—Old Ways in the New World as a way of celebrating the diversity and plurality of American culture—we insisted that the proper nomenclature for an Afro-American presentation was *African diaspora.* Some of our white colleagues who worked in the fields of African, Afro-Caribbean, or Afro-American culture questioned the terminology as one unrecognized by the field. My response then—and it is a view I continue to hold—will serve as the central point of my discussion.

The role of native scholars is very much the process of collecting and analyzing, from the perspective of the cultures they study, as well as from the perspective of the disciplines and methodologies in which they were trained.

3. Information on Imogene Kennedy was gathered by observations of her presentation at the 1975 FAF, the reports of Smithsonian field researcher Leonard Goines, and Olive Lewin, scholar for the Jamaican delegation. African Diaspora Files, Smithsonian Institution, Washington, D.C.

4. Information on Bessie Jones comes from, "Oh What A Time," Southern Folk Cultural Revival Project (SFCRP), Nashville, 1982; and Bessie Jones and Bess Lomax Hawes, *Step It Down: Games, Plays, Songs, and Stories From the African-American Heritage* (New York: Harper and Row, 1972).

The Black Female Presence in Black Francophone Literature

Karen Smyley Wallace

Although the field of women's studies and the topic of black women in literature have recently generated considerable scholarly interest, the black woman has often intrigued and mystified writers of various cultures who have attempted to capture her essense in their literary works. Some of the more well known examples are the black women in William Faulkner's *Absalom, Absalom* (1936); the "mulatresse" Jeanne Duval in Baudelaire's *Fleurs du Mal* (1857); or the sensuous black dancers in Luis Pales Matos' *Poesía* (1915). Although some of these portrayals were flattering, most were distortions of a true image of the black female. They tended to present mere plastic figurines, one-dimensional literary types, rather than full-fleshed individuals. It was significant, therefore, that the greater truth, the more realistic portrayals of the black woman, ultimately come from the pen of the black writer.

Even the most cursory review of the history of a developing image of black women in literature rendered by black writers requires consideration of the Harlem Renaissance in the United States and the *Négritude* movement in black Francophone Africa and the Caribbean. As the progenitor of the two literary movements, the Harlem Renaissance brought about a new sense of solidarity and a fresh commitment to the expression of black values and black realities. The renaissance profoundly influenced the future direction of black literature in the United States and throughout the diaspora, and also influenced the creation of a new black aesthetic. In Paris, during the 1940s, those very seeds

181

which had been cast by African-American artists during the renaissance, blossomed into the *Négritude* movement among black French-speaking literati. What is most significant about these movements is that while black artists were expected to elucidate the values and realities most closely associated with their perception of the world, they were correspondingly required to denounce all cultural and psychological ties with colonial Europe. Thus, their entire thematic portfolio was altered to include a new variety of subjects. The stage was set for the artists to present black feelings, black dreams, black struggles, black joys. For instance, it was with a sense of jubilation that they spoke of black music: Langston Hughes recalled the sound of the jazz trumpet; Leopold Senghor recounted the melody of the distant harp-like kora; Léon Damas revived the notes of Louis Armstrong's trumpet; Nicolas Guillen reveled in the light cadence of the African guitar.

Of the many themes raised and portrayed by these artists, the black woman's image rose majestically above all others. In their poems and stories, mothers, singers, single women, and church women all began to receive new and well-deserved attention. In this regard, perhaps, W.E.B. DuBois's tribute to black women in *The Souls of Black Folk* is notably appropriate:

> For this, their promise, and for their hard past, I honor the women of my race. Their beauty,. . . their dark and mysterious beauty of midnight eyes, crumpled hair, and soft, full-featured faces . . . because I was born to its warm and subtle spell. . . . I have always felt like bowing myself before them in all abasement, searching to bring some tribute to these long-suffering victims, these burdened sisters of mine. . . .[1]

The whole story, however, had still not been told. While the theme of black women in literature was gaining greater importance throughout the diaspora, those images from the French-speaking world remained relatively unexplored and became an intriguing source of new inspiration. In the black Francophone world, African and Caribbean writers, recently released from the yoke of colonial oppression, began to recall and bring forth visions of their own women: on the hills of Martinique, in the towns of Haiti, or in the savannahs of Senegal.

From its inception, the *Négritude* movement brought about significant changes in black literature of French expression. The first literary voices to cry out against the political, psychological, and particularly the cultural oppression of colonial France were the young revolutionary black students living in Paris, far from their native climes. There, ironically, they underwent a type of literary baptism in the black aesthetic. By denouncing their ancestors' strict and blindly obedient adherence to French culture, they were able to wash away the long-range effect of their acculturation. Their aim was not only to present black values to the world but, more important, to revive them for themselves.

Thus, one of the essential vehicles of this new expression of blackness was the portrayal of the black woman. The *Négritude* movement inspired multidimensional roles for black women, ranging from the metaphysical symbol of mother Africa to the embodiment of political leadership engaged in the struggle for African and Caribbean solidarity and liberation. Writers such as Camara Laye, Aimé Césaire, Ousmane Sembène, Aboulaye Sadji, Ferdinand Oyono, Bertène Juminer, and Jacques Roumain found themselves glorifying the physical form, the gestures, the sensitivities, and most important, the spirit of black women in their works.

These portrayals, although somewhat stereotypical, must be acknowledged for their broader literary and cultural intent and impact. Not long before this period, some of these same artists or their associates had taken great pleasure in using the language of the colonizer to sing praise to the chestnut tresses and the fair skin of the colonizer's woman. One of the most significant contributions of the *Négritude* movement, therefore, was this change in literary focus. The writers began to draw from the sources closest to them and created a plethora of images of all the black women who had ever given birth, nursed, taught, loved, chastised, supported, or inspired them. Perhaps one of the most classic praises was offered by the Senegalese poet, Léopold Sédar Senghor. These well-known lines have come to symbolize the timelessness and spiritual quality of black women:

> *Femme nue, femme obscure*
> *Fruit mûr à la chair ferme, sombres extases du vin noir,*
> *bouche qui fais lyrique ma bouche*
> *Savane aux horizons purs, savane qui frémis aux*
> *caresses ferventes du Vent d'Est*

Tamtam sculpte, tamtam tendu qui grondes sous
les doigts du vainqueur
Ta voix grave de contralto est le chant spirituel
de l'Aimée.[2]

Although poetry had originally provided a useful mode of expression for the depiction of the black woman (see David Diop's "A Une Danseuse Noire," *Coups de Pilon* [1957] and Senghor's "Femme Noire," *Chants d'Ombre* [1956]), the novel encouraged the most realistic investigation of the female image. From the period of what is known as the first black novel (René Maran's *Batouala* [1928]) to the late 1950s, black Francophone novelists primarily projected images of women in traditional settings, mainly concerned with home and family life.[3]

In these earlier writings, the female characters often lacked dramatic complexity and depth; however, they consistently represented symbols of strength, whether they were portrayed as earth mothers, dutiful and obedient wives, or as nubile love goddesses.

While the colonial period and French domination left an indelible mark upon black Francophone cultures, in general, the role of the women in these cultures was notably affected. The emergence of Western values regarding education, religion, morality, and trends toward urbanization were duly reflected in the literature. Ironically, it was the colonial system which provided the impetus for the development of more intricate and subtle literary treatment of the black female persona. From the period of the late 1950s and into the early years of independence from colonial rule, a new and problematic female character developed in Francophone literature: a character "whose goal was to redefine the position of the African individual in a changing and developing society."[4] Existing in a world of conflict and forced to struggle with social, political, philosophical or sentimental problems, the black female character was frequently depicted in a climate of anxiety. There, she often found herself cut off from her past, trapped within the confines of a system of alienation, and lost in an intense search for self. Some classic examples of these phenomena may be seen in the heroines of Aboulaye Sadji's *Nini: Mulâtresse du Sénégal* (1947) and *Maimouna* (1958); other examples are N'Dèye Touti in Sembène's *Les Bouts de Bois de Dieu* (1960) and Diouana, in his *La Noire de . . .* (1962).

Ousmane Sembène, a noted contemporary Senegalese novelist and filmmaker, stands out among Francophone writers as one who frequently presents his female characters as real, palpable individuals. By creating women figures who do not merely represent shadows of the male figure, nor echoes of the male voice, Sembène's works reflect the complexities of a changing Africa.[5] His novels abound with portraits of black women who must often break ties with traditional sociocultural mores, and thus, constantly struggle to redefine their perceptions of the world.[6] Through this mirror of social criticism, Sembène reveals two powerful messages. First, women are the repository of Africa's cultural strengths and traditional wisdom. Second, women often provide a vital catalyst for change. Thus, with particular skill and perception, he has crystallized the story of Rama, the young female educator *(Xala);* Tioumbé, the female political activist *(L'Harmattan);* and Penda, the prostitute turned soldier *(Les Bouts de Bois de Dieu).* While these characters experience new problems and new victories, they must also face new dilemmas. Often finding themselves betrayed by these new roles, they must learn to survive without mates (as Maimouna, in *Les Bouts de Bois de Dieu*) or family ties (as Tioumbé, in *L'Harmattan).* This is a compelling and singularly new theme in African literature.

Although male writers have fairly accurately portrayed the black female, their renderings have been somewhat incomplete. Consequently, the black female writer's view has been necessary to complete the picture. Through her perceptions, she has been able to articulate the feelings of the black woman and, thus, to add the necessary flesh and blood to what are, at best, literary skeletons set out by the male writer.

Currently, there exists a veritable choir of major black female voices in Francophone literature. Some of the more well-known novelists are Mariama Bâ, Aminata Sow Fall, Nafissatou (Senegal); Michèle Lacrosil, Maryse Condé, and Simone Schwarz-Bart (Guadeloupe). By telling a tale of women, each of these writers has been able to present a special portrait of black female reality. Some of the more striking themes revealed in their works are the special bonds of female friendships (as in Schwarz-Bart's *Pluie et vent sur Télumée Miracle* [1972] and Miriama Bâ's *Une Si Longue Lettre* [1980]; the pains and joys of motherhood (as in

Bâ's *Une Si Longue Lettre*); women in love (as in Schwarz-Bart's *Télumée*, or Michèle Lacrosil's *Cajou* [1961] and *Sapotille et le serin d'argile* [1960]; women who survive alone (as in Bâ's *Lettre*, and Mayotte Capecia's *Je Suis Martiniquaise* [1948]; women in search of the self (as in Maryse Condé's *Hérémakhnon* [1976] and Lacrosil's *Sapotille et le serin d'argile*).

As these writers penetrate the female psyche, each ponders female identity, questions female expectations, analyzes female deceptions. What is most important is that these and other black female writers have offered a panorama of black female characters, who, in some cases, may be wearied by life (as in Lacrosil's *Sapotille*, or Bâ's *Lettre*), but who are ultimately committed to survival, like the protagonist Télumée in Schwarz-Bart's *Télumée*.

By presenting these realistic yet sensitive tableaux of the black female presence in Francophone literature, these writers are preparing their audiences for the eventual development and expansion of future roles for black women in literature and in society. Their work serves as testimony to their accomplishments throughout a difficult literary past, holds promise for their achievements in a brighter future, and hopefully, will encourage further study of the black female in literature.

NOTES

1. Julius Lester, ed., *The Seventh Son: The Thought and Writings of W.E.B. DuBois* (New York: Vintage Books, 1971), 526.
2. Léopold Sédar Senghor, *Anthologie de la Nouvelle Poésie Nègre et Malgache de langue Française* (Paris: Presses Universitaires de France, 1969), 151.
3. See the depiction of the mother in Camara Laye's *L'Enfant Noir* (1953); the grandmother and wife in Ousmane Sembène's *Les Bouts de Bois de Dieu* (1960); female figures in Aboulaye Sadji's *Maimouna* (1958); Ousmane Socé's heroine in *Karim: Roman Sénégalais* (1948); or Jacques Roumain's female characters in *Gouverneurs de la Rosée* (1946).
4. Sunday Anozie, *Sociologie du Roman Africain: Réalisme, Structure et Détermination dans le Roman Moderne Ouest-Africain* (Paris: Tiers-Monde et Développement, 1970), 27. French text was translated by author.
5. See *O Pays, Mon Beau Peuple* (1957); *Les Bouts de Bois de Dieu* (1960); *L'Harmattan* (1964); *Voltaique* (1962); and *Xala* (1974).
6. For further discussion of this point, see Karen Smyley, "Ousmane Sembène: Portraitist of the African Woman in the Novel," *New England Journal of Black Studies*, 1, no. 1 (June 1981), 23–27.

God's Divas: Women Singers in African-American Poetry

Andrea Benton Rushing

The images of black women created by African-American poets are unique when compared to images of women in verse of
Eurocentric cultures. The single most prevalent image of women
in African-American verse is the image of woman as mother.[1]
That makes this body of literature quite different from British
or Anglo-American poetry, where most verse to women characterizes them as the beloved. The second most statistically significant category of poetry to African-American women is composed of poems to women singers. Again, this is in sharp contrast
with British and Anglo-American poetry. Furthermore, although
African-American literature has many verses to African-American
male instrumentalists, male singers figure much less prominently
in the work. It is not, of course, enough merely to note the number of poems in these various categories. One must attempt to
discern what, if anything, the pattern signifies.

Many of the poems about African-American women singers
use them as symbols of racial and cultural oppression. The artists'
drug habits, unhappy love affairs, and early deaths become em-
blematic of the suffering of an abused people doomed, like the He-
brews in their Babylonian captivity, to sing God's song in a strange
land. An example of this kind of poem is Michael Harper's reflection on the life and death of Bessie Smith, "Last Affair: Bessie's
Blues Song."

Alongside the few poems that depict women singers as symbols
of African-American anguish, there are many poems, by writers as
different as Paul Laurence Dunbar, Sterling Brown, Mari Evans,

187

and Nikki Giovanni, which describe women singers as figures of awesome power. One source of that power is surely the freedom that classic blues singers boldly attested to in their lyrics and lives. Long before Euro-American women articulated their version of liberation, at a time when most women of African descent lived in southern rural towns and toiled as domestics, figures like Ma Rainey, Bessie Smith, and Ida Cox lived glamorous urban lives, earned unparalleled salaries, and proclaimed, "wild women don't have the blues." [2] Since so many of the tributes to women singers depict these figures (and their counterparts in African-American religious music), even a casual reading of the poetry points to parallels between literature and life. The diaspora perspective so forcefully argued in Sierra Leonean anthropologist Filomina Chioma Steady's anthology *The Black Woman Cross-Culturally*[3] impels one to look for the sources of women singers' power in the history and culture African women brought with them to New World slavery.

In precolonial Africa, song was viewed as functional in everyday life and as critical in the sacred life which interpenetrated the secular life. Not only did songs accompany work in the fields and around the house, they also were vehicles for teaching the young, honoring the praiseworthy, summoning the ancestors, and preserving the history of the ethnic group. Their ritual importance is attested to in the saying, "the spirit does not descend without a song." [4] While some African-Americans may be familiar with African solo singers like Miriam Makeba, traditional music in Africa is usually performed by groups of singers.[5] Furthermore, unlike the Judeo-Christian tradition in which the entire Godhead is imagined as male (God the Father, God the Son, and the Holy Spirit, usually conceived as male, despite biblical references to the contrary), indigenous African religions included women not only as healers and priestesses, but also as revered ancestors and potent deities. Those enslaved Africans shipped to Catholic countries like Brazil, Cuba, and Haiti could find counterparts to their African female divinities in Catholic female saints and, of course, in the veneration of the Virgin Mary as the mother of God. The United States is, however, a predominately Protestant country, and the Baptist, Methodist, and Pentacostal practices accepted by African-Americans do not provide their adherents with a comparable range of female saints or a cult of the Virgin. Perhaps the poetic tributes to African-American women singers demonstrate that they often act as "loas" and "orishas" in African-American culture by possessing enormous emotional power, healing their hearer's grief, and mediating between the human and the transcendent. My argument is *not* that the enormous power ascribed to African-American woman singers is on a direct continuum with the role of women singers in traditional or contemporary Africa, but rather that African-American women singers often seem to take on roles ascribed to female deities in Africa. If so, the poets do not invent this role for the singers. Instead, their verses reflect and celebrate the function of women like Gertrude Rainey, Bessie Smith, Dinah Washington, Billie Holiday, Nina Simone, and Aretha Franklin who have been given by African-American popular culture the titles, respectively, "Ma," "Empress of the Blues," "Queen of the Blues," "Lady Day," "High Priestess of Soul," and "Lady Soul."

The earliest African-American poem to a woman singer is "When Malindy Sings," composed by Paul Laurence Dunbar, an Ohio-born poet whose parents had lived during slavery. In creating this fictional singer, Dunbar ignores her appearance and concentrates on her impact. The poem's undramatized narrator juxtaposes Malindy's untutored voice and Miss Lucy's formally trained piano-playing and calls the latter "noise." Furthermore, the bold narrator points out that, confronted by Malindy's resonant voice, banjo players and fiddlers are astounded, and birds are silent with rapt attention. Malindy does not sing to entertain. Her renditions of "Come to Jesus" and "Rock of Ages" convince "hardened sinners" to repent and seek salvation. In the face of Euro-American culture's preference for musicians educated to read the "dots and dashes" of written music, Dunbar's confident speaker asserts that Malindy's "humble praises" ascend to "de very gates of God" and even claims to hear "de bresh of angels wings" when Malindy sings the spiritual "Swing Low, Sweet Chariot." These are large claims, indeed, especially about the music of chattel slaves and their oppressed descendants. Dunbar's dialect poem makes them forcefully and persuasively.

African-American poet and folklorist Sterling Brown was born in Washington, D.C., five years before Dunbar's premature death in 1906. His four-part "Ma Rainey" is technically more complex than Dunbar's nine-stanza poem. While Dunbar uses a regular rhyme scheme and relies on four beat lines and the repetition of the phrase "when Malindy sings," Brown's poem demonstrates more variety: the first and third sections are composed of three-beat lines, the second and fourth are longer, more conversational lines. Dunbar gives us no idea of geography, while Brown refers to actual places like Mobile, Alabama. And, in contrast to Dunbar, who provides no physical description of Malindy at all, Brown sketches Gertrude "Ma" Rainey as "li'l an low" and "a-smilin' gold-toofed smiles." Despite these differences, there are clear parallels in the way the poets present the singers. Malindy's voice hushed instrumentalists and birds; Ma Rainey's version of "Backwater Blues" made her listeners bow their heads and cry. Although one woman sings sacred music and the other sings secular blues, both sing with a force that absorbs and persuades their listeners. And Ma Rainey's effect is further enhanced by the first person voice in which she sings about a disastrous Arkansas flood and by the way she goes outside to join the audience after her song has had its cathartic impact. Section three of Brown's poem offers its most direct statement of Ma Rainey's powers:

> O Ma Rainey
> Sing yo' song'
> Now you's back
> Whah you belong,
> Git way inside us,
> Keep us strong . . . [6]

We see that, though stated in different musical and poetic forms, the redemptive power Brown ascribes to Ma Rainey's songs mirrors the effects Dunbar attributes to Malindy's.

Despite the trace of irony in the narrator's tone toward the poem's subject, "Mourning Poem for the Queen of Sunday," written by the virtuoso Michigan-born poet Robert Hayden, shares common elements with both "When Malindy Sings" and "Ma Rainey." Hayden's poem depicts a fictional singer murdered by four bullets. In calling this singer God's "mockingbird," "fancy warbler," and "diva," Hayden, whose poetry spans the period from the 1940s to the 1980s, reminds us of Dunbar's Malindy. When the Queen of Sunday's voice is brutally silenced by death, the world is left "a-clang with evil," and the poem's undramatized speaker wonders:

> Who's going to make old hardened singer men
> tremble now and the righteous rock?
> Oh who and oh who will sing Jesus down to help
> with struggling and doing without and being
> colored all through blue Monday?
> Till way next Sunday? [7]

African-American churchgoers speak of "singing till the power of the Lord comes down," and a West African proverb declares "the spirit will not descend without a song." Reflecting the central role played by women singers in African-American churches, Hayden's Queen of Sunday is like Dunbar's Malindy in her ability to convince and convert sinners who hear her. Her songs make angels seem visible and inspire the saved to clap and shout. In addition, in the first mention of African-Americans' racial caste status in these poems about women singers, the Queen of Sunday is credited with nourishing the congregation so it can endure and even transcend the day-to-day effects of poverty and racism. While Dunbar's poem portrays a sacred singer and Brown's describes a blues singer, Hayden's reflects African-American life in blurring the line between these two potent streams of African-American music.

In her fourteen-line poem ". . . And the Old Women Gathered," Ohio-born Mari Evans, a product of the black arts movement of the 1960s and 1970s, presents a group of seasoned singers whose voices are "fierce and not melodic." The music of these grim women is unlike the lyrical beauty of Malindy's notes, Ma Rainey's cathartic blues, or the healing and transforming songs of the Queen of Sunday, and the narrator and her companions flee from it. Two things link these fictional gospel singers with the other women singers we have encountered in poetry: they have "seen/everything/and are still Regular Army," and the sound of their music persists in the unwilling hearers' ears. The comparison to supply sergeants not only alludes to militant hymns like

"Onward, Christian Soldiers" but also attests to the singers' endurance in difficult times and extreme conditions. The persistence of their harsh song declares its power. Though these singers are not presented as mediators between the human and the divine, the awe in which the narrator holds them suggests that their forceful music provides a window, revealing mysteries both beautiful and terrible.

Another poet who came to prominence during the black arts movement is Mississippi-born Etheridge Knight. His "To Dinah Washington" is a direct address to the singer. Written in an elegaic tone after her early death in 1963, it does not provide a physical description of its subject nor supply biographical information about her brief life. In line with African-American popular tradition, Knight calls the singer "the Queen of the Blues," and he terms her music "royal and real." The poem asserts that Dinah Washington's music outlives her performances and is such an accurate rendition of African-American life that it is even part of the lives of those who do not know it:

> Children stop their play to listen,
> Remembering—though they have never heard
> you before
> You are familiar to them . . .[8]

Dunbar's Malindy indicts sinners and provides her audience with a glimpse of the divine; Brown's Ma Rainey articulates a community's helpless suffering and provides a healing release for it; and Hayden's Queen of Sunday arraigns the errant, affirms the saved, and nourishes the oppressed. For Knight, Dinah Washington's music is part of the "eternal song" and resounds, though she herself has died. The last three lines of his seventeen-line poem claim immortality for the singer: "Some say you're sleeping/But I say you're singing/Unforgettable Queen."[9] In these compact closing lines, the poem accomplishes several things simultaneously by alluding to one of Dinah Washington's best-known songs, insisting on her majesty, and declaring her timelessness.

Like Evans and Knight, Nikki Giovanni also came to prominence during the tumultuous 1960s and 1970s. Born in Tennessee in 1943, she is the youngest writer in this study. Her

"Poem for Aretha" is much longer than the other celebrations of African-American women singers. Like them, however, this one ignores Aretha Franklin's physical appearance, cites songs she has made famous, and focuses on her relationship to her audience. This poem is more biographical than the others; it mentions Lady Soul's husband, children, tours, and invitation to sing for the Hubert Humphrey presidential campaign. Dunbar referred to Malindy's rendition of "Come to Jesus," "Rock of Ages," and "Swing Low, Sweet Chariot"; Brown described Ma Rainey singing Bessie Smith's classic "Backwater Blues"; and Knight alluded to Dinah Washington's version of "Unforgettable." Giovanni's poem has a wider range of musical allusions. Not only does she cite such Aretha Franklin songs as "Natural Woman" and "Respect," she also compares and contrasts the singer with such other African-American vocalists as Billie Holiday, Dinah Washington, James Brown, Ray Charles, Diana Ross, and Otis Redding.

Two striking features distinguish Giovanni's poem from the shorter ones we have so far considered. No matter what the narrative stance of all the earlier poems, there is a relaxed distance between the narrator and the reader. In contrast, this poem alternately scolds and instructs:

> aretha doesn't have to relive billie holiday's life doesn't
> have
> to relive dinah washington's death . . . [10]

True to the tenents of the black arts movement, Giovanni employs poetry to educate and to exhort; the lack of capital letters and the absence of punctuation marks give her words an air of breathless urgency quite unlike the pace of poems from earlier eras. The second striking thing about "Poem for Aretha" is the scope of the claims Giovanni makes for her. On the one hand, the poet asserts that the singer's fidelity to African-American culture challenged other vocalists to halt their assimilation to Euro-American modes and to reaffirm African-American musical traditions. On the other hand, although Aretha Franklin has never been considered a political singer like Bernice Reagon or Gil Scott-Heron, Giovanni imagines a political role for her:

> the Black songs started coming for the singers
>   on the stage and the dancers
> in the streets
> aretha was the riot was the leader if she had
>   said "come
> let's do it" it would have been done.[11]

Even after the range of powers attributed to Malindy, Ma Rainey, the Queen of Sunday, Dinah Washington, and the anonymous gospel singers, one may be caught off guard by the breadth of the influence the poet declares. Rather than indicting sinners, soothing the care-worn, or providing an avenue to the divine, this singer is seen to possess the latent power to lead an urban rebellion.

The six works discussed constitute the most compelling examples of verse about women singers in the body of African-American poetry. Although only a sample, they reveal a pattern of similarities that extends past these six works and seems to reverberate with significance for other aspects of the study of women in the African diaspora. Despite the differences in their dates of composition and literary styles, the poems demonstrate several pronounced likenesses. They prefer direct statement to irony or ambiguity and, except for comparison between Malindy and the Queen of Sunday and birds, they make little use of such figures of speech as similes and metaphors. In addition, they allude to the singers' repertoires, de-emphasize their appearance, and are less concerned with the musical details of their performances than with their impact on their audiences. The spectrum of powers these poems attribute to their subjects is impressive indeed: Malindy converts sinners and provides believers with a glimpse of the divine; Ma Rainey articulates a community's anguish to the face of a catastrophic flood; and Aretha Franklin both challenges other artists to return to the folk roots of African-American music and has the potential to ignite urban political action. Notice that the awesome potency of these artists does not seem to depend on their wealth or fame and is always exercised on their listeners' behalf. Though part of the real world of natural disasters, racism, and sin, these singers also seem to shimmer above its quotidian cares.

African-American popular culture provides honorific titles like

"Ma," "Lady," and "Queen" for women singers whose bold personal style and superlative music impress their audiences as extraordinary. In writing about these performers, poets as disparate as Paul Laurence Dunbar and Sonia Sanchez reflect the seminal role of song in African-American life which, true to its African origin, values music as the central sacred and secular art form. In the past, studies of African-American women from the diaspora perspective have generally focused on their social role as mothers, their economic role as producers, or their political role as activists. This overview of women singers in poetry indicates, however, that there is a vibrant nexus connecting African ideas about women and song with the depiction of women in African-American poetry.

In a comparative study of women protagonists in contemporary African and African-American novels, I analyzed the umbilical connection between African and African-American ideas about women.[12] My examination of the portrayal of women singers in African-American poetry reveals that another manifestation of that tensile web of connections is the widespread reverence shown for women whose renditions of secular or sacred music earn them a praise-name like "high priestess" or "empress." The number of poetic tributes to women singers and the terms in which these artists are celebrated seem to indicate a family resemblance between the female healers, priestesses, ancestors, and deities in precolonial African cultures; female loas and orisha in Brazil, Cuba, and Haiti; and singers like Ma Rainey, Dinah Washington, and Aretha Franklin. Though the singers' devotees do not worship at altars, they do venerate the artists, depend on them for emotional succor, and partake in a larger, sacralized world through the intervening medium of their music.

Future research will reveal whether or not the pattern of similarities discerned in the poetic presentation of women singers is also present in other genres of African-American literature. Comparative studies of literature in Creole, English, French, and Portuguese by writers of African ancestry in the Caribbean, Central America, and South America will examine congruences and contrasts among depictions of women singers in Africa's New World diaspora. For now, this preliminary study demonstrates that women singers are consistently characterized as figures of numinous power. No mere entertainers, these potent women voice their audiences' deepest emotions and modulate the distances between temporal and transcendent spheres. Acting with an authority and efficacy that reminds us of African deities like Oshun and Yemanja, the women singers in African-American poetry are indeed God's divas.

NOTES

1. In *The Afro-American Woman: Struggles and Images,* ed. Sharon Harley and Rosalyn Terborg-Penn (New York: Kennikat, 1978), 74–84.
2. This memorable phase is the title of a 1924 Ida Cox blues lyric. Daphne Duval Harrison notes the difference between the reality and the idealized urban life of black women blues singers in "Black Women in the Blues Tradition," in *The Afro-American Woman: Struggles and Images,* 65–66.
3. Filomina Chioma Steady, *The Black Woman Cross-Culturally* (Cambridge, Mass.: Schenkman, 1981).
4. As quoted by LeRoi Jones in *Blues People* (New York: Morrow, 1963), 41.
5. See the extensive liner notes from *Traditional Women's Music from Ghana,* produced and recorded by Verna Gillis, Ethnic Folkways, FE4257, 1981.
6. Stephen Henderson, ed., *Understanding the New Black Poetry* (New York: William Morrow, 1972), 134–36.
7. Ibid., 153–54.
8. Ibid., 329.
9. Ibid.
10. Dudley Randall, ed., *The Black Poets* (New York: Bantam, 1971), 328.
11. Ibid., 329.
12. Andrea Benton Rushing, "Family Resemblances: A Comparative Study of Women Protagonists in Anglophone-African and African-American Novels, 1965–1980" (Ph.D. diss., University of Massachusetts, 1983).

Images of Black Women in New World Literature: A Comparative Approach

Martha K. Cobb

Literature is created, listened to, read, and enjoyed not only because it is put into entertaining form but because people discover in its legends, poetry, songs, and stories a way of interpreting the human experience and of finding meaning and values in the struggles of ordinary life. This literary perspective can be applied to the way individuals assess the lives of black women. Thus, in his masterwork, *The Souls of Black Folk,* W.E.B. Du Bois recalls the song his grandfather heard his slave grandmother sing in the cold valley of northern New England, where she had been sold by a slave trader. The strange language she used was of her recollected African past:

> *Do bana coba, gene me, gene me!*
> *Do bana coba gene me, gene me!*
> *Ben d'nuli, nuli, nuli, nuli, ben d'le.*[1]

Du Bois suggests, as he heard the song handed down in the family from his slave foremother, that "this was primitive African music; it may be seen in larger form in the strange chant which heralds "The Coming of John" and the voice of exile—

> You may bury me in the East,
> You may bury me in the West,
> But I'll hear the trumpet
> sound in that morning.[2]

197

In this sense the slave grandmother was herself the subject of the verse she chanted. She defined her consciousness, her image of self within the song, and the language that she very dimly remembered; it was *her* voice, *her* self, and *her* language that she recalled from another time and another distant place.

Traditionally, however, the definition and images of black womanhood have been seen through male voices. The following nineteenth century folk song from Argentina has a black man addressing his sweetheart:

Morenita, morenita	Black girl, black girl
Tu amor me mata;	Your love is killing me;
Quereme morenita	Love me, black girl
No seas ingrata.[3]	Don't be so mean.*

Here the young woman being addressed is silent, but from the man's point of view she stands as an object of his love; she is a presence that has meaning for the suitor who composes his song for her.

The pattern of expressive love in another part of the African diaspora has its folkloric counterpart in the song "Choucoune," originally sung in the late nineteenth century and early twentieth century Creole patois of Haiti, which the Haitian poet Oswald Durand transferred to the printed page. Later translated from French to English, this early example of the woman as love symbol has become a popular song still heard today in parts of the Caribbean to the tune of the distinctive melody "Yellow Bird." Symbols often become stereotyped, as with the female presence as an image of mother, home, sweetheart, authority figure, or even as sole provider; however, symbols must be taken into account where fictional characterization often mirrors real life and becomes an essential element in the portrayal of black women in fiction. It is not too sweeping a statement to say that the black woman, as someone else's symbol or as an image, is the conception—and one might even say the invention—of male myths and the underlying male psyche cross-culturally. This is not to say that the black female protagonist is not a positive person,

---

*Translated by Martha K. Cobb.

even when stereotyped, but that with the advancement of women writers in Europe and the Americas in the nineteenth and the twentieth centuries, it becomes enlightening to meet the woman as poetic voice or as the protagonist, rather than as the object of someone else's perceptions. This female point of view in literature is long overdue, since, traditionally, male writers have dominated the literary scene throughout the diaspora.

One can gain an indepth understanding of black women's lives throughout the diaspora by looking at their writings cross-culturally. Examples of a literary female point of view can be analyzed by reviewing two novels and one collection of poetry by black women from three New World societies — Alice Walker, *The Color Purple* (United States), Marie Chauvet, *Amour, Colère Et Folie* (Haiti), Virginia Bundis De Sales, *Cien Carceles De Amour* (Uruguay). These works, which were published between the 1940s and the 1980s, illustrate a level of consciousness that evolves from events and characters and in the images shaped by them Alice Walker's work, published in the 1980s, will serve as the point of departure for comparing and assessing the consciousness level of a Haitian writer who wrote in the 1960s and a Uruguayan writer who wrote in the 1940s. Although over a generation exists between the publication of these three works — written in three different languages — they all reflect the consciously active subject of the female person.

ALICE WALKER, *THE COLOR PURPLE*

Alice Walker, a black American writer, was born in Georgia, and before the publication of *The Color Purple,* in 1982, she had written and published collections of stories and poems, and two other novels—one of them, *Meridian,* a novel about a young woman named Meridian who went south to risk her life in the civil rights movement of the 1960s.

The major voice in *The Color Purple* is that of the protagonist, Celie, who has two children by the man who rapes her—who she also believes to be her father. Nettie, Celie's younger sister, is rescued from similar experiences when she is befriended by a missionary couple who take her with them to Africa, where they remain a number of years. Meanwhile, Celie finds an outlet for her misery when she begins writing letters to God in which the poignant story of her unhappy life unfolds. She writes, for example:

> Dear God, My mama dead. She die screaming and cussing. She scream at me. I'm big. I can't move fast enough. . . . By time I git the tray ready the food be cold. By time I git all the children ready for school it be dinner time. He don't say nothing.[4]

The letters unveil Celie's sense of hopelessness, her fears, and her shame. She doesn't know where to write her sister Nettie or the missionaries. However, with the arrival in the household of Shug, a loving woman, a singer, and an entertainer who befriends Celie, life improves and changes color—the metaphoric royal purple—through a mutually rewarding relationship with Shug, who teaches Celie something about women's mutual, supportive love and about her worth as a woman. Finally, amidst all the cruelty and degradation, life takes on new meaning for Celie, which she communicates to the God to whom she still writes letters and to her sister Nettie, whom she finally sees again, after many years, when the missionaries come home from Africa. This is a story that is both poignant and powerful, full of probings and meanings that are communicated through the language, consciousness, and the emerging image of a poor young, southern, black girl who, in the end, senses her own womanliness and can articulate it in her communications with God, with Shug, and with her sister Nettie. In effect, Celie learns to become the central unifying subject of her own destiny, which she illustrates in a positive feminine image and feminine voice. Appropriately, Alice Walker received the 1982 Pulitzer Prize for this novel.

MARIE CHAUET, *AMOUR, COLERE ET FOLIE*

Haitian writer Marie Chauvet, who died in 1969, is the author of the next novel under consideration. Like Alice Walker, she was a prize winner, receiving the Prix de l'Alliance Francaise in 1935 for her first novel, *Fille d'Haiti.* However, her later novel, published in a single volume in 1968 with two other novels under the title *Amour, Colère et Folie (Love, Anger and Folly)* concerns us here. It is a work of fiction depicting the bitter consciousness of an "old maid" *(vieille fille)*, Claire, as she reaches the age of thirty-nine and realizes that she has not known love and that she will, in all probability, spend the rest of her life a virgin. As the oldest sister in this upper-class Haitian family, Claire is in charge of the home that she shares with two younger sisters. Felicia, married to Jean Luze, and the unmarried youngest sister, Annette—all of whom, with both parents deceased, Claire resents bitterly. The story is told from Claire's point of view. Moreover, Claire is very conscious of being the dark-skinned sister, unattractive, in her society's opinion, in contrast to her younger sisters, who inherited light complexions from their parents. Claire deceives her sisters and is determined to wreck the marriage of Felicia and Jean Luze, using as an instrument the youth and beauty of the youngest sister, Annette, with whom Jean Luze is supposed to fall in love. The opening sentences of the novel underscore Claire's deep bitterness and her determination to gain her own ends:

> *J'assiste au drame, scene apres scene, efface comme une ombre. Je suis la seule lucide, la seule dangereuse et personne authour de moi ne la soupconne. La vieille fille! Celle qui n'a pas trouve de mari, qui ne connait pas l'amour, qui n'a jamais vecu dans le bon sens du terme.*[5]

> I watch over the drama, a scene after scene, self-effacing as a shadow. I am the only lucid one, the only dangerous one, and no one around me suspects it. The old maid! The one who has not found a husband, who does not know love, who has never "lived" in the best sense of the word.*

As Claire's frustrations increase when she is unable to engender a love affair between the youngest sister Annette and Jean Luze, she begins to perceive that she was entrapped by circumstances over which she had no control; circumstances pertaining to the family, the stiff social codes imposed on women of the upper classes in Haiti, and the moral obligations toward church and

---

*Translated by Martha K. Cobb.

family that had kept her tied to the home and a virgin up to thirty-nine years of age. Left alone after her sister Felicia's second child is born and Jean Luze returns to the company of his wife, Claire caresses a doll as though it were her own child, and at night she imagines the act of love as she stimulates sexual dreams by eagerly inspecting a set of pornographic postcards that she had ordered from France. In her unhappy fantasy Claire considers taking the life of Felicia, expecting to escape punishment by making it look like suicide, and dreaming that Jean Luze will marry her because she would be needed to care for his two children, whom she has made motherless.

Unable to murder her sister, she decides in despair to commit suicide, but at the moment of taking her own life, the cruel and hated Chief of Police, Caledu, a killer of innocent men and a mutilator of women, is being driven down the street toward her house by angry beggars, and at that moment Claire becomes the actor, rather than the observer, in her own life-drama; she kills Caledu with the knife destined for herself.

This novel by Marie Chauvet presents a strong picture of a woman who, even when wrong, was the consciously active subject of her own person. Unhappy, frustrated, hating her spinsterhood, and hemmed in by all the prohibitions of the bourgeois Haitian society in which she grew up, in the end she redeemed herself by ridding the people of a dictatorial chief of police who was especially cruel to women and to the poor.

VIRGINIA BRINDIS DE SALAS, CIEN CARCELES DE AMOR

Literary critic Richard Jackson has stated, very appropriately, that the poet "Virginia Brindis de Salas comes closer to shaking the famous black fist" than other poets in her country, Uruguay.[6] There is little doubt, on reading her poetry, that the black female poet-voice within the poem proclaims her race, her African heritage, and the struggle of black women and men in Uruguay in the mid-twentieth century, when she and a few others were trying to establish their writing from a black point of view. In her justly famous early work, Cien Carceles de Amor (One Hundred Prisons *of Love)*, 1949, Virginia Brindis de Salas confronts the black experience in Uruguay and makes a point in identifying herself with it, in order to spread the meaning of the black presence as she perceived it. Thus, in the poem "Abuelito Mon" ("Old Grandfather"), she speaks out:

Poco paga el yanqui ya	Little does the Yankee pay now
por este million de canas	for these million sugar canes
que el negro sembro y corto	that the black sowed and cut
Mas no me trago este trago	But I won't swallow this dose
porque es trato de sudo[7]	because it is a question of my own sweat.*

A closely related theme of "blackness" follows in her poem "Negro: siempre triste" ("Black Man, Always Sad"), in which African deities and other aspects of the African-Hispanic world are called upon to sustain a sense of freedom from shame and a sense of pride in black heritage.

Yo negra soy	I am a black woman
Porque tenga la piel negra	because my skin is black
Esclava no!	But a slave woman no!
Yo naci de vientre libre	I was born of a free womb
Badagris Badagris, Dictador	Badagris, Badagris, ruler
de la punalada y el veneo.	of the sharp sword thrust and the poison
Espiritu vuelto de los canaversales	Spirit returned from the Carnival
del Tafia. Padre del rencor	Tafia, Father of animosity
y de la ira,	and of anger
negro: implora al	Black man: call upon

---

*Translated by Martha K. Cobb.

Legba, Dembola, Uedo,	Legba, Damballah, Ouadah,
Avida	Avida.
Yo negra soy	I am a black woman,
porque tengo la piel	Because my skin is black
negra.	
Esclava no![8]	But a slave woman, no!*

Virginia Brindis de Salas represents one of the few, published, black women writers in the Spanish American diaspora, and another who is following Brindis de Salas's footsteps, the younger, Cuban writer, Nancy Morejón, also embraces her blackness in her work. Both women are poets, and in their understanding of black history and the black experience they appear to surpass some of their male counterparts in the themes that they treat and in their conception and characterization of the meaning of black life in Spanish America.

In the poem "Negro siempre triste," both the title and the body of the work suggest that the poet is addressing the black man in defining and elaborating on her proud sensitivity to the historic black experience. Hers is a militant voice calling upon the black man to raise his consciousness and his courage in the repeated lines from a woman's point of view: "I am a black woman, because my skin is black/But a slave woman, no!" The significant thing about these crisp lines is that Brindis de Salas does not mask her slave ancestry or allow that skein of her past to define her. She proclaims that being black is more than merely having the legacy of chattel slavery. It is also being a woman whose cultural heritage encompasses African cultural traditions which survived the ravages of slavery and provided building blocks for African-based cultures in the New World.

CONCLUSION

In the context of the historic and cultural settings in which these three literary works were written, one observes distinctively feminine points of view in black perceptions of life. Although

*Translated by Martha K. Cobb.

the literary traditions and genres are different, the works are similar because each contains a feminine consciousness of self that is aesthetically crafted into the structure of the literature. The feminine voice is inseparable from the narrative and poetic designs that are built around new and enlightened feminine images: There is young African-American Celie's search for her real identity in her letters to God in Alice Walker's novel; there is the sense of barrenness that the Haitian spinster Claire is conscious of and fights against in the upper-class black milieu portrayed in Marie Chauvet's novel; and there is the black feminine rage that shapes and shouts out defiant new images of the black experience from Uruguay in Virginia Brindis de Salas's poem. In Chauvet's 1968 Haitian novel, an upper-class woman suffers sexual repression and emotional and spiritual violence, which she finally turns outward by killing a man—the hated chief of police. In Walker's 1982 novel, the young, poor, rural protagonist finds a way to express her search for identity by writing letters to her long-lost sister in Africa and to God; by going into an economically profitable business; and by experiencing a loving relationship with a bold woman who teaches her much about self-esteem and emotional courage. The fiery speaker in Virginia Brindis de Salas's poem does not seem to need lessons in self-worth or assertiveness. Her defiant declaration depicts a woman who has, through her connection with African deities, already claimed her status as a proud and liberated woman. Each of these works marks another stage in the evolving relation between literary images and the reality of black women's lives during the second half of the twentieth century.

A major comparative study of women writers of African descent in the New World diaspora seems the next logical step. It would include such disparate African-American writers as Phillis Wheatley, Frances Harper, and Gayle Jones, as well as the sub-set of African-American authors of West Indian descent, like June Jordan, Audre Lorde, and Paule Marshall. It would also encompass such Caribbean authors as Guadeloupe's Maryse Condé, Haiti's Jacqueline Thebeaud and Marie Blanchett, and Jamaica's Sylvia Wynter. Carolinia Maria de Jesus is *the* famous Brazilian writer of African ancestry; since Brazil contains the largest number of people of African ancestry in the New World, it is probable that other women of African descent are writing there too. Discovering authors of African descent in Spanish-speaking sections of South America is more difficult. Historical and cultural factors have combined to make absorption of people of African ancestry into the general population the rule in Spanish-speaking South America: in those countries racial ascriptions are rare. In contrast, on many Caribbean islands, very specific distinctions are made between Europeans, Africans, and people of mixed race; and in the United States, racial categories are strictly defined as "white" and "black" and are considered of primary importance in identifying people.

In addition to encountering stumbling blocks related to the race of the writers studied, scholars who undertake a broad comparative analysis must have fluency in several languages. They must know English to be able to examine the literature of Canada, Guyana, some Caribbean islands, and the United States; they must be fluent in Spanish to study authors whose heritage is from Spanish-speaking countries in the Caribbean, Central America, and South America; fluent in French to read writers from Guadeloupe and Martinique; fluent in Creole for Haitian authors; and fluent in Dutch and Papiamento for the neglected writers of Surinam and Curaçao. As a task too large for any one scholar, the important work of juxtaposing the themes and styles of women writers in the New World African diaspora clearly calls for long-term research by a committed group of specialists in the various geographic and cultural zones of this "strange and terrible Babylon," this "brave new world."

NOTES

1. W.E.B. Du Bois, *The Souls of Black Folk: Essays and Sketches,* 9th ed. (Chicago: A.C. McClurg and Co., 1911), 254–55. Same material available in later editions.
2. Ibid.
3. Sources for this and other samplings from Caribbean and Latin American countries are: Jose Arrom, "Presencia del negro en la poesia folklorica Americana," in *Certidumbre de America* (Havana, 1959); Ramon Guirao, *Orbita de la poesia Afro-Cubana* (Havana, 1938); Ildefonso Pereda Valdes, *Cancionero popular Uruguayo* (Montevideo, 1947); Jean

Price Mars, *Ainsi Parla l'Oncle* (Port-au-Price, 1928). For a secondary source, see Martha K. Cobb, *Harlem, Haiti and Havana: A Comparative Critical Study of Langston Hughes, Jacques Roumain, and Nicolas Guillen,* Chapters 1 and 2 (Washington, D.C.: Three Continents Press, Inc., 1979), 13–16, 35.

4. Alice Walker, *The Color Purple* (New York: Harcourt, Brace, Jovanovich, 1982), 4.

5. Marie Chauvet, *Amour, Colère et Folie* (Editions Gallimard, 1968), 9. For my analysis of Haitian women in literature, I wish to extend my acknowledgment to the excellent scholarship of Régine Latortue, Yale University, whose work "The Image of the Haitian Black Woman in Contemporary Haitian Literature" led me to the study of Marie Chauvet, *Amour, Colère et Folie,* from which I drew my own conclusions.

6. Richard Jackson, *Black Writers in Latin America* (Albuquerque: University of New Mexico Press, 1979), 108–109.

7. Virginia Brindis de Salas, *Cien Carceles de Amor* (Montevideo, 1949), 21–22.

8. Ibid., 31–32.

Conclusion—
Research Priorities for the Study of Women in Africa and the African Diaspora

Sharon Harley

As an area of scholarly research, the study of women in Africa and the African diaspora is relatively new. Most of the published literature in the field dates from the late 1960s and early 1970s; cross-cultural studies of women in African and New World societies are even more recent.[1] The burgeoning interest in the study of black women cross-culturally, including this publication, can be attributed to a number of factors, such as the recent women's rights movements in the United States and Europe; the rising female consciousness of Third World countries, the advancement of such academic disciplines as black studies, women's studies and diaspora studies; the increasing attention being paid to women by international development agencies; the United Nations Declaration of 1975 as International Women's Year and the start of the U.N. Decade for Women; and, finally, the growth in the number of black and female social scientists and humanists.[2] Clearly, more and more scholars and development "experts" are recognizing the futility of discussing African and Afro-American communities without considering the role of women.

While there has been a rapid growth within the last decade and a half in the scholarly literature, in a variety of disciplines, focusing on women in Africa and the African diaspora, this field of study is still in its infancy; consequently, tremendous gaps still exist in the published literature. The paucity of readily available data, the inadequacies of conventional research models, and the financial expense often required in conducting cross-cultural or comparative analysis help to explain the small number of truly comparative works focusing on black women in Third World societies. The primary purposes of this paper are to suggest aspects of black women's lives still in need of inquiry from a cross-cultural perspective and to discuss research approaches which, hopefully, will result in a more complete and realistic picture of these women's lives.

Until recently, most studies and development policies involving African, Latin American, and Caribbean societies that did not ignore women entirely, frequently depicted black women as inferior, nonproductive and, generally, as passive members of society. The tendency to exclude women or to perpetuate negative images of them in past studies is due to a number of factors: (1) the Western and "male" perspective of the researcher or development planner, (2) inappropriate research models and approaches, (3) reliance on male members of the society and often biased sources for information about women, and, finally, (4) the use of inadequate concepts and research questions.

In general, when social scientists and development agencies studying non-Western women and non-Western societies rely on analytical models based upon Western modes of thought and behavior, their analysis tends to be flawed. Concomitant with the lack of an appropriate perspective in conventional research designs for the study of non-Western women, there has often been an inadequate use of terminologies and concepts. In the past, researchers have not always considered whether the concepts they use have any validity for the group being analyzed, whether they have the same meaning for the group as they do for the researcher, or whether they have been defined such that they incorporate the activities of women. For instance, depending upon how the concepts *power* and *authority* are defined, according to Latin American historian Ann M. Pescatello, women can be perceived as either powerful individuals or as "pawns" in a male-dominated world. Furthermore, researchers have not always been alert to possible racist use of certain concepts. Anthropologist Sidney Mintz and others have pointed out that depending upon how such terms as *development* and *modernization* are used, they can have racist and ethnocentric overtones. Clearly, it is nearly impossible to unravel the complexities of women's lives, especially African and other women of color when inappropriate or racist concepts are used.[3]

One way to assure a better understanding of the roles and status of women in Africa and in the African diaspora is for researchers and development analysts to adopt an "insider's" perspective. This research approach dictates that the researcher study the experiences and perspectives of the group being analyzed based upon that group's reality, rather than his or her own reality, when the two are distinct. Researchers cannot assume that non-Western women and men share the same experiences and world view as Westerners. Western assumptions and preconceived notions about women's roles have little significance for the study of women in Africa or black women throughout the diaspora. For example, intense poverty and racism force the majority of black women (and men) throughout the world to identify with impoverished members of their community, male and female, rather than with women exclusively. June Nash and Helen Icken Safa, editors of *Sex and Class in Latin America,* argue that:

In Third World countries . . . class inequalities take priority over sexual inequalities, since only a basic structural change aiming at a more equitable distribution of wealth and income, coupled with the recognition of the need for sexual equality, will benefit working-class women as well as their more privileged sisters.[4]

At this point, it seems that the researcher who seeks to untangle the intricacies of women's lives in African and New World societies would be advised to employ an "insider's" perspective and interdisciplinary research methods. In doing so, the scholar or development planner would benefit from the research findings and methodologies representing a variety of academic disciplines, which is especially important due to the paucity of scholarship in any one discipline dealing with Third World women.

In addition to the cross-disciplinary method that an increasing number of scholars in the field are using, the very nature of the subject—black women cross-culturally—dictates the use of a comparative approach. Determining the roles and status of black women across societies, requires examining the situation of female members in two or more societies. To do more than a superficial comparison, the researcher or developmentalist must be fully knowledgeable about the historical, cultural, economic, and political dynamics of each of the societies under examination. As

Barbara Brown demonstrates in her essay on women in Botswana, the current situation facing Botswanan women is "not the result of some Biblical or 'traditional' ordering, but is the result of a confluence of historical, cultural, ecological and economic factors."[5] It is this unique set of circumstances that must be analyzed in terms of its impact on the roles and status of women. Despite the similarities among cultures within Africa and the African diaspora, the uniqueness of each society must be taken into account when undertaking cross-cultural studies.

Whether engaging in single- or multi-societal studies, more and more scholars and development specialists are involving indigenous women in their research projects from the beginning to the final stages. The assistance of local women has been sought in formulating the research design, collecting data, and in evaluating and distributing the results of various research projects. The level and structure of indigenous women's involvement varies from study to study, but the recognition of their importance to the overall success of the research project is becoming an increasingly accepted fact, especially among female and black researchers. Through the Association of African Women for Research and Development (AAWORD) and the Women in the Caribbean Project (WICP), respectively, black female anthropologists Filomina Chioma Steady and A. Lynn Bolles are representative of academic researchers engaged in studies involving both scholars and local women. Not only are the scholars likely to gain from the involvement of local women because it reduces local resistance to the project and because it lessens the chances for misinterpretation, but the local groups of women are more likely to benefit when they are involved in the formulation and implementation of research projects. Since interest in the effects of research studies and development policies on local groups exists among a growing segment of the scholarly and development community, the benefit to the women studied will not be merely incidental but an inherent part of the research design.[6]

In order for academic research to be beneficial to local groups, it must also spread beyond the academic community and be shared with international development agencies. Apparently, one reason development policy often is so unenlightened—at least, toward Third World women—is that, for one reason or another, it has not benefitted greatly from current scholarly research findings. To reduce the lag time between the publication of scholarly research findings and their implementation by policy analysts would require more joint research projects involving academicians and developmentalists, as well as greater sharing of data bases. Maybe then academic research will have a more positive impact on women's lives.[7]

In summarizing the discussion about research methods and approaches, the following observations can be made about contemporary research in the field. Recent studies focusing on black women in Africa and the Americas (1) use a myriad of approaches in order to capture the "insider's" perspective; (2) rely on scholarship and methodologies from various disciplines; (3) depend upon original, innovative research methods and research questions; (4) involve local people in some or all phases of the research project; and (5) reflect an interest in how the research project benefits local groups. As a consequence, women of color, both within and outside the African diaspora, are depicted differently in contemporary literature than they have tended to be portrayed in the past. Today, these women are frequently viewed as active, rather than passive, members of society, as powerful, rather than powerless, and as productive, rather than unproductive, members of society. With the proper approach and appropriate research questions, the future is much brighter for those academicians whose research focuses on women in Third World societies, as well as for the women they study.

Yet, despite the recent surge in published scholarly works on non-Western women, most notably by anthropologists, sociologists, and economists, and, to a lesser extent, historians, many aspects of their lives have escaped the purview of scholars. The remainder of this paper will be devoted to exploring research priorities for the study of black women cross-culturally. This section will also include research suggestions that emanated from the ABWH Conference on "Women in the African Diaspora: An Interdisciplinary Perspective."

In her introduction to *The Black Woman Cross-Culturally,* Filomina Chioma Steady suggests the following topics to researchers for cross-cultural analysis, since they reflect commonalities among black women in Africa, the Caribbean, and the

United States. They are: (1) a common African heritage, (2) economic exploitation and marginality, (3) negative literary images, (4) self-reliance, (5) creation of survival imperatives, and (6) a less antagonistic feminism. Other frequently mentioned research themes in need of initial or additional investigation by scholars interested in black women in African and New World societies are: (1) the impact of race, gender, and class on women's values and behavioral patterns, (2) the impact of modernization and urbanization on women's social status and roles, (3) the relationship between ideologies of male domination and women's actual status in the family and society, (4) the dynamics of female migration, and (5) male-female relationships. Other scholars in the field believe also that female friendships, female perceptions, and the dichotomy between myths and ideals about women and their actual status and role in society deserve scholarly attention.[8]

The research conference, "Women in the African Diaspora: An Interdisciplinary Perspective," sponsored by ABWH represented an effort on the part of social scientists and humanists in a variety of disciplines to further their understanding of women in Africa and in the diaspora. Based upon their own research, the panelists and members of the audience were cognizant, as are others in the field, that the cross-cultural investigation of black women is a fertile area for research. Since the focus on women in Third World countries is in the beginning stages and the lives of women in these countries are so complex—reflecting both traditional and modern influences—there are so many aspects of women's lives that have yet to benefit from systematic analysis. Therefore, in addition to presenting the results of their research, panelists and other conferees made a point of suggesting areas of research that are greatly in need of future investigation.

In the first session—"Conceptual Frameworks for the Study of Women in the African Diaspora"—participants suggested research priorities and approaches. According to recorder William Alexander, the general sentiment of the group was that

the phenomenon of women in the African diaspora should be conceptualized and studied on a vast stage, beginning with the situation and condition of women in African society, proceeding next to the circumstances and patterns of their migrations, and then to the multiple dynamics of the different societies in which Black women have found themselves.

At this session, as well as in the published literature in the field, the importance of detailed studies of women in particular diaspora societies was emphasized. Specific topics recommended by panelists for immediate examination included the development of survival strategies among women, self-reliant female networks, and black female self-perceptions.

Contrary to the general assumption prevalent in traditional studies of women in Third World countries about female subordination and powerlessness, participants in conference session two—"Research Techniques for the Study of Women in the African Diaspora"—emphasized female authority and power and called for a better understanding of the female power base in these societies. Historian Cynthia Neverdon-Morton informed the audience that the current interest in Third World women would benefit from a fuller understanding of the dynamics of one organization in particular—the International Council of the Women of the Darker Races—a Pan-Africanist women's organization established in the 1920s. Since research techniques were the focus of this particular session, more suggestions were offered about such techniques than about topics for future investigation. Yet, the two—research techniques and research priorities—are clearly interrelated.

Panelists pointed out that the advancement of psychological and sociological research in the field is very much dependent upon the development of appropriate psychological and sociological instruments of evaluation. In addition, conferees stressed the importance of the comparative research approach and the need for academic researchers to become more personally involved in the lives of the groups that they study. On this point, recorder Neverdon-Morton added that researchers must "move [their] research, whenever possible, from a theoretical, intellectual level to a level of action." It may be necessary for scholars to explore ways in which middle-class black and white researchers, especially aliens, can establish rapport with often illiterate working-class and peasant women and men of developing nations.

Despite the importance of religion in the lives of men and

women in Africa and the diaspora, the religious roles of women are just beginning to benefit from the scholarly interest of researchers in the field.[9] According to Professors Janette Hoston Harris and Maricela Medina Cruz, recorders at the "Religious Experiences of Women in the African Diaspora" session, future research on the subject needs to address the following questions that conferees raised: (1) What impact does religious "conversion" have on women today, especially in terms of their child-rearing practices? (2) What was and is the perception of African women and men of Afro-American missionaries? and (3) How have Christianity and religious cults affected women's cultural values and self-perceptions?

In her summary of the fourth ABWH conference session, "Family Structure and Women's Roles," recorder Noralee Frankel listed the following themes as suggestions for further study: (1) the dynamics of the extended family today, (2) the relationship between urban and rural kin, (3) the changing family structure and traditional values in Africa and the diaspora, and (4) women's roles as mothers, wives, and daughters.

Despite the proliferation of studies dealing with slavery in the Americas, especially during the last two decades, little is known about the experiences of slave women or about the legacy of slavery as it affected the status and role of women in slave societies. A common historical link between black women in Africa and throughout the diaspora, "Slavery," was the subject of conference session five. The somber truth, as the panelists indicated, is that slavery specialists have tended to ignore the female dimension of slavery and, when they do mention women, they focus on female fertility and sexuality exclusively. Consequently, scholars in the field and members of the audience were urged to begin critical analyses of every aspect of slavery, as it encompasses the female experience. Specific research topics recommended at the "Women and Slavery" session, according to recorder Sharon Harley, were (1) the importance of women to slave economies throughout the diaspora, (2) the relationship between slave women's productive and reproductive lives, (3) the relationship between slave women and white women, especially in Latin American and Caribbean societies where there was considerable racial intermixing, (4) the impact of plantation size, absenteeism, and the organization of the plantation work force on female slave experiences, and (5) the role of women and women's networks in survival strategies and resistance activities during slavery. It was frequently noted that women's lives in particular New World societies today are, in part, a reflection of their slave past.[10]

Future research in the study of "Images of Black Women in New World Literature," as recorder Deborah McDowell indicated, seems to fall into two major groupings: "the logistics of diaspora studies in literature and the specifics of black female characterization." Two research topics germane to these groupings are the relationship between the changing images of women cross-culturally and the emergence of black women writers and the relationship between the treatment of black female characters and the "point-of-view" and narrative technique.

In addition to the themes suggested by panelists and conferees, there are still other aspects of black women's lives cross-culturally that are worthy of analysis. Surprisingly, few studies at present focus on female and male socialization patterns, health conditions, sex roles, or female poverty in Africa or in New World societies. So much of women's lives has yet to be examined that the field is extremely rich in possibilities for future research.

Future research is needed to divulge more about the private, or domestic, lives of women and about the relationship between their "public" and "private" lives. The editors of *Women in the World: A Comparative Study,* Lynne B. Iglitzin and Ruth Ross, argue that the private lives of women in the home and the family have failed to keep pace with the changes in their public lives. Is this observation equally applicable for black women throughout the diaspora and Africa? There also is a demand for more studies focusing on women in rural societies. Anthropologist Achola Pala and other social scientists have maintained that there has been an overemphasis in the literature on urban women to the practical exclusion of rural women. In *African Women in Rural Development: Research Trends and Priorities,* Pala offers specific topics on the subject of rural women that need future examination.[11]

While some of the suggested research topics have been the subjects of previous scholarly review, they have not always been examined from either a comparative or cross-cultural perspective, nor have they benefitted from critical, systematic analysis.

Cross-cultural studies of women enable researchers to examine the lives and expectations of women in diverse cultures and, simultaneously, to uncover the common concerns and situations of women, in spite of their cultural and historical diversity. The underlying assumption of most cross-cultural or comparative studies of women is that there are a number of gender-defined experiences that women share, despite their cultural differences. By uncovering these commonalities, it is possible to determine the role of gender in diverse societies. If development agencies do not design separate strategies for each nation, which they are not likely to do and, in fact, which it may not be necessary to do, an understanding of women's common experiences and situations will enable them to design and implement policies that improve the lives of women, regardless of cultural and regional differences. On a more personal level, the use of cross-cultural examinations will likely promote a common identity among Third World women, which will ultimately foster a greater sense of sisterhood.

For the reasons mentioned at the outset, the conclusions reached in many of the earlier studies may be in need of revision. For instance, in their study of twenty-nine African and seventy-nine non-African societies, contrary to the general assumption about African socialization, Michael Welch and Barbara Page Miller, coauthors of "Sex Differences in Childhood Socialization: Patterns in African Societies," found little difference in these societies when it came to assigning dissimiliar values and behavioral expectations to female and male children.[12] Indeed, current scholarship in the field must involve not only the investigation of new research topics but also the reevaluation of earlier findings.

Some recent English works, besides those previously mentioned, that warrant the special attention of scholars interested in cross-cultural studies of women are: *Women and Poverty in the Third World,* ed. Mayra Buvinic et al., (Baltimore: The Johns Hopkins University Press, 1983); *Women's Roles and Population Trends in the Third World,* ed. Richard Anker et al., (London: International Labour Organisation and Crown Helm Ltd., 1982); *Women and World Development,* ed. by Irene Tinker et al., (New York: Praeger Publishers, 1975); and *Women Cross-Culturally: Change and Challenge,* The 9th International Congress of Anthropological and Ethnological Sciences, Chicago, 1973, ed. Ruby Rohrlich-Leavitt (The Hague: Mouton Publishers, 1975). A must reading for individuals interested in women and development is the 1982 issue of *Development Dialogue: A Journal of International Development Cooperation* published by the Dag Hammerskjold Foundation, Sweden. This issue is largely devoted to publishing the papers delivered at the 1982 Dakar Seminar on "Another Development with Women," jointly organized by the Association of African Women for Research and Development and the Dag Hammerskjold Foundation.

Recent dissertations focusing on women in Africa and the African diaspora that will broaden our understanding of women in Third World countries and that will likely influence future policy decisions include: "Modernization by Decree: The Role of Tunisian Women in Development," by Nahla Sherif-Stanford (University of Missouri-Columbia, 1984); "Women and Rural Development in Africa: A Case Study of Women's Income-Generating Activities in Swaziland," by Hasrin Tabibian (University of Massachusetts, 1985); "The Emergence of Liberian Women in the Nineteenth Century," by Debra L. Newman (Howard University, 1984); "Women's Income Generation and Informal Learning in Lesotho: A Policy-Related Ethnography," by Louise B. Cobbe (The Florida State University, 1985); and "Migration of Caribbean Women in the Health Care Field: A Case Study of Jamaican Nurses," by Marteen Nicholson (City University of New York, 1985).

In conclusion, it is hoped that the Association of Black Women Historians Research Conference and this publication will bring us, at least, one step closer to developing more accurate measurements and, thus, better assessments of women's lives in Africa and in the African diaspora. The research conference and the publications mentioned have focused on black women. However, these research findings should be informative concerning the general history and study of African and New World societies. If conducted properly, this research, even with its focus on women, should enhance our understanding of the social, cultural, economic, and political structures of various nations in Africa and the diaspora. Furthermore, contemporary research in the field will likely encourage scholars to reexamine traditional social science models of analysis, to raise new research questions, and to perceive the importance of involving native groups in the formulation of research designs.

Once completed, the current research should lead scholars to reevaluate many traditionally accepted theories in African, Afro-American, and women's studies and to revise development policy toward Third World societies. Most important, critical studies based upon an "insider's" perspective should result in improvements in the status and roles of women in Africa and the diaspora.

NOTES

1. Most of the recently published literature in the field focuses on black women either in the United States or in Africa, rather than throughout the diaspora or in the Caribbean or Latin America. To date, only two books have as their focus black women in Africa and the African diaspora: Filomina Chioma Steady, ed., *The Black Woman Cross-Culturally* (Cambridge, Mass.: Schenkman Publishing Co., Inc., 1981) and Beverly Lindsay, ed., *Comparative Perspectives of Third World Women: The Impact of Race, Sex, and Class* (New York: Praeger, 1980). Bibliographic references on this subject appear in both Steady and Lindsay's publication. Also consult: Doris Hull, *African Women in Development: An Untapped Resource—A Selected Bibliography* (Washington, D.C.: Moorland-Spingarn Research Center, Howard University, 1983); *The Journal of Development Studies*, vol. 17, Special Issue on African Women in the Development Process (April 1981); Joycelin Massiah, comp., *Women in the Caribbean: An Annotated Bibliography; A Guide to Material Available in Barbados* (Eastern Caribbean: Institute of Social and Economic Research, 1979), Occasional Bibliography Series, no. 5; Carolyn J. Matthiasson, ed., *Many Sisters: Women in Cross-Cultural Perspective* (New York: The Free Press, 1974); Alice Schlegel, ed., *Sexual Stratification: A Cross-Cultural View* (New York: Columbia University Press, 1977); and Suzanne Smith Saulniers and Cathy A. Rakowski, *Women in the Development Process: A Select Bibliography on Women in Sub-Saharan Africa and Latin America* (Austin: University of Texas, Institute of Latin American Studies, 1977). Cross-cultural studies have been aided by the publication of such journals as the *Journal of Cross Cultural Psychology,* the *Journal of Development Studies,* and *Signs: The Journal of Women in Culture and Society.* In addition, the University of Denver recently opened the Womankind Cross-Cultural Museum.

2. It should not be concluded that all development agencies have altruistic motives. Much of the extant comparative work in the field has been initiated by Third World women scholars, particularly black women.

3. See Sidney Mintz, "Men, Women, and Trade," *Comparative Studies in Society and History: An International Quarterly* 13 (July 1971): 247–69; Ann M. Pescatello, *Power and Pawn: The Female in Iberian Families, Societies, and Cultures* (Westport, Conn.: Greenwood Press, 1976); Nancie Solien Gonzalez, "Household and Family in the Caribbean: Some Definitions and Concepts," in the *Black Woman Cross-Culturally,* ed. Steady.

4. June Nash and Helen Icken Safa, eds., *Sex and Class in Latin American* (New York: Praeger Publishers, 1976), xi.

5. Barbara Brown, "Women, Migrant Labour and Social Change in Botswana," (Boston: Africana Studies Center, 1980).

6. See Steady's and Bolles's papers in this anthology. Also see Gloria A. Marshall (Niara Sudarkasa), "In A World of Women: Field Work in a Yoruba Community," in *Women in the Field: Anthropological Experiences,* ed. Peggy Golde (Chicago: Aldine Publishing Co., 1970).

7. For a brief discussion about incorporating research into development studies, see Achola Pala, *African Women in Rural Development: Research Trends and Priorities,* OLC Paper, 12 (1976), Moorland-Spingarn Research Center, Howard University.

8. Steady, *The Black Woman Cross-Culturally.*

9. On this subject, see, for instance, Sheila Walker's "African Gods in the Americas: The Black Religious Continuum," *Black Scholar* 11 (November/December 1980): 25–36.

10. An excellent recent contribution to the study of Afro-American slave women is a dissertation by Deborah White, "Ain't I A Woman?: Female Slaves in the Antebellum South" (Ph.D. diss. University of Illinois–Chicago Circle, 1979). This dissertation was revised and published as Deborah Gray White, *Ar'n't I A Woman: Female Slaves in the Plantation South* (New York: W.W. Norton Publishing Co., Inc., 1985). For a recent anthology about female slavery in Africa, see Claire C. Robertson and Martin A. Klein, eds., *Women and Slavery in Africa* (Madison: The University of Wisconsin Press, 1983).

11. Pala, *African Women in Rural Development.*

12. Michael Welch and Barbara Page Miller, "Sex Differences in Childhood Socialization: Patterns in African Societies," *Sex Roles* 7 (December 1981): 1163–1173.

Contributors

A. Lynn Bolles, Ph. D., is an Associate Professor of Anthropology and the Director of the Afro-American Studies Department, Bowdoin College. Her publications include "Economic Crisis and Female Headed Households in Jamaica," in *New Directions in Sex and Class in Latin America* (1985) and "Kitchens Hit by Priorities: Employed Working Class Jamaica Women Confront the IMF," in *Men, Women and the International Division of Labor* (1982). She was the 1985–86 President of the Association of Black Anthropologists and was a 1985 Smithsonian Institution Visiting Associate.

Martha K. Cobb, Ph. D., is Professor Emeritus of Modern and Comparative Languages, Howard University. Among her publications are "Ortiz, Glissant and Ellison: Fictional Patterns in Black Literature," in *The Afro-Hispanic Review* (1982) and *Harlem, Haiti, and Havana: A Comparative Critical Study of Langston Hughes, Jacques Roumain, and Nicolas Guillen* (1979). In 1983 she received the College Language Association (CLA) Creative Scholarship Award. She has served on numerous CLA committees and is the former Chairperson of the Department of Romance Languages, Howard University.

Sharon Harley, Ph. D., is an Assistant Professor of History, Afro-American Studies Program at the University of Maryland, College Park. Among her publications are "Black Women in a Southern City: Washington, D.C., 1890–1920," in *Sex, Race and the Role of Women in the South* (1983) and *The Afro-American Woman: Struggles and Images,* with Rosalyn Terborg-Penn (1978, 1981). During 1983–84 she received a National Endowment for the Humanities Summer Stipend and in 1986–87 a Rockefeller Post-Doctoral Fellowship for Minority Group Scholars. She has been an active member of the Association of Black Women Historians

(ABWH), serving as Assistant National Director from 1982–86. In addition, she is a member of the teaching division of the American Historical Association and a Consulting Editor for *Feminist Studies*.

Joseph E. Harris, Ph. D., is an Associate Dean of Liberal Arts and former Chairperson of the Department of History, Howard University. Among his major publications are *Global Dimensions of the African Diaspora* (1982) and the *William Leo Hansberry African History Notebook* (1977). During 1981–82 he was a Woodrow Wilson Fellow. Among his numerous professional activities, he was Project Director for the two African Diaspora Studies conferences held in Washington, D.C. (1979) and in Nairobi, Kenya (1981). He is currently Editor of the *African Diaspora Studies Newsletter*.

Sylvia M. Jacobs, Ph. D., is a Professor of History at North Carolina Central University. She is the author of *Black Americans and the Missionary Movement in Africa* (1982) and *The African Nexus: Black American Perspectives on the European Partitioning of Africa, 1880–1920* (1981), for which she won the 1984 Letitia Woods Brown Prize from the Association of Black Women Historians. Her other awards include a Rockefeller Post-doctoral Fellowship for Minority Group Scholars (1987–88). She was the Southern Regional Director of the Association of Black Women Historians, 1979–84, and now is currently the National Director (1984–86, 1986–88). In addition, she is a member of the Executive Council, Association for the Study of Afro-American Life and History.

Bennetta Jules-Rosette, Ph. D., is a Professor and Chairperson of the Department of Sociology, University of California, San Diego. Her major publications include *Message of Tourist Art* (1984) and *Symbols of Change* (1981). In 1982 she received a Fulbright Hays Faculty Research Abroad Grant for studies of women in Kenya and Zambia. In 1985 she received a Guggenheim Fellowship to teach and to do research in Paris. In addition, she is a member of the Board of Directors of the African Studies Association, and a member of the Executive Council of the Association for the Scientific Study of Religion.

Harriette Pipes McAdoo, Ph. D., is a Professor and the former Acting Dean of the School of Social Work at Howard University. Her major publications include *The Black Child* (1985) and *Black Families* (1981). Among her awards is the National Institute of Mental Health grant she received during 1980–81 to study black single mothers. She is on the Board of Directors of the Grooves Family Conference and she was Vice President of the National Council on Family Relations (1985).

Saundra Rice Murray, Ph. D., is the Director, Office of Field Services Operations of the United Planning Organization, Washington, D.C. Her publications include Part V, "Overview: Sex Equity Strategies for Specific Populations," in *Handbook for Achieving Sex Equity Through Education* (1985) and "Who is that Person: Images and Roles of Black Women," in *Female Psychology: The Emerging Self* (1981). She was a member of the National Advisory Committee of the Black Women's Educational Equity Network, 1981–82, and she is on the Editorial Boards of the *Journal of Negro Education* and of *Sage: A Journal of Black Women.*

Bernice Johnson Reagon, Ph. D., is the Director of the Program in Black American Culture, Museum of American History, Smithsonian Institution. Among her publications and productions are "My Black Mothers and Sisters or on Beginning a Cultural Autobiography," *Feminist Studies* (1982) and the album "Riverside of Life, Harmony: One" (1987). In 1984 she received the Thomas Merton Award for Social Ministry for Peace and Justice. She is the founder and leader of Sweet Honey in the Rock, an Afro-American women's vocal ensemble.

Andrea Benton Rushing, Ph. D., is Professor of Black Studies and English, and formerly Chairperson of the Black Studies Department, Amherst College. Her publications include "Lucille Clifton: A Changing Voice for Changing Times," in *Coming to Light* (1985) and "Images of Black Women in Afro-American Poetry," in *The Black Woman Cross-Culturally* (1981). Her awards include a 1983–84 Fulbright Fellowship to the University of Ife, Ife, Nigeria. She is a current member of the Advisory Board of the

Institute of the Black World and a Consulting Editor for *Feminist Studies.*

Filomina Chioma Steady, Ph. D., is Executive Director, International Women's Research and Consulting Institute, Madison, Wisconsin. Among her publications are "African Women, Industrialization and Another Development," in *Development Dialogue* (1982) and *The Black Woman Cross-Culturally* (1981). She has taught at the University of Sierra Leone and at Boston, Yale, and Wesleyan universities. From 1984–1986 she was on assignment with the United Nations as Deputy Director of the Branch for the Advancement of Women in Vienna, Austria, and was an executive member of the Nairobi Conference Secretariat. In 1982 Dr. Steady received the Otelia Cromwell Distinguished Alumna Award from Smith College "for outstanding contributions to the Black community by a Smith College alumna."

Niara Sudarkasa, Ph. D., is President of Lincoln University and former Associate Vice-President of Academic Affairs, University of Michigan. Among her major publications are "Interpreting the African Heritage in Afro-American Family Organization," in *Black Families* (1982) and *Where Women Work: A Study of Yoruba Women in the Market Place and in the Home* (1973). During the 1981–82 academic year she received a Fulbright Research Grant to study West African Women in Nigeria, Ghana, and Benin. In 1983 she served as the planning committee chairperson for the International Conference on Immigration and the Changing Black Population in the United States, at the University of Michigan.

Rosalyn Terborg-Penn, Ph.D., is a Professor of History and the former Chairperson of the Department of History and Georgraphy, Morgan State University. Among her publications are "Black Women in Resistance: A Cross-Cultural Perspective," in *In Resistance* (1986), and "Survival Strategies Among African-American Women Workers: A Continuing Process," in *Women, Work, and Protest* (1985). She is an editor of *Feminist Studies.* During the 1980–81 academic year she received a Ford Foundation Postdoctoral Fellowship for Minorities, and in 1984 she received a Berkshire Fellowship for Women Historians to the Bunting Institute, Radcliffe College. She is a founder of the Association of Black Women Historians, serving in several offices since 1979 and as Project Director for the 1983 conference, Women in the African Diaspora: An Interdisciplinary Perspective.

Karen Smyley Wallace, Ph.D., is an Associate Dean of Liberal Arts at Howard University. Her publications include "Women and Identity: A Black Francophone Female Perspective," in *Sage A Journal of Black Women* (1985) and "Women and Alienation: Analysis of the Works of Two Francophone African Novelists," in *Odyssey: A Journal of the Humanities* (1984). During the 1976–77 academic year she received a Mellon Foundation Doctoral Dissertation Fellowship. She was on the Curriculum Advisory Committee of the College Language Association, 1982–84 and was a coordinator for the 1982 African Literature Association conference at Howard University, Washington, D.C.

Miriam Were, Dr. P. H., is a Professor in the College of Medicine, University of Nairobi. She is also a pediatrician, and her public health speciality is International Public Health, focusing upon maternal and child health. In 1985 she was one of the official Kenyan government delegates to the United Nations Conference on the Decade of Women, held in Nairobi, where she wrote and presented the Kenyan position papers related to health. In addition to her medical and public health scholarship, she is a published poet and novelist.

Index